A PRIMER OF PHYSIOLOGICAL PSYCHOLOGY

HARPER'S PHYSIOLOGICAL PSYCHOLOGY SERIES
UNDER THE EDITORSHIP OF H. PHILIP ZEIGLER

A Primer of Physiological Psychology

ROBERT L. ISAACSON
University of Florida

ROBERT J. DOUGLAS
University of Washington

JOEL F. LUBAR
The University of Tennessee

LEONARD W. SCHMALTZ
The University of Wisconsin

HARPER & ROW, PUBLISHERS
NEW YORK, EVANSTON, AND LONDON

A Primer of Physiological Psychology

CONTENTS

A NOTE TO STUDENTS

This book is an introduction to physiological psychology. We believe this area of research and knowledge may some day provide the information necessary to understanding behavior, both normal and abnormal. It is an area with which most students of behavior should be familiar even though they may not become physiological psychologists. Undergraduate courses in physiological psychology are offered in most universities and colleges but often are elected by only a relative handful of students because most students are afraid they cannot do well in them without a strong background in the physical and biological sciences. Certainly a firm grounding in the basic biological sciences is necessary for graduate work in physiological psychology. Many physiological psychologists are specialists in biochemistry, neurophysiology, or anatomy, as well as psychology, and competence in these other areas is important for their research. Nevertheless the basic information of physiological psychology can be understood with a less complete background. We have tried to write this book so that it will be intelligible to the reader with the equivalent of a sound high school course in biology. We hope the writing style allows rapid comprehension and will afford a clear overview of much of the work going on today in physiological psychology.

Most textbooks written for advanced courses in physiological psychology are weighty documents with considerable detail. We have tried to minimize certain details which we have judged to be less than essential to the major ideas presented. References to comprehensive articles and advanced textbooks are given at the end of certain chapters. Some students reading this book will, we trust, experience the excitement and understand the challenges in the field and be motivated to prepare themselves for advanced courses. In any event, the material in this book should be of value in other courses in psychology and in the other sciences.

R.L.I.
R.J.D.
J.F.L.
L.W.S.

Chapter 1

INTRODUCTION

CHAPTER 1

WHAT IS PHYSIOLOGICAL PSYCHOLOGY?

Physiological psychology is that body of knowledge which attempts to explain behavior from a biological point of view. Physiological psychologists believe that man's behavior can be understood only in terms of accepted facts and theories of biology in general. They seek to discover the relationships between behavior and the underlying physiological mechanisms.

Physiological psychologists do many things. They investigate the relationship of biochemistry to memory. They explore the behavior of lower organisms to find the biochemical changes occurring in them as learning progresses and as memories are formed and stored. They examine the changes in the electrical rhythms generated by aggregates of the millions or even billions of single nerve cells during particular episodes of behavior. They study the patterns of activity found in individual nerve cells. To study the reactions of a single cell involves an entirely different approach from that required to study the summated electrical activities of millions of nerve cells. Some physiological psychologists look into the reactions of the blood vessels and sweat glands in the skin and try to relate the changes to feelings of emotion and emotional behavior; this kind of work calls for yet another approach. The point is that physiological psychology cannot be defined in terms of one approach or one particular set of methods. It must be defined in accordance with the attitudes and goals of those who are actively engaged in this area of science and the belief that an understanding of behavior will ultimately come from an understanding of the physiological nature of the organism.

APPROACHES TO THE STUDY OF PHYSIOLOGICAL PSYCHOLOGY

Let us consider some of the various approaches to physiological psychology. First, it should be emphasized that the approach used by a physiological psychologist is dictated by the problem he is investigating. That is, he chooses the approach he feels is most likely to shed light upon the problem. Although he makes his decision as a scientist, many techniques and approaches are used because of historical tradition. Any particular scientist has a history of training and past experience in research which he tends to use and to capitalize upon. However, as new research problems arise, the creative scientist changes his methods accordingly. He refuses to be limited in his procedures or attitudes. Human ingenuity is the key to success.

The Comparative Approach

The first broad approach to the study of physiological psychology is the comparative approach. When one wishes to evaluate the effects of a certain type of brain lesion or the effects of electrical stimulation of a particular region of the brain, it is often necessary to experiment on animals. The results obtained may or may not be similar to those from comparable damage or stimulation in the human. The work of physiological psychologists is directed toward the understanding of human behavior, yet it is often impossible to study the human organism directly. Recourse must be had to the study of experiments upon animals. On the basis of these experiments and what is known about the relationship between the brain and behavior of man and animals, certain inferences can be drawn and tested in a limited fashion upon the human organism. There is, in fact, no other way to proceed in most cases. Consider the difficulties of evaluating the effects of damage to the human brain. Usually the damage results from a gunshot wound or an automobile accident or some other tragic event. In all cases the degree and location of injury is hard to assess with any clinical technique. The effect of a bullet entering the brain is not restricted to the area of entrance or the area in which the bullet finally lodged. Repercussions in terms of brain damage can be found at remote places throughout the entire brain. Most often the damage is unknown since very few cases are studied in detail after death to determine the extent of the damage.

Therefore, to know the contribution made to behavior by any particular region of the brain, we must study animals in which known damage can be produced and the effects compared with the results of damage to other regions. The brain is made up of many discrete parts each interacting with others but each adding its unique contribution to behavior. What we know of the role of each part has come, primarily, from the study of animals.

A comparative approach to brain function or to behavior means that *comparisons* must be made among several species of animals. When we compare the effects of stimulating a brain region in one species with those produced by stimulating the same region in a different animal or the human, we are trying to generalize about brain structure, function, and behavior across species. The comparative approach does not rest merely with evaluating the differences between two species but searches for the principles governing these differences and their implication for the study of human behavior.

Thus, it should be recognized that while most physiological psychologists study the nervous system of animals many do so out of sheer necessity. Others study the behavior of animals before, during, and after some manipulation of the nervous system with the aim of discovering the principles controlling the specialization and development of animal life more generally.

Although there are many people who continue the exacting and difficult work of making comparisons of animal behavior, much of the early interest in the behavior per se has lessened. Instead, comparative psychologists examine in detail the fine-grain behavior of animals considering its relation to events in the internal environment of the animal and to the changes in the external environment. The effect of this line of inquiry has been a healthy movement toward recognizing the dynamic interplay of the many forces constantly influencing behavior. Let us consider some examples.

SPONTANEOUS ACTIVITY. Today we know that spontaneous activity is found in all living organisms—quite a change from earlier views which described animals as inert except when responses were evoked by particular environmental stimuli or internal drives. Even animals as primitive as the sea anemone show spontaneous activities, and differential amounts of such activities can be demonstrated in various muscle groups. As in many other forms of activity, there are more or less regular rhythms associated with spontaneous activity.

DAY-NIGHT CYCLES. If the sea anemone is observed for long periods of time, it is seen that daytime and nighttime activities are not the same. This differential responsiveness is not limited to lower forms or to changes in "spontaneous activities." Some animals are nocturnal; others are most active during the day. Not only do activity levels change from one kind of animal to another when the transition is made from light to dark, but responsiveness to stimuli and the ease with which animals can be conditioned also change. In addition, animals come to "anticipate" their periods of light and dark. The sea anemone begins to expand before dark—that is, before the stimulus event of darkness occurs.

Those interested in animal behavior have been responsible for our increased awareness of the importance of looking at behavior in terms of definite goal-directed episodes, as well as at the relation of such episodes to longer chains and cycles of behavior.

Behaviorally oriented investigators are interested in daily fluctuations and rhythms. (Daily rhythms are sometimes called *circadian,* from *circa,* meaning "about," and *diem,* meaning "day.") Sleeping, eating, drinking, and other activities reflect these cycles. Of special interest to physiological psychologists is the fact that animals with surgically induced brain lesions may show quite different reactions in the daytime and at night. For example, rats with damage to certain parts of the *limbic system,* a set of brain structures lying deep in the brain, are more active and sleep much less at night than normal animals. They also run mazes faster at night than in the day. During the day the differences in activity and sleep between the brain-damaged and normal animals are much less. In fact the animals with this kind of brain damage are slightly slower in maze running than normal animals during the daylight hours.

In general, the daily rhythms of living creatures depend upon both the external cues or signals associated with the time of day and some essentially unknown internal mechanisms. Experiments on several species have demonstrated that normal patterns of daily activities will continue even when the normal signals of the correct time have been changed. The animals will, however, more or less rapidly adapt to altered day-night cues and establish new circadian cycles.

OTHER BEHAVIORAL CYCLES. Cycles of behavior can be classified in many ways. In fact, the entire period between birth and death is one long cycle—too long, however, to be of much value in understanding behavior. More significant is the study of shorter cycles which have identifiable and usually periodic patterns. Some sea animals respond in different ways during different tidal periods of the ocean and continue to do so, sometimes for several months, even when removed from the sea and placed in laboratory aquariums. A common example of cycles of long duration at higher animal levels would be the many physiological and emotional changes associated with the monthly cycle of the mammalian female.

The behavioral rhythms exhibited by animals are due to genetic mechanisms, the details of which have yet to be established. But while most animals receive the rules for their daily rhythms from heredity, there are variations in inherited information in even closely related animals. It is likely that considerable differences exist among an animal's siblings, although little work has been done on individual differences in cycles of behavior. Physiological psychologists too often tend to ignore differences among animals, especially when using animals from the same supplier, breeding colony, or litter. Individual differences do exist from the start and should be considered in any experiment.

INTERNAL FACTORS CONTROLLING BEHAVIORAL CYCLES. The study of behavioral rhythms leads to recognition of the strong contribution of internal factors in the regulation of behavior. Among internal factors of undoubted significance to behavior are the *hormones* secreted by the ductless glands of the body, the *endocrine glands.* Secretion occurs cyclically and yet is regulated in part by events occurring in the environment. For example, the development of eggs in female birds is controlled by hormones from the pituitary gland at the base of the brain. However, an isolated female dove will ordinarily not lay, but only minimal cues associated with another dove will induce her to do so. In a series of extremely interesting experiments Professor Daniel Lehrman of Rutgers University has shown that the courtship behavior of doves speeds up subsequent nest-building behaviors. This activity is related to the secretion of estrogens, a type of female hormone, from the female dove's ovaries. Moreover, the cues received by the female may be subtle. Female doves secrete much less estrogen when only allowed to watch a castrated male dove than when allowed to watch a normal "courting" male dove. In doves the stages of nest building, egg laying, and incubation are closely related to complicated changes in hormone levels. At each stage the release of hormones is controlled in part by stimuli impinging upon the organism from the environment and arising from the animal as a result of its own behavior.

Although hormones probably have less direct control over behavior at higher animal levels than at lower, they unquestionably influence behavior at all levels. Moreover, the amounts of hormone secreted are affected by environmental factors bearing on the central nervous system. Recognition of the significant influence of hormones on behavior is important for physiologi-

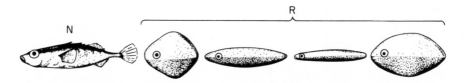

FIGURE 1-1–Models of stimuli used by N. Tinbergen in his studies of "sign stimuli" used to elicit instinctive behaviors. (From N. Tinbergen. *A study of instinct*. Oxford: Clarendon Press, 1951. By permission of the author and the Clarendon Press.)

cal psychologists. Often damage to, or stimulation of, the nervous system affects hormone levels in the body; behavior caused by the brain manipulations could be secondary consequences of hormone changes. Such potential effects can be measured by testing animals while they have more normal hormone relationships established through supplementary hormone administrations.

Behavioral Episodes   Both internal hormone levels and external circumstances help determine the beginning and end of behavioral cycles. To this point we have talked mainly about recurring cycles of activity or other common behaviors, but the idea of recurring *episodes* in behavior is of general importance. All behavior sequences can be considered episodes which have more or less well-defined beginnings, middles, and ends. Manipulations of the central nervous system by physiological psychologists can affect any of these, as well as determining whether or not an episode will occur at all.

Sexual behavior in many lower animals is organized into episodes which are initiated by hormonal and external stimuli, have an intermediate period of ritualized activity or play, and lead to the terminal events, usually copulation. This is followed by an episode of sexual inactivity. Throughout each episode the patterns of behavior are constantly under the guidance and support of external stimuli.

As a rule, each species has highly specific stimuli to which it attends during any particular behavioral episode. The aspect of the environment which acts to "release" or begin a particular behavioral episode has been called a *sign stimulus* by some ethologists, including the British scientist N. Tinbergen. He studied the "zigzag dance" of a fish, the three-spined bony stickleback, exhibited by males when a female fish enters its territory. However, not all female shapes are equally effective in eliciting the dance. To determine the precise nature of the fish figure responsible for production of the zigzag dance, Tinbergen introduced into the male's waters many artificial patterns roughly resembling the female. An example of the figures used is given in Figure 1-1. Tinbergen found that the form need only approximate that of a female fish to elicit the dance, the significant aspect of the stimulus being the protruding underbelly of the figure, whether real or artificial. The underside of the figure is the sign stimulus for that particular type of behavior. It is also possible to make stimuli which have more releasing power than any naturally occurring fish figure.

In general, factors (such as hormones) of internal environment and sign stimuli interact to begin a behavior sequence. The more frequently zigzag dances are elicited, the more exaggerated will be the sign stimulus required to call them forth in the future. If a zigzag dance has not been elicited for some time, a minimal underbelly protuberance can begin the dance.

The same thing can be said for responses aimed at satisfying hunger. The hungrier an animal is, the less strong a stimulus will need to be to evoke food-getting responses.

THE DURATION OF BEHAVIORAL EPISODES. Not only are the inherited and relatively fixed patterns of behavior organized into episodes but most behavior falls into a category of shorter or longer episodes. Often these are definable in terms of the end result of the behavior, as in sexual and food-seeking episodes. Animals and man have periodic episodes organized around almost all of the biological motives. There is considerable variance from one species to another and in even from one society to another.

Once an animal is engaged in a behavioral episode, it tends to persist in the sequence until the goal of the episode is obtained. This behavior represents something analogous to inertia. Once a ball begins to roll down a plane, inertia keeps it going. Thus in studying the effects of training stimuli, motivation, or what have you, on an animal's behavior one must remember that the stimuli are often imposed upon an ongoing episode, and the animal's reactions will depend upon the behavioral episode at that time. The "force" required to disrupt the episode is determined by the internal conditions of the animal, the inherent strength of the episode, the stage of the episode when the stimulus is introduced, and the stimuli in the environment which are supportive of the particular sequence.

When Training Is Begun   What happens when an animal is placed in a training situation? Frequently rats are used in experiments on learning and memory in the laboratories of psychologists interested in these phenomena. Animals are commonly trained in the daytime, but the rat is a nocturnal animal and some 80 percent of his day is spent in naps or more prolonged periods of sleep. When the time for training arrives, the behavioral episode centered around sleeping is disturbed by the experimenter's removing the animal from its cage and placing it in an unfamiliar environment. Naturally the transfer from home cage to training environment is traumatic for the animal.

The first time an animal is handled and placed in a new environment, of course, it is subjected to the greatest trauma, as is reflected in reactions of the heart and gut, as well as a tendency to hide from the possible dangers in the new environment. The animal often urinates and defecates, two signs of turmoil in the portions of the nervous system controlling the internal organs. But more than the internal organs are reacting. Almost all parts of the nervous system respond to intensive stress. In extreme reactions, the animal may even "tune out" the environment and assume a "catatonic posture" evidencing an attempt to withdraw from the situation. After repeated experiences with being picked up and transported to the training situation, the traumatic reactions diminish. As the extreme fright reaction dissipates, the animal begins exploratory movements in the new environment.

ORIENTING RESPONSE. One of the first reactions of an animal to new and unfamiliar stimuli is a complicated response involving both the general body muscles and the internal organs. As a rule, *orienting reactions* will occur in response to minor or subtle changes in the environment, or after stress reactions to the completely new circumstances have subsided through adaptation. Each animal species has an individual style of exhibiting the orienting reaction. A monkey tends to orient to a stimulus by movements of the eyes and head. In a rat more total bodily adjustments are found. The end purpose of whatever movements are made by an animal serve to "tune" the animal toward specific events occurring in the environment.

The entire orienting response is quite complicated and includes a redistribution of blood flow to certain regions of the body and changes in the *autonomic nervous system* (that part of the nervous system controlling the internal organs). These changes are much less intense than the reactions which follow severe trauma or stress. One other aspect of the orienting response is of special significance. This is the cessation of ongoing behavior. The orienting response interrupts whatever pattern of behavior the animal is following when the stimuli eliciting the reaction are presented. If a whistling sound is made while a dog is in the middle of its dinner, the animal will stop eating and look around for the source of the sound. The unexpected signal has interrupted an ongoing behavioral sequence. Depending upon the nature of the sound, the hunger of the animal, and a number of other factors, the animal will more or less quickly return to its food.

Returning to our rat in a training situation: After it has adapted to the trauma of being handled and placed in a new situation and the associated fright response has decreased, the rat exhibits many orienting responses. These lessen as it begins to move about, exploring the environment. Effective training of an animal in a behavioral task can occur only after the initial stress and orienting responses have subsided.

THE INTRODUCTION OF REWARDS. The learning of any behavioral problem presented is based upon the appropriate use of rewards or incentives, given at appropriate times. Rewards can be of a positive type, as when food is given to a hungry animal, or of a negative type, as when an "incorrect response" is punished. For example, if the animal is being trained in an *operant conditioning* chamber it will be placed there when mildly hungry. In this case internal factors associated with hunger will also influence the animal's general behavior. An operant conditioning chamber is simply a box which has a small bar or lever extending from one wall and a device, close to the bar or lever, for delivering a food pellet to the animal when appropriate (see Figure 1-2). In the early training ("shaping") of the animal to press the bar, food pellets are delivered whenever the animal approaches the bar. As it nears the bar during the course of exploring the box, the arrival of a food pellet, an event not experienced before in the situation, will evoke an orienting reaction that temporarily interrupts exploratory activities. The animal will move toward the food pellet, smell it, and perhaps eat it. Probably, however, the animal will sniff it, then return to its explorations for some time before going back to the food pellet and eating it. Subsequent training involves waiting until the animal gets closer and closer to the bar before giving it the

FIGURE 1-2–An operant conditioning chamber. The animal is placed in the chamber and learns to depress the lever at appropriate times to obtain food or water or other rewards. (Photograph, courtesy Lehigh Valley Electronics Corporation.)

food pellet reward. At first the food pellets produce orienting responses, but, like the reaction to handling, the orienting responses themselves will adapt, and with enough experience they will, to all intents and purposes, disappear. The animal will begin pressing the bar to obtain its food pellets in a regular and systematic fashion. When it is working the bar or lever with skill and apparent "singleness of purpose," it has developed a new behavioral episode which starts when it is placed in the training situation, has as a middle period the regular continued operation of the bar, and terminates only with satiation from food or with removal from the training compartment.

While we have discussed the situation of the animal as it is introduced into an operant conditioning chamber and subjected to this particular type of training regime, many similar reactions will occur in any training situation: fear and stress reactions to the trauma of being handled and placed in a new situation, orienting responses which are progressively replaced by exploratory activities, and orienting reactions transiently reintroduced by rewards. The orienting responses elicited by the rewards used in training must themselves be overcome in order for a smooth and integrated response system to be developed which allows the animal to perform the tasks efficiently.

If the animal is being trained in a situation in which it must avoid or escape from electrical shocks, the overcoming of the fear response elicited by the electrical shock may be much more difficult than the establishing of a smooth performance by means of incentives (positive rewards like food or water to a deprived animal).

It should now be clear that training an animal in even a simple type of learning situation is complicated. When the physiological psychologist investigates the effects of brain stimulation or lesions or other physiological manipulation upon performance, the obtained results can be due to all sorts of behavioral changes. It is important for physiological psychologists to keep in mind that many different kinds of changes may affect an animal's performance in any training task.

Differences Among Animals   Not only do species of animals differ in the ways they adjust to a learning task, but differences are found among animals within a species. Several times in this chapter we have mentioned differences in the performance of animals in the same species: *individual differences*. What do we mean by this term? For one thing, we mean that animals are not identical in their physical characteristics or behavior. Although one may look much the same as another, close examination would reveal small physical differences, due, at least in part, to differences in their genetic compositions. Yet individual differences among animals amount to more than differences in genetic endowments. Animals born in the same litter, or even identical twins, may be influenced by their positions in the mother's uterus and by each individual's access to the air and nutrients crossing the placenta from mother to offspring. In addition, they are differentially affected by their early experiences after birth. Their body size and weight influence their ability to succeed in the struggle among littermates for mother's milk. Such things as allover activity and energy levels also help determine how successful they will be in competition with their brothers and sisters. Often peculiar accidents in their home environment early in life influence later behavior.

The physiological psychologist must recognize that any manipulation he undertakes with a group of animals will not have exactly the same effects on each one. The animals are different to begin with and will often react differently to apparently similar treatment.

GENETIC INFLUENCES. The ways in which an animal's genetic endowment affects its behavior are varied. The most drastic influences, perhaps, are exerted by congenital neuropathologies such as microcephaly (small head and brain), anencephaly (failure of brain to develop fully), and hydrocephaly (large fluid-filled brain chambers). However, because of relatively rapid weeding out by professional breeders of animals, these types of devastating neural deformities are infrequent in most laboratory populations of animals. It is important to recognize that on commerical breeding farms and in laboratories associated with universities and medical schools the less fit animals are constantly weeded out. In addition, animals which are docile and easy to handle are favored for breeding, a reflection only of the natural desire of the breeders and caretakers to deal with the more pleasant members of a particular species. Thus manipulations performed upon animals bred from generations of laboratory stock often cannot be replicated in the same way in animals of the same species which are less removed from their natural or wild states.

Through the use of selective breeding of animals for certain characteristics, it has been possible to show that many behavioral traits have a genetic basis. These include, for example, overall activity level and the relative dependence on visual, as opposed to other cues, in maze running. Studies

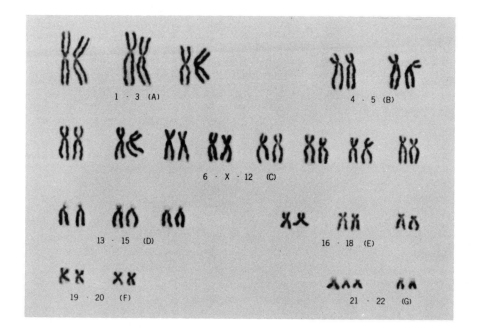

FIGURE 1-3–Karyotype of the chromosomes of a mongoloid child. Note that there are three "21" chromosomes which gives rise to the more modern name for the condition, trisomy 21. (From C. P. Francisco. Genetics investigations and family counseling in mental retardation. *Modern Treatment,* 1967, *4,* 837.)

with the laboratory rat show that it cannot be bred specifically for a general learning ability. Rather, its ability to learn is apparently very much related to the specific situation. In short, an animal may learn to run mazes quickly, but this ability is not highly related to an ability to learn other tasks. It should also be remembered that different tasks used by those studying animal behavior often require different amounts of adjustment to handling and the apparatus, different occasions for the elicitation of the orienting responses, and different degrees of motivation and reward. For these reasons a general animal intelligence factor will perhaps never be discovered if it does exist.

GENETIC DISORDERS IN PEOPLE. We are beginning to recognize the vast importance of genetic factors in certain forms of mental retardation, criminal behaviors, and some mental disorders. One of the clearest types of a genetically based form of mental retardation is *mongolism.* Children suffering from mongolism are found to have an additional chromosome; they have 47 instead of 46 chromosomes. The extra chromosome is one of the type which is given the designation 21. Thus, the disease is now often referred to as trisomy 21 (3 chromosome bodies of the type labeled 21). (Pairs of chromosomes are numbered from 1 to 22 according to size, the smallest being 22.) The third chromosome of the size 21 related to mongolism can be found in one of several different positions, but in all cases in which it appears the patient exhibits severe mental retardation and other bodily characteristics associated with mongolism.

Recent investigations into the chromosome patterns found among male prisoners of various state and federal penitentiaries have revealed the surprising finding that a substantial proportion (10 to 15 percent) of the habitual criminal offenders have extra chromosomes. Typically these are extra sex chromosomes. We do not yet know how this extra genetic inheritance influences behavior. However, it is an extremely exciting observation and one which at present is being intensively investigated.

Genetic Mechanisms   Research into the biochemical nature of genetic materials is progressing at an unprecedented rate. Today we know that the basic genetic material found in the chromosomes is *deoxyribonucleic acid (DNA)*. The DNA exists in two strands and has four organic compounds which connect the strands like the rungs of a ladder. Most of the information governing the biological inheritances of the individual, and hence his development and behavior, is encoded in the order of these four organic compounds. That is, the genetic code is made up of the pattern of the four connecting compounds in the DNA molecule.

A related compound, *RNA (ribonucleic acid)*, is an active mechanism for transporting the genetic information from the chromosomal DNA in the nucleus of the cell to the protein production sites in the cell body. RNA is constantly being synthesized in the body, while DNA is a fixed quantity in adults. The RNA of a cell interacts with the protein building blocks (amino acids) found in the extranuclear portions of the cell to put together the proteins which govern the structure and function of the cell. Because RNA is always changing in the brain, whereas DNA is not, people have considered the RNA molecule a likely mechanism for storage of memories. In theory the DNA molecule represents a source of information for the manufacture of proteins which is fixed and immutable and the RNA a source which can be modified by experience. This modification is of presumed significance for the mechanisms of memory.

Whether the brain's method of storing information does involve the RNA molecule is uncertain at the present time. Nevertheless, the work directed toward its evaluation as a basis for memory represents an example of how basic information derived from the study of genetic mechanisms may bear on the understanding of behavioral processes more generally.

Genetic Contributions to Behavior   The differences in genetic endowment between one animal and the next express themselves in a myriad of forms. Behaviorally oriented psychologists have paid most attention to the studies in the possible inheritance of learning, memory, or performance. Often forgotten are the vast numbers of physiological attributes which come to an individual through heredity also. Animals and people inherit information which allows greater or less metabolic efficiency, greater or less efficiency of the chemicals involved in the action of the brain, increased or decreased tendencies toward certain types of glandular reactions, especially the reactions of the ductless (endocrine) glands, and so on. Many of these physiological reactions directly or indirectly influence the behavior of animals studied in typical laboratory tasks.

In preceding pages we have stressed differences among individuals and the origins of these differences in heredity and environment. Yet numerous aspects of behavior are similar among animals in the same species and across several species. If it were not for the similarities, the study of behavior and of the nervous system would be useless since generalizations could not be made which would apply to other individuals. The similarities do exist, generalizations can be made, and endeavors have not been futile.

Similarities Among Individuals In terms of the nervous system, great similarities of structure exist among all the vertebrates and especially among the mammals. Even the principles of neural activity found among some insects are much the same as those found in the mammals. Despite the resemblance of the nervous systems at the cellular level, the insects have progressed along completely different lines in terms of the organization of the nervous system. Yet below the mammalian level, organization of the nervous system is very much like that found at higher levels. As will be discussed in Chapter 4, the basic design of what is thought to be the crowning neural achievement of man, the neocortex, can be observed even in the reptiles. Differences do exist, of course, in the neural mechanisms found at different animal levels, but among mammals they are not gross and often, indeed, are differences in degree rather than in kind. It is almost as if certain elementary patterns of nervous system functions are supplemented in various ways as the evolutionary scale is ascended. Even this generalization is hard to document because existing life forms are not laid out along straightforward evolutionary lines. Man did not descend from the apes. Rather, both may have had a common ancestor and each followed divergent evolutionary courses ever since, including many branching processes and with intermediate forms which are completely lost now.

Anatomically no two animals are exactly alike, but, once again, the differences among animals of the same species are differences in degree, not qualitative differences. The extent to which animals with similar genetic endowments display similar behavioral patterns can be seen in Figure 1-4. The performances of four groups of mice learning a two-way active avoidance task are shown. At the left the individual performances of a group of genetically heterogeneous Swiss mice are represented. The other graphs show the individual performances of animals from genetically pure strains of mice. Note the superior performances of the strain next to the Swiss mice graph, the extremely poor performances of animals of the strain represented on the right-hand graph, and the relatively consistent levels of performance within each strain.

Anatomical differences in the brain (in size or in overall appearance) can be found among species and among strains within a species. One prominent external feature is the "hills and valleys," the *gyri* and *sulci,* of the neocortical surface. Rodents and rabbits have only a few minor sulci; the surface of the brain is almost smooth. Cats and dogs, on the other hand, have many prominent sulci. Yet even the convolutions of the brain surface are notorious for their variability from one animal to the next, and even from one side of a brain to the other. We know little of the bearing of convolutions of the neocortex on behavior. At the other extreme: although microscopic evaluation of brain tissue reveals significant variations in the tiny "processes"

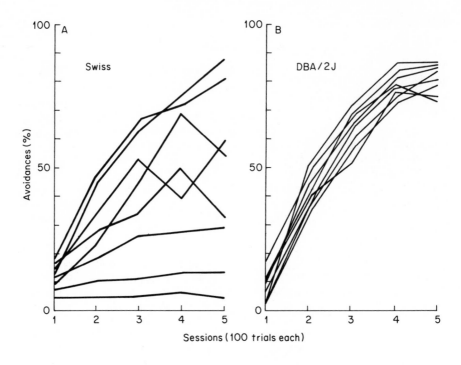

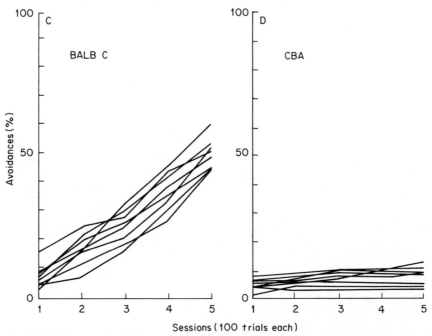

FIGURE 1-4–Learning curves showing the percent avoidance responses made by individual animals in a two-way active avoidance problem in successive sessions of 100 trials each. Four groups of mice are shown. On the left is a genetically assorted group of Swiss mice while the other graphs show the performance of animals in genetically purer strains with the specialized names give the left corner of each graph. (From D. Bovet, F. Bovet-Nitti, and A. Oliverio. Genetic aspects of learning and memory in mice. *Science,* 1969, *163,* 139–149. Copyright 1969 by the American Association for the Advancement of Science.)

arising from the single cells of the nervous system, how these differences are related to differences in behavior is highly uncertain. The establishment of hard correlations between differences in anatomy and behavior is one of the major goals of those working in physiological psychology.

The Developmental Approach

Physiological psychology has gained valuable information from scientists who approach problems from a developmental point of view. Any problem in any of the life sciences can be studied developmentally. The question of how learning early in life differs from that later on has held special fascination. One behavior found in certain animals, especially some types of birds, which has been studied vigorously by psychologists and ethologists is called *imprinting*. Its potential importance lies in the fact that it may describe a phenomenon applicable to behavior of other, higher species and give a clue to how the nervous system of young animals differs from that of older animals.

Imprinting refers to the tendency of the animal to become behaviorally "attached" to an object which is presented to it at some early stage of development. This was observed by Lorenz in the greylag goose, a precocial bird (able to move about and navigate in its environment shortly after hatching). This type of bird has often been used in research on imprinting because of the ease with which a *following response* can be observed as the measure of imprinting. Birds which are not mobile shortly after birth and must be pampered by their parents have been studied much less.

Figure 1-5 is a picture of Dr. Lorenz being followed by a brood of young greylag geese. Dr. Lorenz arranged it so that he himself was the object present at the critical moment, and the geese responded later by following him in preference to other objects, even their own mother. The imprinting of the following response can be made to occur to any one of a large number of objects and can be modified in many ways—strengthened or weakened.

Imprinting in a sense represents a very rapid form of learning. Often only one exposure is required for the baby birds to become attached to an object, but some birds might require repeated exposures. Imprinting only happens at a particular stage of early life. Although some people consider the imprinted reaction irreversible and permanent, this is probably not the case. Imprinting depends in part upon the nature of the stimulus and may be limited to certain types of birds.

Whether or not the phenomenon of imprinting, per se, has general implications for behavior in particular avian species, its study has led us to reevaluate the importance of critical periods during development in all species. By *critical periods* we mean those stages when the animal is especially receptive to certain kinds of stimuli. Experiences provided earlier or later are less effective in producing the behavior in question. Moreover, if for some reason the appropriate stimulation for the behavior under study is not available, it will be more difficult for the animal to develop the behavior later on. Actually, perhaps the term "optimal period" better describes the time during which the animal exhibits a preference for specified stimuli, and "critical point" may be applied to the point up to which stimuli will be effective in producing the behavior but after which they will not.

FIGURE 1-5–Goslings following Dr. Konrad Lorenz after having been imprinted upon him at an early developmental stage. (Thomas McAvoy, LIFE Magazine © Time Inc.)

In any event, the quest to discover those changes in the nervous system which represent the differential sensitivities of the organism at different times and the various abilities for responding associated with the changes will be exciting. We know next to nothing about the neural and physiological bases of imprinting in birds or about critical periods in other animals. As more and more information comes to light about the great specificity with which the nervous system develops, we shall better understand behavior.

Cellular Changes During Brain Development During development, cell division in the central nervous system goes on at a tremendous rate, but the rate is not constant. Moreover, cells with specific functional and ana-tomical destinies are formed at the same time, often to migrate in groups over considerable distances to take up their final, or almost final, positions in the nervous system of the adult organism.

In mammals, cells are formed in the internal regions of the fetal brain and migrate outward, in successive waves, to become the layers of the neocortex covering the brain. The first layers formed are those which will be the deepest layers. Subsequent cell divisions produce cells which migrate through the layers already made to positions closer to the outer surface. We can keep track of cells undergoing cell division and their routes of migration by administering to the embryo radioactive substances which are taken into cell nuclei *only* at the time of cell division. The radioactive cells, then, will be ones which had been undergoing cell division when the substance was given. By processing sections of brain tissue to detect the radioactivity, examine the progress and ultimate fate of cells maturing at different embryologic stages. Examination of material processed this way has revealed a great specificity of migration. Each developing cell moves along tiny tendrils or processes of preceding cells through the bottom layers of cortex to almost its final location in the neocortex.

Views of the Developing Organism Our view of the developing be-havior of organisms in the past 30 to 40 years has been of a progressive development of specific behaviors and structures from a more general type of development. This picture arose primarily from observations of the de-velopment of lower animals, particularly the salamander. Reactions to stimuli introduced into the environment were at first general and diffuse; then they were modified and perhaps replaced by more specific reactions as the animal matured.

A better view of the developing nervous system is that proposed by the Russian physiological psychologist Anohkin, who argues that we should regard the organism as developing, sequentially, a vast number of sensori-motor systems. Depending upon the requirements of the animal before and after birth, systems reach their mature, functional states at different times. They involve certain sensory components, central components, and response components, which all differentiate together, at the same time, independ-ently of the overall maturational state of the organism.

A kind of timetable allows some functional systems to become func-tional before others. The timetable seems to be based on the impending need for the parts to be used in systems required for life processes or de-velopment.

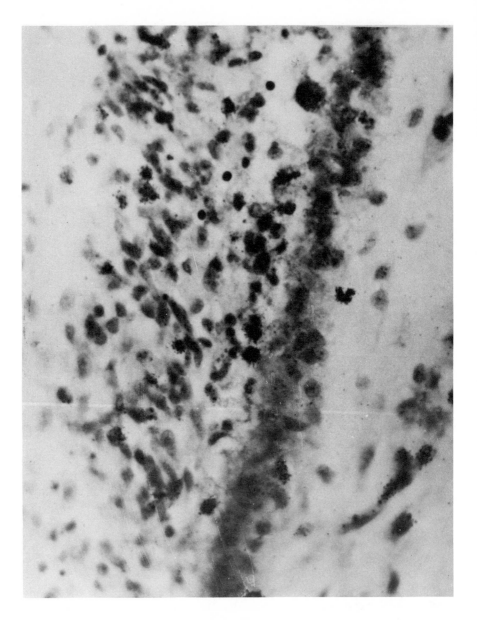

FIGURE 1-6–Photomicrograph of radioactively labeled cells in brain of two-day old rabbit. The little black granules are the results of radioactive thymidine which was incorporated by the cells lying underneath the granules just before cell division. Since the thymidine had been administered 24 hours previously, cells which appear black or with black granules on top of them were ones which were in an active cell division phase in the 24 hours prior to the time this preparation was made. Cells without the black or granulated appearance were not undergoing cell division during this time. (Photograph, R. L. Isaacson. About 300x, H^3 thymidine treatment and thionin.)

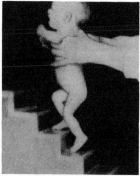

FIGURE 1-7–Three photographs showing some well-developed, premature reflexes of the neonate. The illustration . . . (Peiper, Figure 87) shows the stepping movements of the neonate which can be demonstrated when the neonate is tilted forward. The illustration . . . (Peiper, Figure 88) shows the motor movements which are available for climbing and the illustration . . . (Peiper, Figure 90) shows that these climbing movements can be elicited even when the baby is held in an inverted position. (From A. Peiper. *Cerebral function in infancy and childhood.* New York: Consultants Bureau, 1963.)

Development of Behavioral Reflexes A curious observation by the German pediatrician Peiper and his colleagues may indicate the complexities of development in man. In examining the behavioral abilities of premature fetuses they have found that the response systems required for walking and climbing are present at or before birth, as Figure 1-7 shows. After birth these reflexive acts are lost for a time, then reappear as the stage for walking occurs later in development. We do not know whether these responses are temporarily suppressed only to reemerge later or whether entirely new reflexive systems replace the prenatal ones. The point is that the movements represent a complicated and sophisticated set of responses which emerge at some maturational stage, all at once, as a functional system. In this case the functional system is ready prematurely and must be stored or replaced for later use; the "wisdom of the body" is less than perfect.

As mentioned before, we know as yet little about the neural and morphological correlates of developing behaviors. One line of promising investigation concerns the role of the hormones secreted by the ductless (endocrine) glands in governing development. We have pointed out the importance of these substances in certain cyclic changes in the adult; they have an equally prominent role in the developing organism. For example, the part of the brain most responsible for the motivational systems (the hypothalamus) seems to be sexually neutral at birth and has available to it both male and female behavior patterns for aggression, sex, urination, etc. Which type of behavior will prevail, i.e., male or female, depends upon the presence of male hormone in the blood system of the animal at a critical stage of development. The male hormone plays the active part in differentiating male behavior. If it is absent, female patterns of behavior emerge. The presence of female hormone administered at a critical period to males can disrupt the typical male behavior patterns but does not have an active differentiating role in behavior. Of course, the next exciting step in this research direction will be to discover how the male hormones come to cause the preferential development of male behavior patterns in the brain.

After the early postnatal period, developmental processes continue, possibly throughout the life of the organism. These certainly are modified and controlled by hormone levels, especially at puberty, but the developmental history of the animal is also affected by the interaction of the animal or person with the environment. The interaction of the nervous system of a maturing organism with the environment is the hardest to investigate. We know that the areas of the brain concerned with language usually differentiate on the left rather than the right side of the brain. On the other hand, we know that both sides of the brain have language capacities at birth and yet the left comes to predominate at adulthood. If the left side is damaged early in life, the right can serve as the language region. If the left side is damaged later in life, language functions can be lost permanently. One important job for the future is determining why certain regions of the left side of the brain are chosen for language and why the comparable regions of the right side gradually lose their capacities for these functions.

As we have seen, problems of interest to physiological psychologists can be studied in animal or human development or both.

Clinical Contributions While physiological psychologists have worked in collaboration with people in many different fields, especially physiology, neurophysiology, biochemistry, and anatomy, a new combination of research interests has recently become prominent. This is exemplified by clinical psychologists who investigate patients with brain damage, using methods drawn from experimental and physiological psychology as well as from classical neurology and neurosurgery. Clinical psychologists, with their special training in personality theory, attempt to help people exhibiting "abnormal behaviors." (Clinical psychologists also work in personality research and teaching.)

Some clinical psychologists believe that the information and methods of experimental and physiological psychologists can be applied to the study of human patients to derive new data about the human nervous system. These can then be used to generate new theories of brain function and possibly new ways to treat troubled patients.

Historically the usual methods of clinical psychologists stem from the theories and patterns of treatment developed by Sigmund Freud, the founder of psychoanalysis. Although Freud was biologically oriented early in his career as a physician, this orientation waned as he began to elaborate the principles of psychoanalysis. The diagnostic tools derived from his theoretical framework include the Rorschach (inkblot) test and various tests designed to reveal one's associations to words, pictures, and other stimuli. Clinical psychologists also use methods rising out of the mental measurement movement which originated in Binet's attempts to predict performances of French schoolchildren. Therefore, their techniques are those which are aimed at evaluating the mental states and abilities of people, and they can be applied to patients who have known neurological disorders or are undergoing surgery or stimulation of the brain. In short, clinical psychologists attempt to understand the functions of man's behavior in terms of central nervous system function, applying whatever methods best suit the problem, including those from the traditions of personality theory and mental measurement. To be most effective, clinical psychologists must include in their training the best from both the clinical-personality area and the experimental-physiological area.

Some of the most exciting work has been done in the evaluation of sensory and perceptual disorders experienced by people with bullet wounds and other damage to the areas of the brain concerned with visual sensations. More recent investigations include the evaluation of verbal deficits found after injury to the left temporal lobe, a region of neocortex lying on the lateral surface of the brain, and the comparison of these alterations with changes found after damage to the right temporal lobes. Apparently language usage and higher mathematical abilities are somehow stored on the left side of most brains although the ability to comprehend the spoken word is represented on both sides.

Today it is not uncommon for clinical psychologists with an interest in central nervous system functions to join a research team studying patients undergoing brain surgery. The team effort is aimed both at better understanding of the particular patient and at better understanding of the brain in general. For example, if a patient has convulsive disorders which do not respond to drugs or other medical treatments, the convulsive state is so debilitating as to impair behavior severely, and the focal region of brain disturbance causing the convulsions can be localized, surgical removal of the damaged area may be elected by a competent neurosurgeon. Typically, the operation is performed while the patient is under only mild sedation and local anesthetics to eliminate pain from the skin, the skull, and the sensitive coverings of the brain. The brain itself is not pain-sensitive. When it is exposed, minute amounts of electrical current may have to be applied to localized regions to determine the diseased area. At time of surgery the mental reactions produced by the stimulation can be observed and recorded. Often several different studies can be made of the brain's control of mental and behavioral processes during a single operative procedure without endangering or hurting the patient. Information acquired from electrical stimulation of the brain during surgery could be obtained in no other way.

OVERVIEW

By now it should be clear that physiological psychologists study a wide range of phenomena by an equally wide range of techniques. The following chapters provide, first, the background information essential to understanding the basic structure and functional principles of the body and brain most related to behavior, and, second, samples of research and knowledge in the area. Eager to convey some of the exciting research without the dryness of the usual textbook format, we have tried to present general knowledge and have placed general references, in which the details of the various studies and data can be found, at the ends of some chapters. Also, we have minimized the use of names of scientists in the text, including only those of historical importance or those with whom certain facts or observations are identified. Finally, we have provided, we hope, a reasonably consistent approach stressing fact more than theory. Surely theories do the work of science—they explain and predict behavior—but unfortunately no adequate theory of brain-behavior relations exists. This is the reason so many facts and observations are found in the area today. No one knows yet which ones will be vital to a comprehensive understanding of behavior.

The study of brain-behavior relationships represents a frontier as real as that faced by our astronauts on their way to the moon. Each journey in space produces new information and new theoretical suggestions. Each study in the laboratory contributes its data and advances the understanding of man. There are many similarities between ventures into space and into the physiology of behavior, including the technological support of computers, ultrasonic devices, and sophisticated electronic equipment and the collective efforts of thousands of people. True, the scientist does not share the personal danger of the actual voyagers into space, but he shares with all mankind the danger that we may not come to adequate understanding of man, his motives and behavior, until it is too late.

SUGGESTED READINGS

Isaacson, R. L. (Ed.). *The neuropsychology of development.* New York: Wiley, 1968.

Marler, P., & Hamilton, W. J. *Mechanisms of animal behavior.* New York: Wiley, 1966.

Scott, J. P. *Animal behavior.* Chicago: University of Chicago Press, 1958.

Stevenson, H. W., Hess, E. H., & Rheingold, H. L. (Eds.). *Early behavior: Comparative and developmental approaches.* New York: Wiley, 1967.

Tavolga, W. N. *Principles of animal behavior.* New York: Harper & Row, 1969.

Chapter 2

THE CELL

CHAPTER 2

The nervous system, like the body in general, is composed of tiny functional units called cells. It is well for the student of the behavioral sciences to know all he can about the cell because in the final analysis all mental and behavioral processes are based on cellular activity and interactions between cells. Unfortunately, however, there is much that is *not* known about the structure and function of cells at the present time. For this reason no feature of cellular anatomy or physiology can safely be dismissed as unimportant. Future research may show that what is ignored today is actually crucial to understanding the processes underlying behavior. As one example, many investigators such as Hydén (1961) and Corning and John (1961) are now convinced that memory storage is related to changes in RNA which normally produces proteins in the cell.

All true cells have a basic structure consisting of a *nucleus* embedded in a viscous liquid called *cytoplasm.* The cytoplasm is, in turn, enclosed in a bag or *membrane.* The cytoplasm is not a uniform homogeneous substance, however; it contains many recognizable parts or *organelles.* Some of these are shown in schematic fashion in Figure 2-1. Most organelles (little organs) are constructed of either folded membrane or long fibers composed of protein.

In order to grow, maintain itself in good health, and reproduce, a cell carries out chemical transformations in which substances from the external environment are eaten or ingested, taken apart, then reformed into products useful to the cell. These substances include particles containing carbohydrates, fats, and "foreign" protein. Carbohydrates, in the general sense, include starches, cellulose, and sugars. A carbohydrate is composed of carbon plus two parts of hydrogen for every part of oxygen. Cellulose is a hard-to-digest form of starch, while a starch is merely a string of sugars. A fat is basically a sugar with some oxygen squeezed out. The carbohydrates and fats are used mainly as fuel, along with oxygen. As long as oxygen is freely available, fats are thus a more concentrated form of energy than sugars. Proteins, in contrast, are used both as structural elements of the cell and as secretory products in complex organisms. They are constructed of parts known as *amino acids.* There are 22 common amino acids, and they can be put together in a vast variety of ways. As a rule the foreign protein taken in by the cell has its amino acids put together in a manner which

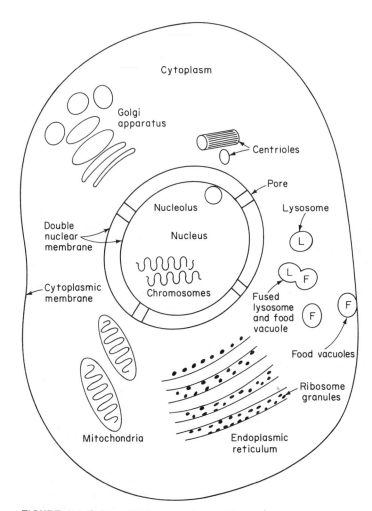

FIGURE 2-1–Schematic diagram of the cell.

makes them useless to the ingesting cell. Thus, the foreign protein is broken down or dismantled and the parts are combined "properly."

The breakdown of foreign protein is accomplished by the *lysosome*. A lysosome is a minute body full of enzymes or digestive chemicals. An enzyme is an organic compound (often a protein) which facilitates chemical transformation while not actually being incorporated into the end product. A digestive enzyme breaks the bonds between the amino acids. The lysosome floats free in the cytoplasm until it collides with a food vacuole. A food vacuole is formed when part of the cell's membrane engulfs a food particle. It then "pinches off," forming a membrane-enclosed glob of food. The lysosomes gravitate toward this food vacuole, and the membranes of the two particles

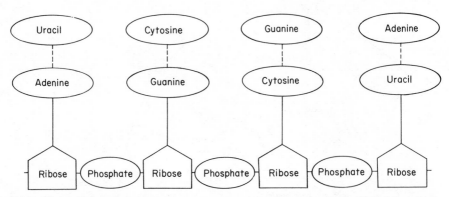

FIGURE 2-2–RNA chain. The four bases shown at the top are not part of the chain. They are included to show how each base has a complementary base which becomes attached by a very weak hydrogen bond (*dotted line*). In RNA uracil and adenine are complements, as are cytosine and guanine.

become fused, with the digestive enzymes turned loose to dismantle the protein while physically separated from the rest of the cell by the membrane. If the digestive enzymes were to escape from the confines of the little bag, they would digest the cell itself. This sometimes happens as a result of injury caused by radiation, and it may also be a normal mechanism for the disappearance of body parts. An example of the latter is the absorption of the tail by the growing frog. After digestion, the amino acids from the food are released into the cytoplasm, where they will eventually be converted into the proteins required by the cell.

Protein manufacture is accomplished with the help of *ribonucleic acid (RNA)*. RNA is composed of sugar (ribose) and phosphate molecules plus four basic compounds: adenine, guanine, cytosine, and uracil. These are arranged in the general pattern shown in Figure 2-2.

Of course, in any sequence of these bases guanine does not have to follow adenine, nor uracil follow cytosine. They can be arranged in any combination along their sugar-phosphate backbone. It is precisely this feature which makes RNA useful, as will be seen later. There are several kinds of RNA, and we have been discussing a type known as *messenger RNA*. The bases arranged along the messenger RNA contain a triplet code. That is, three consecutive bases make up a unit, like uracil-cytosine-uracil. Amino acids become attached to the messenger RNA at the appropriate triplet code region. For every one of the varieties of amino acid there is a code that "suits" it. The amino acids themselves do not, however, recognize the code. Instead, another type of RNA called *transfer RNA* does the recognizing. That is, the transfer RNA (a smaller molecule than the messenger RNA by far) contains a code which is the complement or opposite of the one in the messenger RNA. Although adenine, guanine, cytosine, and uracil can be strung out in any combination, they do not usually interact chemically with other substances which are not the complements. Uracil, for example, is the only base which becomes attached to adenine, while cytosine and guanine, have an affinity for each other (see Figure 2-2). If there is a string of uracil-cytosine-adenine, it will become attached to a complementary string of adenine-guanine-uracil and to no other sequence. For every triplet code sequence in the messenger RNA there is a molecule of transfer RNA with the complement triplet. This complex coding system would be of little use if it were not for the amazing fact that each variety of transfer RNA somehow "knows" which amino acid to seize. A variety of transfer RNA with a certain triplet code will become attached to only one type of amino acid. It will then transport that amino acid to the site of protein synthesis, the messenger RNA. At that point the triplet code end of the transfer RNA will fit precisely into its complement string on the messenger RNA, like a key in a lock. When a number of amino acids are arranged side by side along the messenger RNA they join together to form a complex protein, which is nothing but a string of amino acids. The protein then breaks loose from its messenger RNA mother and floats off to where it is needed. One string of messenger RNA appears to be capable of synthesizing one protein, after which it is dismantled or breaks apart. A schematic diagram of protein synthesis is shown in Figure 2-3.

Protein synthesis does not appear to take place at random locations throughout the cytoplasm but is generally localized along folds of the membrane which are called endoplasmic reticulum. The messenger RNA molecules are attached to particles called ribosomes. The ribosomes also contain a variety of RNA (ribosomal RNA), but it is far more robust, and a given ribosome is used for the manufacture of many strings of protein.

Like most other cellular processes protein synthesis requires energy. This is mostly supplied by adenosine triphosphate (ATP). Because of the nature of its chemical bonds, a great deal of energy is released when the last trailing phosphate is broken off. ATP is manufactured through a long process of chemical transformations of carbohydrates and fats which takes place within an organelle known as the *mitochondrion* (plural: mitochondria). These transformations mainly involve the serial removal of hydrogen, carbon, and oxygen atoms from the primary fats and carbohydrates, ATP being the end product. ATP is physically very similar to one of the bases of RNA (adenine) with its sugar and phosphate. The manufacture of ATP results in the harmless waste products of water and carbon dioxide. ATP can be considered the fuel of the cell; the mitochondrion, the power plant. Mitochondria are invariably found in cellular regions where the greatest energy expenditure is required. They resemble oblong balls composed of an outer membrane and a very wrinkled inner membrane, and the chemical transformations take place on the surface of the inner membrane.

THE MEMBRANE

One of the most important features of the cell is the molecular membrane which encloses it. Without this membrane the organelles and chemical substances necessary to cellular life would be scattered in all directions. The membrane creates an internal environment favorable to life

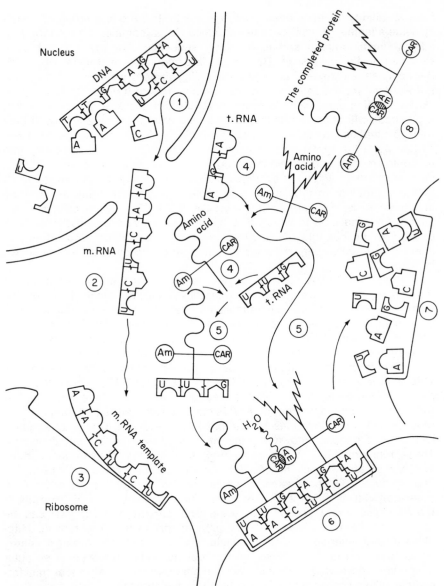

FIGURE 2-3–Protein synthesis. (1) Messenger RNA formed from component parts assembled on DNA template inside the nucleus. (2) Messenger RNA leaves nucleus via pore and enters cytoplasm. (3) Messenger RNA becomes attached at site on a ribosome. (4) Meanwhile, in the cytoplasm transfer RNA becomes attached to its characteristic amino acid. (5) Composite of transfer RNA and amino acid migrates to exact site on messenger RNA which has the complement of its triplet code. (6) Transfer RNA triplets fill sites on messenger RNA, and the attached amino acids join to each other, releasing water. (7) The transfer and messenger RNA molecules break up into component parts as: (8) The joined amino acids (a completed protein) break loose from the transfer RNA.

Outside of cell

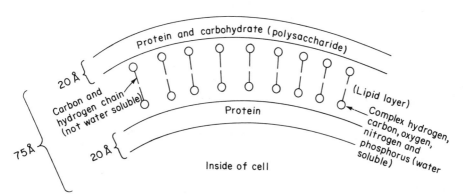

FIGURE 2-4–The unit membrane.

through the selective exclusion of certain substances and the active transport of others into or out of the cytoplasm.

The membrane is so thin that it cannot be seen even under the highest magnification of light microscopes. However, chemical analysis, x-ray diffraction techniques, and electron microscopy have shown that it is composed of three layers, as can be seen in Figure 2-4. In the inner and outer layers, composed primarily of protein, the molecules are organized horizontally. The center layer, composed of a kind of fat called lipid, has a vertical or radial organization. The thinness of the membrane can be better appreciated when one realizes that over 50,000 separate membranes stacked in a pile would be no thicker than a pencil line. The three-layered membrane discussed here is referred to as a *unit membrane.* It was once thought that membranes in different regions of the cell were of different thickness (and possibly construction), but it is now known that in many instances the thickness is a multiple of the unit membrane and that extra thickness must therefore be due to folding.

An example is the case of the nuclear membrane. The nucleus has long been known to be surrounded by a double layer of membrane (two unit membranes). Between the layers is a space which is continuous with one phase of the endoplasmic reticulum. *Endoplasmic reticulum* is the term applied to the mazelike regions of cytoplasm shown in Figure 2-1. Now, it has often been observed that if ribosomes are arrayed along one side of one of these "walls" there will be no ribosomes on the opposite side. Thus, there are said to be two phases. The space between the two nuclear membranes is continuous with the phase of the endoplasmic reticulum which does not contain ribosomes. The nuclear membranes are frequently interrupted by pores through which large molecules can pass, and the so-called pores communicate with a phase which does contain ribosomes. All of these puzzling features can be readily explained by the theory of Robertson (1962), who believes that the endoplasmic reticulum and the nuclear membrane are

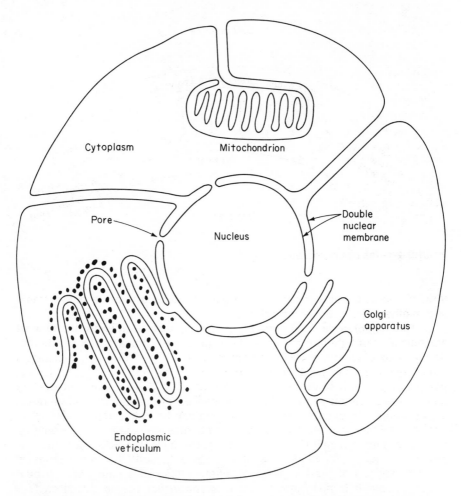

FIGURE 2-5—Folded-membrane theory of cellular construction. Note that all parts are constructed of a single continuous membrane. (Robertson. The membrane of the living cell. Copyright © 1962 by Scientific American, Inc. All rights reserved.)

really just infoldings from the membrane surrounding the cell, as can be seen in Figure 2-5. According to this theory the nonribosomal phase is actually *outside* the cell. Both the wrinkling of the individual cell and the convolutions of the cerebral cortex with its billions of cells could be due to the same inexorable law of mathematics: As the radius of a sphere increases, its surface increases as the square of the radius while the volume increases as the cube of the radius. Now, if there is a constant relationship between a unit of volume and a unit of surface, the surface area of a growing glob must increase relatively faster than its volume. In short, it must become wrinkled. Thus, we would expect larger cells and brains to be more wrinkled than smaller ones, all else being equal, because there are in fact many constant relationships between units of surface and volume. For example, the chemical reactions taking place in a given volume of fluid require a given surface area for dissipation of the heat generated by the reactions and for the transfer of oxygen or other substances into or out of the region of action. These factors are extremely important in governing the size and shape of all organisms.

Membranes can apparently be manufactured inside the cell. A region known as the *Golgi organ* is a site where secretory products are encapsulated in membrane bags or vesicles. This packaging always takes place within the cell body and not in its extensions such as the dendrites or axons of neural cells. The vesicles must then be transported to the region where they are secreted. The Golgi organ looks peculiar because it is essentially a pile of flattened bags in various stages of completion and filling.

THE NUCLEUS

The nucleus is more or less sealed off from the cytoplasm by a double membrane. Communication between the fluids of the nucleus and the cytoplasm occurs through the "pores," regions where the folding membranes do not quite meet. A cell deprived of its nucleus cannot divide or reproduce, but it can live for a short time. It eventually dies because its stores of RNA get used up and protein synthesis can no longer occur. One vital function of the nucleus is to supply the cytoplasm with fresh messenger and transfer RNA so that protein synthesis can continue at a proper rate. The nucleus contains the master template from which RNA is constructed. This template is very much like RNA and even has a similar name: *deoxyribonucleic acid* (*DNA*). It, too, has a backbone of sugar and phosphate molecules, but the sugar lacks one oxygen atom, as is signified by the "deoxy" part of the term. It is also composed of four bases, three of them the same as in RNA: adenine, guanine, cytosine. Instead of uracil, however, DNA has *thymine.* The thymine is the complement of adenine, just as uracil is in RNA. A string of DNA produces a string of RNA through the attachment of complements. In this event the RNA will have a uracil wherever the DNA has an adenine. When a string of such messenger RNA has been made, it migrates out through a pore into the cytoplasm and eventually becomes attached to a ribosome, where it forms a template for protein synthesis.

DNA has one property which is important to the survival of the species, not merely the individual: it periodically makes a copy of itself. When DNA is not being directly used in synthesis, it is arranged into a spiral consisting of two complementary strands: where one strand has adenine, the other has thymine. When the cell is ready for reproduction or division, the strands unwind and each makes its complement, so that the cell ends up with two identical pairs of strands. A similar use of both strands may occur during RNA manufacture, one strand making messenger RNA and the other transfer RNA, with its complementary code. In any case, the DNA code is what differentiates butterflies from men. It must not be regarded, however, as anything like a blueprint for construction. Instead, it should be thought of as an initiator of a sequence of events. The DNA produces RNA, which then produces specified proteins and enzymes, which interact to produce still other substances, etc. We are the end result of a great many such interactions between manufactured and ingested products, and the interactions need not be specified in a code. They are inevitable in a given biochemical environment.

If any segment of the DNA code is disrupted or changed by radiation or other means, a different chain of events will ensue. In a single cell, any change is usually lethal. But worse, the DNA will reproduce itself in the changed form, provided that the cell is not killed outright. This is called a mutation. Not all aberrant individuals are the result of mutation, however. Often a strange or deformed individual is due to an improbable combination of genes which are carried by many individuals in the population.

Finally, the reader is probably wondering why the cells of a given individual look so different if each is supposed to have the same DNA. The answer to this question is not entirely known, but it is suspected that various portions of the DNA are masked or inhibited in different types of cells. No single type of cell would use all of its DNA.

THE CENTRIOLE

The last common organelle to be discussed here is the centriole. It consists of a pair of cylindrical structures usually located near the nucleus. They appear to be inactive in the intervals between cell division, but just prior to cell division they spring into action. First they divide into two pairs, and one of the pairs migrates to the opposite side of the nucleus. Each pair then becomes a focal point of radiating fibers which attach at certain locations on the chromosomes, the complex structures which contain the DNA. Half of the chromosomes are then drawn by the contracting fibers to each side, and the nucleus disappears while the cell is pinched into two parts. Centrioles may also be involved in the production of the very thin tubules or fibers which are found in such great numbers in nerve cells. The axon is literally a tube full of still smaller tubes. Many of the specialized structures of cells seem to be made of centrioles, as they have an almost identical basic construction. In the sensory receptors called *hair cells* at least one so-called "hair" is a modified centriole. A modified centriole also connects the receptive part of the rods and cones (visual receptors) to the portion of the receptor which generates electrical activity. Centrioles may turn out to be of far greater importance than is currently thought, and the reason why some cells do not divide may be that these organelles have become adapted to other functions.

CELLULAR ACTIVITIES

Single cells which are not highly specialized components of a complex organism have certain primitive capacities that appear to be basic properties of living organisms. Single-celled organisms (protozoa) are irritable or sensitive to a variety of external stimuli such as heat, light, and chemical concentrations. They selectively take in (eat) some substances and excrete others. Cells get about in a number of ways: by lashing tail-like structures (the flagellates), by rowing with tiny oarlike processes (the ciliates), and by extension and retraction of the cell mass itself by means of false feet or pseudopods (the amebas). Through these primitive capacities the cell manages to feed itself, rid itself of waste products, avoid danger, and reproduce itself. It is even suspected that protozoa modify their behavior as a result of past experiences, but this ability has not yet been decisively demonstrated.

The protozoa of the present time have had hundreds of millions of years in which to evolve, and it is likely that they represent the ultimate development of abilities in a single cell. Any improvement in one ability would probably be coupled with a decrement in others. By analogy, an athlete training for the decathlon can improve his performance in the shot put by gaining weight, but his high jump or pole vault performance will consequently suffer. Since the athlete, like the protozoon, must perform many different tasks, he must settle upon an optimal weight and not deviate from it.

A way out of this apparent dilemma appeared when cells began to form cooperative colonies or societies. Some cells became concerned with movement (prototypes of muscle cells), others with secretion (prototypes of glands), others with sensitivity or irritability (prototypes of sensory receptors), and so on. Along with specialization of function came a reduction in the capacities of individual cells. The specialized cells became dependent for certain functions upon other cells. In this manner the total collection of cells gained in its overall ability to deal with the world, but at the expense of the independence of the individual members. We seem to have benefited by the trade.

The increase in size and complexity of the colony presented many new requirements. The group needed to move as a whole, and better organization was required to do so efficiently. The multicellular organism must have a means through which decisions among possible courses of action can be made and carried out. In very primitive organisms these decisions, such as whether to move in one direction or the other, could be made by the receptor cells. An organism might, for example, have a built-in decision rule always to move in the direction corresponding to the location of those sensory receptors which detect light. Even here, however, there must be communication with the effector cells which actually accomplish the movement; it is carried out by a cell specialized in the ability to conduct excitation: the nerve cell or neuron. The neuron developed as a communication link between receptors and effectors, and for this purpose it became greatly elongated in order to span long distances.

Primitive communication functions are performed by a network of nerve fibers such as that covering the penumbra or "umbrella" of the jellyfish. This situation can be pictured if one imagines an umbrella with a fishnet thrown over it. The fibers cross over one another and make numerous contacts. The nerve net is stimulated by receptors, which in our analogy would be arranged around the edges of the umbrella. When the receptors are stimulated (by touch, for example), the nerve net is stimulated at that point, and excitation travels in a wave spreading to all other points of the penumbra. The effectors nearest the point of stimulation are excited first and the ones farthest removed at a later time as the wave of excitation spreads spatially. A nerve net communication system is characteristic of only the most lowly animals. Probably the "highest" animal to retain a nerve net is the flatworm (Platyhelminthes). The flatworm is also thought to be the lowest animal form to possess the beginnings of a central nervous system, a system differing in many respects from the primitive nerve net.

The central nervous system developed when animals, and their behavior, became more complex. In the higher animals a course of action depends less upon a single type of stimulation than upon an overall picture provided by many different specialized receptors. An organism might, for example, approach food which is both warm and slightly acidic, but not cold and acidic or warm and alkaline. Of course, even the lowest animal must make decisions much more complex than this, and the nerve cell became specialized not only for transmission but also for complex decision making. It is interesting that as the mammalian nervous system develops from the embryo to the adult state it is the long-axon neurons which evolve first from the generalized neuroblasts. The interneurons, which probably perform the integrative functions, are quite tardy in their development and continue to divide and differentiate (assume adult shape) long after the larger cells have ceased to divide. A central nervous system appears in animals that have become elongated and acquired bilateral symmetry (have nearly identical right and left halves). These animals tend to move in one direction and thus possess a head and tail end. The head end, meeting the environment, is the logical location for the distance receptors. A mass of integrative neurons then develops near the distance receptors, or those receptors that guide the animal's movements into new territory. This head ganglion (or primitive brain) extends long fibers down into the tail end of the animal, in a bundle analogous to our spinal cord in some respects. In the flatworm there are two such fiber bundles, connected in numerous places so that this portion of the central nervous system is said to resemble a ladder. The head ganglion also is paired, like our cerebral or cerebellar hemispheres, with some connecting fibers uniting the two members.

Another form of intercellular communication is by signals or hormones secreted into the bloodstream. This is a most ancient system but persists in the higher animals such as man. Our glands of internal secretion (endocrine glands) are controlled by the pituitary, which is in turn controlled or modified by the neural cells of the hypothalamus. Thus, even this form of communication is ultimately directed by the decision-making cells of the central nervous system.

THE NERVE CELL

One of the basic components of a neuron is the cell body (soma), which generally has a large number of protoplasmic extensions known as *dendrites* (see Figure 2-6). Since the material inside the dendrites is much like that

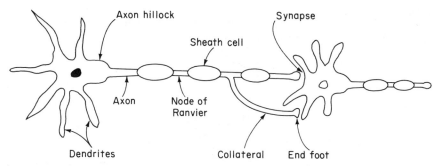

FIGURE 2-6–Schematic nerve cell.

inside the cell body cytoplasm, the dendrites can be considered extensions of the cell body. Both the dendrites and the surface of the cell body are receiving areas for incoming impulses from other neurons or from receptor cells. The cell body also has a bulge or swelling known as the *axon hillock* because a long slender tubelike fiber known as the *axon* extends from it. The interior material of the axon differs considerably from that of the dendrites or cell body. Chemical synthesis, for example, does not occur in axons. The axon, however, is in need of the products of this synthesis, and they are transported from the cell body all the way out to the very end of the axon, where swellings are formed known as boutons or *end feet.* Excitation is normally conducted in a direction from the cell body and axon hillock down the axon to the end feet. The end feet are in very close proximity to the next cell in the chain (neuron, muscle, or gland) but stop just short of making physical contact. A narrow space of 100 angstrom units separates the end foot of one neuron from the dendrite or cell body of another. This space, the *synaptic cleft,* is so narrow that roughly two and a half million such spaces would be required to make up 1 inch. Transmission across the synapses is polarized. That is, excitation passes from the end foot to the dendrite or cell body and not vice versa.

The above description is an oversimplified composite picture of a "typical" neuron. There are a great many different kinds of neurons, however, and at least three general classes, as can be seen in Figure 2-7. These main classes are sensory, motor, and internuncial (interneurons). Here the term "sensory neuron" refers to the type of neuron which is often the first neural link in a sensory chain of communication from the periphery to the central nervous system. Those cells which form later portions of the chain have distinctly different shapes. The sensory neuron either contacts a receptor cell or has a bare ending which acts as a receptor. Some sensory neurons are called *bipolar* cells; others, *unipolar.* A unipolar cell appears to be merely a more developed version of a bipolar one, and all grades between the two extremes can be found. What makes these neurons unusual is that they have no true dendrites; their extensions or processes all have the physical structure of axons and conduct electrical potentials characteristic of axons, as will be discussed later. That portion of the fiber which contacts a receptor and conducts excitation toward the cell body has been called a

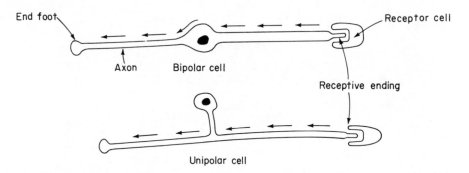

First-order sensory neurons

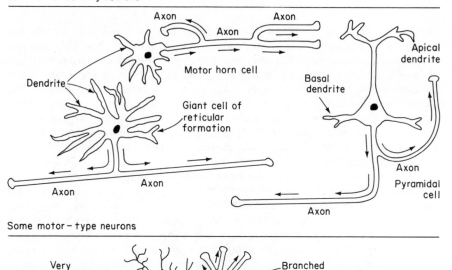

Some motor – type neurons

Some interneurons

FIGURE 2-7–Some types of neurons. Arrows indicate direction in which impulses travel.

functional dendrite. The true receiving or sensory portion of the "functional dendrite," however, is the very tip. This tip is not surrounded by a sheath, as is most of the rest of the fiber, and thus is a bare ending. Even when the fiber contacts a sensory receptor, it still has a bare ending, which is inserted into the receptor. Impulses are initiated at this ending and transmitted up the axon toward the cell body, and they continue on past the cell body and into the central nervous system. In this case the bare ending functions as a dendrite. The portion of the fiber entering the central nervous system then makes a synapse with the next neuron.

There are also two types of motor neuron. The first, found in the spinal cord, has many branching dendrites and a long axon, much like the cell pictured in Figure 2-6. The axon extends out to a skeletal muscle. It should be noted at this time that neurons rarely, if ever, have a single unbranching axon. After the axon proceeds for a short distance from the hillock it generally branches into a main axon and a smaller *collateral* axon, which often loops back to the cell body region. In addition, many axons ramify or branch into numerous fibers before synapsing with the next cell.

Another type of motor cell, found in the cortex, is termed a *pyramidal* cell because its cell body is pyramid-shaped. A long "apical" dendrite extends upward from the peak (apex) of the pyramid and, after traveling a relatively long distance, branches profusely. Basal dendrites extend from the bottom "corners" of the pyramid. Pyramidal cells are located in two different layers of the cerebral cortex (layers III and V), and are present in great concentration (and with the largest size) in the motor regions of the cortex. Although we are referring to these cells as motor, perhaps they are better thought of in terms of size. They are the largest cortical cells and thus capable of having very long axons. (The length of a neuron's axon is largely determined by the volume of its cell body.) Thus, it might be more accurate to view these cells as long-distance transmitters.

While both sensory and motor neurons may have extremely long axons (sometimes more than 3 feet long), the remaining neural type, the interneuron, is characterized by its short axon with numerous collaterals. The dendrites (also profusely branched) and axons of interneurons usually are confined to a very restricted part of the brain, such as a particular nucleus. Interneurons are found everywhere in the brain and spinal cord and are especially concentrated in sensory cortex, where they are called *granule cells.* These are most densely packed in the cortical layers (II and IV) which receive incoming sensory impulses.

GLIAL CELLS

Any discussion of neurons is incomplete unless their close relatives and allies the glial cells are included. The central nervous system of man contains an estimated 10 billion neurons but 5 to 10 times as many nonneural or glial cells. These cells do not appear to transmit excitation but they do seem to perform many functions vital to the nervous system. They provide structural support and they line the blood vessels to form an impassable barrier (the blood-brain barrier) to noxious chemicals. They also may pass vital chemicals over to the neurons. Several varieties of glial cells are shown in Figure 2-8. Glial cells also keep the brain tidy by removing (ingesting) dead tissue and are very important for insulating axons.

The axon is not bare. It has satellite cells wrapped around it at intervals, giving its microscope structure the appearance of a string of sausages (see Figure 2-6). The "links" are known as the *myelin sheath;* the relatively

Schwann's cell (peripheral nervous system) or oligodendroglial cell (CNS) wrapped around single axon. The axon is said to be heavily myelinated.

One sheath cell surrounding many small- diameter axons. These are the so-called unmyelinated or lightly myelinated fibers.

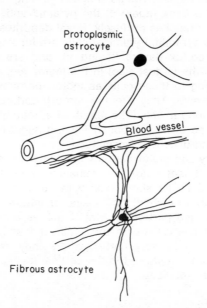

Protoplasmic astrocyte

Blood vessel

Fibrous astrocyte

Note : Both astrocyte types surround the blood vessels.

FIGURE 2-8–Some types of glial cells. (Adapted from Robertson. The membrane of the living cell. Copyright © 1962 by Scientific American, Inc. All rights reserved.

bare spots between links, the *nodes of Ranvier.* The satellite cells within the brain and spinal cord are known as one form of *oligodendroglia.* Similar sheath cells which wrap the axons found in nerves (outside the central nervous system) are called *Schwann cells.* The myelin of the myelin sheath is a fatty substance thought to provide electrical insulation. Actually, myelin is merely the middle layer of the membrane shown in Figure 2-4. The myelin sheath is composed of a great many layers which are left behind as the sheath cell winds itself around the axon. Although a single layer of membrane is nearly transparent, many layers together have a white appearance. The parts of the brain called gray matter have relatively few heavily myelinated axons while white matter is packed with them.

By now the reader is probably wondering what is meant by excitation, reception, decision making, and the transmission of excitation. All of these functions have been related to electrical and chemical changes across the membrane of the neural cell body, dendrites, and axon. We shall examine them next.

TECHNIQUES OF ELECTRICAL RECORDING

Most of what is now known or inferred about excitation or transmission in neurons is based upon studies of the electrical potential of the nerve cell. The interior of the neuron is electrically negative, and the decision-making and transmitting properties of neurons are related to changes in this potential. Before the reader can evaluate this evidence, he must know something of the nature of electrical potentials and the way they are recorded.

Electrical phenomena are due to charged particles and movements of charged particles. Atoms consist of a nucleus, containing positively charged protons, and uncharged or neutral neutrons. In the Niels Bohr theory of atomic structure, which is more than adequate for our purposes, negatively charged electrons are located in concentric orbits around the nucleus. An electron has one unit of negative charge; a proton, one unit of positive charge. Positive and negative charges attract each other, and two negative or two positive charges are mutually repulsive. In an atom the number of positive charges exactly equals the number of negative.

Chemical and electrochemical events are mainly due to the arrangement of the orbiting electrons in "shells." There are a series of shells (or possible shells) around the nucleus, and an electron never orbits halfway between two shells but always in one or the other. In addition, each shell has a fixed number of electrons which can occupy it. For instance, the shell closest to the nucleus, the inner shell, can accept only 2 orbiting electrons. If an atom has more than 2 electrons, then some must occupy outer shells. The next shell has room for 8 electrons. When this is filled, the electrons begin occupying the third shell, and so on. It is obvious that if the number of protons in the nucleus of an element ranges from 1 (hydrogen) to well over 100 (in the very heavy elements) most atoms will not have fully occupied shells. In sodium (Na), for example, there are 11 protons in the nucleus and thus 11 orbiting electrons: 2 in the first shell, 8 in the next, and only 1 in the outermost shell, which has a capacity of 8. When the number of electrons in the outermost shell is less than half of capacity, they tend to be loosely held and easily lost. Metals are composed primarily of atoms with loosely held electrons, which therefore tend to move about freely and to respond quickly to potential differences. For example, if a metal wire is connected to the positive and negative poles of a battery, the loose electrons of the metal will rush to the positive pole. Electrons from the negative pole of the battery will enter the wire (which has become positive because of the loss of electrons). The entering electrons collide with those in the wire, which then collide with others, etc., until there is a flow of current through the wire. Such a flow or wave of collisions travels with nearly the speed of light, but the individual electrons do not.

When an atom loses its loosely bound electrons it becomes a *positive ion*. The ion as a whole is positively charged because it has more protons in its nucleus than it has electrons orbiting in its shells. A positive ion is signified by the same symbol used for the atom but with a number of plus signs equal to the excess of protons. The sodium atom, for example, is Na while the sodium ion is Na^+.

Atoms having an outermost shell more than half full of electrons tend to accept extra electrons rather than give them up—just enough electrons to fill the outer shell. Chlorine, for example, is one electron short in its outer shell. When it seizes that electron, it becomes the negatively charged chloride ion Cl^-. The extra electron gives chloride a net negative charge of -1.

When atoms of substances such as sodium and chlorine are placed in a water solution they tend to become rapidly ionized into charged particles, and the particles tend to become equally distributed in all parts of the container. In any restricted portion of the container there will be equal numbers of positive and negative ions and thus no potential differences anywhere in the solution.

The term *electrical potential* is used to describe a condition in which all charged particles are *not* evenly and uniformly distributed. An electrical potential exists between two points when they differ in the balance between positive and negative charges. If one point is neutral and the other has more negative than positive charges, the excess negative charges in the latter region will have a tendency to move toward the first point. If they do not, it is because there is no path between the two points along which the charges can flow. Such a path is called a *conductor*. When it does not exist, the two points are *insulated* from each other. For example. if you rub an amber bead, you remove some electrons. The bead is then positive because it has more protons than electrons. Since the ground is assumed to be electrically neutral, some electrons should flow from the ground to the bead because the bead has a positive potential. They do not do so, however, because the air between the bead and the ground is an effective insulator. If the bead is actually touched to moist ground, the moisture acts as a conductor. Exactly enough electrons will then flow into the bead to make it neutral again.

Whether an electrical potential is positive or negative depends, of course, on whether there is a relative excess of positive or negative charges in one region as compared to another. Potentials are always relative—one point has a potential relative to the other. If one of two points is neutral (such as a point connected to ground by a good conductor), the potential between them can be considered absolute, for all practical purposes. If both points are insulated from ground, however, one point is negative only *in comparison* to the other. Actually, both points might well be negative as compared to ground, but one might have a larger excess of electrons than the other.

PROCESS OF ELECTRICAL RECORDING

For the most part we will be concerned with recording or detecting differences in electrical potential, as measured in volts (V.) or thousandths of volts (millivolts or mV.). The electrical potential at a given point can be measured by connecting that point, by way of a good conductor such as a metal wire, with a reference point or ground. If the point is negative, electrons will flow down the wire from that point to ground. If the point has a potential of −100 volts, many more electrons will flow in the wire than would if the potential were −50 volts. To record the exact potential we need only insert a measuring device somewhere along the wire. The most accurate and commonly used measuring device is the oscilloscope. An oscilloscope is much like a television set. It has a cathode-ray tube coated with phosphors on its face. When the phosphors are struck by electrons, they emit photons or visible light. At the opposite end of the tube is a filament from which electrons are "boiled off" and repelled. A positively charged grid starts them streaming in a beam toward the face of the tube, where they strike at one point and produce a dot of light. This beam is made to move regularly back and forth across the face of the scope by means of horizontal plates placed on either side of the tube. When the left-hand plate is positive, the beam is attracted to the left since it consists of electrons, which are negatively charged. As this plate is gradually made less positive until it reaches neutrality and then gradually becomes negative (while the right plate becomes positive), the beam sweeps from the left side of the scope to the right side. Oscilloscopes are made so that when the beam sweeps across in this way it instantly flicks back to the left as soon as it reaches the extreme right. The speed of the sweep can be varied, but at any setting a given distance of travel represents a given amount of time. Thus, horizontal distance is a *time axis.*

The reader has probably already guessed how this device could be used to record potentials: simply by the introduction of another set of plates in the vertical dimension. One plate can be used as a reference, or connected to ground, while the other can be connected by wires with the point from which we want to record. If this point is positive, the beam traveling across the scope face will be deflected upward (if we have made the top plate our "hot" one). If the recording point is negative, it will make the top plate negative and the beam will be repelled downward. The direction of the deflection then indicates the positivity-negativity of the point recorded from, while the distance of the deflection indicates the magnitude of the potential. Because the horizontal sweep is a time axis, we can even say how long our point retained its potential. Some biological electrical potentials appear and disappear in much less than the twinkling of an eye (a thousandth of a second or less), and thus our horizontal sweep speed must be so fast that a thousandth of a second represents an appreciable distance along the sweep. The horizontal sweep can also be set so that it does not begin until a signal is received. If the experimenter is studying the reaction of a nerve cell to electrical stimulation, for example, he might set the scope so that the beam remains at the left side until he stimulates. The stimulation then starts the beam sweeping at a set rate of speed, and the electrical response of the neuron will deflect it after it has traveled some distance. By measuring how far the beam has traveled, he can say how long it took the neuron to respond.

Finally, if we wish to record a potential at a given point, we must be sure to record from only that point. Our wires must be insulated everywhere but at that point. If the point happens to be very small, such as the inside of a neuron, the wire electrode must be sharpened (usually by acid) until it is less than 1 micron (1 μ = 1/1000 mm.) in diameter. It can then be insulated by being dipped in varnish or plastic and dried. When the insulated material dries, it contracts and pulls away from the very tip of the electrode. Strangely, it is easier to penetrate and record from neurons by using a glass tube filled with a conducting salt solution as the electrode. The glass tube or pipette (which is actually the insulator, not the electrode itself) is heated and pulled until it snaps. It is then filled with a solution containing ions, and this solution is connected with the plate of an oscilloscope by wires.

We are now ready to record the electrical potential of a neuron. Very slowly the electrode is inserted into the brain or spinal cord in a region where cell bodies are grouped together. As a reference point we would probably attach one wire (connected to one plate of the oscilloscope) to a muscle or other wet body tissue, since this can be assumed to be neutral. As the tip of the recording electrode is lowered, it records a potential of zero for a long time, indicating that the extracellular fluids are neutral. Finally, there is a sudden change and the electrode tip records a steady potential of about −70 mV. The cell body has been penetrated, and what we are recording is the *resting potential* of the neuron. The electrode tip, fine as it is, is still too thick to get inside an axon or fine dendrite. With luck, the membrane of the cell body will form a seal around the electrode and we will be able to record for hours. With bad luck, the membrane will be ruptured and the cell will sputter and die as it loses its fluids. The name "resting potential" refers to the fact that even though the electrical potential fluctuates so that the cell is sometimes less negative than usual (less *polarized*) and sometimes even more negative than usual (*hyperpolarized*) it tends unless stimulated always to return to the base level of −70 mV.

ELECTRICAL PROPERTIES OF THE NEURON

In addition to the resting potential, the neuron is characterized by several types of short-lived changes in its intracellular potential. These changes (and the resting potential itself) are related to changes in concentration of various ions inside and outside the cell membrane. Before discussing them, however, we will first examine the event which is actually measured: the electrical potential. If we watch the face of our oscilloscope for some time, we see that the internal potential does not hold steady at −70 mV. It might jump to −61 within a couple of milliseconds and then drift back to the resting potential level after perhaps 10 milliseconds or so. At other times a similar deflection might occur but in the other direction so that the internal potential is more negative than usual for a short period. These changes are called *graded potentials* because they can take any value between the resting potential and roughly 10 mV. to either side—between −80 and −60, in other words. The peak deflection of the change might have been 1 or 2 mV., or maybe 3.1416.

When the neuron becomes hyperpolarized by a graded potential (more negative), it eventually drifts back to the resting level. When the graded change is in the other direction (depolarization), however, it can trigger another type of potential. In order to do this the deflection usually must be about 10 mV. of depolarization, bringing the cell interior to −60 mV. This is the threshold level for the initiation of an explosive change in the membrane potential known as the *action potential* or spike. An action potential consists of a sudden change in which the membrane potential not only goes to zero but overshoots so that the cell interior is actually about 40 mV. positive for an instant. From this peak the potential quickly returns to a level even more negative than before, as can be seen in Figure 2-9a. When this course of events is displayed on an oscilloscope, with positive up (the usual convention), the beam seems to trace out a sharp spike, origin of the nickname "spike" for action potential. During the hypernegativity which immediately follows the spike it is more difficult than usual to fire another action potential, but with relatively intense stimulation the neuron can fire again during this period. Consequently the hypernegative state has been termed the *relative refractory period.* The period of rapid change or the spike has been termed the *absolute refractory period* because, as a rule, another action potential cannot be generated at the same location until the cell interior has returned to a level somewhere near the resting potential. (Some brain cells appear to be exceptions to this rule.) The action potential, unlike the graded changes previously discussed, either occurs or does not occur. When it does, its peak is always at the same value, usually +40 mV. For this reason the spike or action potential is said to be *all-or-none* instead of graded.

Action potentials are generated somewhere on the surface of the cell body or dendritic membrane. There is persuasive evidence that in some types of neuron spike generation occurs at the axon hillock, a bulge in the cell body which is the root of the axon. The action potential, after initiation, travels down the axon from the hillock region to the end feet with no detectable loss in size along the way. In strong contrast is the spread of graded potentials from the site of their initiation on the receiving side of a synapse; they lessen in size as they spread or travel along a membrane. When the action potential reaches the end feet which synapse with the next cell (muscle, gland, or neuron) in the chain, it does not simply jump the gap or synaptic cleft; there is a "considerable" delay (.5 msec.) before the initiation of a response (graded potential) by the next cell. Although it appears short, this delay is sufficiently long to rule out the likelihood that transmission involves a simple electrical or electrochemical change acting across a small (100 Å) synaptic cleft. Transmission across a synapse depends upon the secretion of a chemical transmitter substance by the end feet, which acts to produce a graded potential change in the postsynaptic cell, as will be

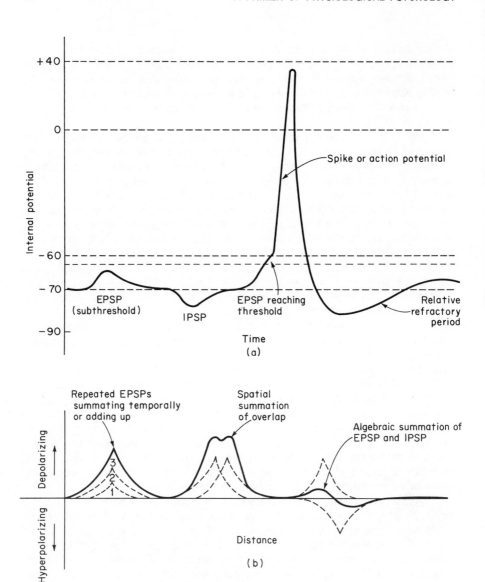

FIGURE 2-9–(a) Potential changes over time in the graded and action potentials. **(b)** Spatial and temporal summation of the graded potentials.

discussed more fully later. For the present, we will examine the electrical activity recorded in a cell when it is stimulated across a synapse by the end feet of other neurons.

The cells on the ventral or belly side of the spinal cord are very large and relatively easy to record from. Their axons run out to the skeletal muscles and cause these to twitch or contract. The location of these neurons is termed the ventral horn of the cord, so they are known as *ventral* or *motor horn cells.* Since motor horn cells are vital components of spinal reflexes, they have sensory fibers synapsing on them. The sensory fibers enter the cord in bundles on the back or dorsal side of the spinal cord and are called *dorsal roots.* Some synapse directly with motor horn cells; others synapse with small interneurons which then synapse with the motor horn cells. For any given motor horn cell it is possible to locate fibers in the dorsal root which activate or inhibit that cell either directly or via interneurons. By stimulating these fibers artificially (electrically) we can activate the end feet synapsing with the neuron from which we are recording. In this way it is possible to examine the changes that occur when a neuron is stimulated across synapses.

THE EXCITORY POSTSYNAPTIC POTENTIAL

If we stimulate fibers making direct contact with the neuron from which we are recording, the result is a slight depolarization. The interior of the neuron becomes less negative and then drifts back to its resting level. If the intensity of the stimulation is very low, it will produce only a very small change. If the stimulation is more intense, a larger change will be produced. We know, however, that arriving at each end foot synapsing with our neuron are only all-or-none action potentials. Thus, the relation between the intensity of the stimulus and the magnitude of the graded potential response must be due to the recruitment of more end feet by the more intense stimulation of the sensory nerve. In any event, the type of change in which the cell interior becomes depolarized so that it falls somewhere between −70 and −60 mV. is called the *excitatory postsynaptic potential* or EPSP. It is called postsynaptic because it occurs on the receiving side of the synapse. It is excitatory because if it is large enough to cause the cell interior to reach a threshold value of about −60 mV. the action potential or spike occurs. The EPSP, in other words, is excitatory because it can trigger a spike if it reaches a certain critical size. Such an effective EPSP is rarely generated across a single synapse by only one end foot. Although some neurons appear to be capable of being fired by the activation of one end foot on their dendrites or cell bodies, most threshold EPSPs are the combined result of hundreds or even thousands of end feet which cover the surface of the postsynaptic neuron.

There are two ways in which EPSPs that are individually ineffective in triggering spikes can be made to trigger them in combination. Both ways depend upon the fact that EPSPs can summate in both time and space (see Figure 2-9b). When an end foot is activated, it produces an EPSP which has a maximum value right under the synapse. At that point the postsynaptic membrane is maximally depolarized. Neighboring regions of the membrane are, however, also depolarized to some extent, but the farther they are removed spatially from the activated synapse, the less depolarized they are. The graded potential travels spatially or spreads out, but with a decrement or loss in size. It is thus distinctly unlike the action potential, which might travel a yard or more and still be of the same magnitude. Now suppose that an EPSP produced across one synapse is not large enough to trigger a spike. A spike may still be generated if a closely neighboring synapse is activated at the same time as the first. At a point halfway between the two synapses the separate EPSPs overlap and combine additively. The process is called *spatial summation.* If, for example, each of two neighboring end feet produce EPSPs of 8 mV. maximum, at a point halfway between them this might decline to, let us say, 5 mV. The halfway point would then be depolarized 5 mV. from each of two sources, and these would summate to produce a combined depolarization of 10 mV., enough to generate an action potential.

EPSPs also summate over time, or *temporally.* When a synapse is activated, it takes a few milliseconds for the consequent EPSP to reach maximum value, and then it gradually dies down over the next 10 msec. If another impulse arrives at the synapse before the first EPSP has faded, it will be built upon the remains of the first. A synapse which produces an EPSP of only 5 mV. maximum may be made to trigger a spike if it is stimulated many times in rapid succession, at interstimulus intervals so short that the preceding EPSP does not have time to disappear before the succeeding one is generated.

THE INHIBITORY POSTSYNAPTIC POTENTIAL

A second type of graded potential has many properties of the EPSP but is inhibitory instead of excitatory. If we stimulated sensory fibers which synapsed with interneurons, which in turn synapsed with our motor horn cell, we might see something quite the opposite of the EPSP. The cell interior would become hyperpolarized by anywhere between 1 and 10 mV., so that it might reach a level of -80 mV. for a short time. This *inhibitory postsynaptic potential* or IPSP never triggers a spike except under very unusual experimental conditions. Instead, the IPSP diminishes the probability of a spike's occurring by making it more difficult for the cell to become depolarized enough to reach threshold value for an action potential. IPSPs can summate both spatially and temporally, like EPSPs. They also summate or interact with EPSPs, but the summation is algebraic. An IPSP, in other words, subtracts from an EPSP. Thus, we have two types of graded potentials. One acts to stimulate a neuron into generating an action potential; the other acts to prevent action potentials from occurring. Each can vary in size within its limits, and each is proportional to the number and location of activated synapses of that type (as we shall see later, some locations are more strategic than others).

In contrast, the action potential is an all-or-none event. That is, it is the same size no matter what the magnitude of the stimulus which produced it, and the distance it travels has no direct bearing on its size. While the graded potential spreads passively, with a decrement in size, the travel of the action potential is active and nondecremental, involving a process in which energy stored at each point along the way is released. It is the interplay between excitatory and inhibitory potentials on the postsynaptic membrane that produces the decisions of the cell. The presence or absence of an action potential in effect *is* the decision. The neuron produces its effects by activating the axon, and the axon is that portion of the neuron which is specialized for the conduction of all-or-none spikes.

Action potentials travel at different speeds in the axons of different neurons. As a general rule, the thicker the axon, the faster the conduction speed. Obviously an animal with relatively fast conduction speed (and hence quicker reflexive movements) is better equipped to survive than one with sluggish conduction of action potentials. The squid has evolved the thickest axons possessed by any animal and hence has the fastest conduction speed in a bare axon. Its thick axons are a factor in the very quick escape reflexes of the squid in which water is expelled from the siphon and movement is by jet propulsion. There is a limit, however, to how big a cell can be and to the thickness of an axon. The squid has, in fact, "cheated" in that its giant axons are composed of many fused cells which were once separate. Thick axons are bulky and take up so much space that the number in a bundle must be reduced as the diameter increases.

Vertebrates have used an entirely different method of speeding up conduction. Rather than being a bare tube, the vertebrate axon is covered at intervals by sheath cells, as described on p. 37. Each sheath is a cell in its own right, either a Schwann cell in the case of peripheral nerves or a type of oligodendroglia in the central nervous system. The sheaths are roughly 1 mm. in length, the bare nodes being much shorter. The exact method by which these sheaths speed up axonal conduction is unknown, but there is firm evidence that the action potential jumps almost instantly from one side of the sheath cell to the other. That is, the action potential moves at a speed characteristic of its axon diameter only while it travels in the very short node of Ranvier. When it reaches the next sheath cell it skips or jumps to the next node. This is called *saltatory conduction,* and it is by this means that some heavily myelinated axons can conduct action potentials at a velocity of 100 yards per second. In axons of very thin diameter, those with small or widely spaced sheath cells, or those which have one sheath cell to insulate many axons, the conduction speed is much slower. In exceptional cases the speed might be measured in seconds per yard rather than yards per second.

Conduction in a series of neurons is said to be polarized. That is, excitation passes from an end foot to a cell body or dendrite; it passes from the cell body out the axon to the end foot. Conduction in the opposite direction is not known to occur in nature.

However, much of what we know about the generation of action potentials is based on the results of artificially "backfiring" neurons. When axons are artificially stimulated, an action potential travels *toward* the cell body and eventually invades it. This is called *antidromic* stimulation, while the normal direction of transmission is *orthodromic.* When one records in the manner previously discussed it is nearly impossible to follow what happens when spikes are initiated because the spike itself obscures it. If we have an electrode inside a motor neuron, however, we can note an interesting series of events which occur as an antidromic spike speeds up an axon and invades the region from which we are recording, for current flow can be recorded at some distance from the potential differences which produce it. This is called *volume conduction.* Of course, the farther one is from the source, the smaller the apparent voltage change. Eccles has exploited the antidromic stimulation technique brilliantly, and his results will be presented here in simplified form. We have been assuming that our electrode placed within the cell body is faithfully recording all of the potential changes occurring on any part of the cell membrane. This is not quite true, however. Eccles (1957) argues that the intracellular electrode is essentially blind to any potential changes occurring more than 200 microns out on the dendrites. He has divided the neuron into portions from which it is possible to detect changes using a centrally placed microelectrode. The soma-dendritic (SD) region includes the cell body (soma) and the nearest 200 microns of the dendrites. An initial segment (IS) region consists of the axon hillock plus the nearby portion of the axon which is not covered with a myelin sheath. Finally, it is just barely possible to record activity in a third region, that part of the axon directly under the first sheath cell, the M portion of the neuron.

If the axon is stimulated at some distance from the cell body, then the cell body electrode will "see" some of the following events. First, it will detect a tiny M spike corresponding to the arrival of the impulse at the first myelinated segment. The M spike has an amplitude of 3 or 4 mV. and is all-or -none in any one cell. The spike itself would, of course, have a total amplitude of 110 mV. (from -70 to $+40$) *if* the recording electrode were in the activated portion of the axon. Sometimes the M spike is not followed by any other event, probably because the spike has died out without activating the initial segment. Usually, however, the arrival of the M spike triggers an initial segment (IS) spike which is about 40 mV. in amplitude. It is larger than the M spike because its source is closer to the electrode. If nothing further happens, it is assumed that the IS spike has failed to invade the SD region. But often the IS spike will be closely followed by an action potential of the full 110-mV. size which sweeps over the cell body and out the dendrites. The size of this SD spike indicates that it is generated in the immediate vicinity of the electrode. It travels over the cell body surface, including synaptic regions, and washes out whatever EPSPs and IPSPs might have been in progress. Precisely because this spike erases graded potentials, it is thought to be localized on the SD membranes. The M and IS spikes do not cancel out ongoing graded potentials but sum algebraically with them. This phenomenon supports the idea of their locations, because there are few or no synapses in either region. Thus, our cell body electrode simultaneously picks up the results of synaptic activation and the distant M and IS spikes. The initial segment spike can occasionally be detected even with orthodox synaptic triggering of spikes. It is then seen as a slight inflection in the rising phase of the action potential. For all of these reasons the axon hillock region is now believed to be the actual trigger area for action potentials. It has a lower threshold for spike initiation than does the SD surface, and synapses located near the hillock are more effective than those farther removed.

CHEMICAL PROCESSES
UNDERLYING ELECTRICAL POTENTIALS

The electrical events discussed earlier are the end result of movements of electrically charged ions. That is, the cause of potentials and their changes is basically electrochemical, rather than simply electrical. The resting potential of -70 mV., for example, is the result of different concentrations of various types of ions on the inside and outside of the cell. The electrical potential and the concentration differences represent compromises between opposed chemical and electrical tendencies which cannot be simultaneously satisfied. These are (1) osmotic pressure, or a tendency for particles of a given type to be equally distributed in space, and (2) the attraction of unlike charges and the repulsion of like charges. If the cell membrane were a sieve with very large holes, both tendencies would eventually be satisfied, with no electrical potential across the membrane and no concentration differences. The membrane is *not* a large-holed sieve, however. It has small pores, not large enough for all sizes of ions to pass back and forth freely. The word "pore" is used here to signify any property of the membrane which has a selective effect, whether this is due to actual holes of a given size or to some other, as yet unknown, factors. In any event, the membrane is *selectively permeable;* it lets some particles through, but it forms a barrier for others.

The results of this selectivity can best be illustrated by the example of a tank of water separated into two compartments by a semipermeable membrane. Suppose that we place a mixture of one part sodium (Na^+), one part potassium (K^+), and two parts chloride (Cl^-) in one side of the tank, which we will call the original side. The two sides start out being electrically neutral, so there is no electrical force involved in moving the ions. The original side would, however, contain three types of particles, and osmotic pressure would result in a tendency for each type to move in all directions in space. Now let us further suppose that the membrane dividing the tank into two equal parts has holes large enough to allow Cl^- and K^+ to pass through easily but not large enough for Na^+ to pass. This is theoretically possible because even though the sodium ion is actually smaller than the potassium ion, water molecules cling to sodium in such a way that its hydrated diameter (which includes the water) is larger than that of hydrated potassium. The random movements of Cl^- and K^+ ions would then result in their passing through the holes to the opposite side of the tank, but the Na^+ ions would remain confined to the original side. If osmotic pressure alone were involved in this case, there would eventually be equal numbers of Cl^- and K^+ ions on either side of the membrane and the original side would contain 1½ parts positive ions for every one part negative. This tremendous electrical imbalance would then simultaneously attract back some of the Cl^- and repel some of the $K+$ from the original side. The tug-of-war between osmotic pressure and electrical attraction would finally reach a compromise state in which neither force would be completely "satisfied" or "denied." The opposite side of the tank would have more than half of the $K+$ and less than half of the $Cl-$

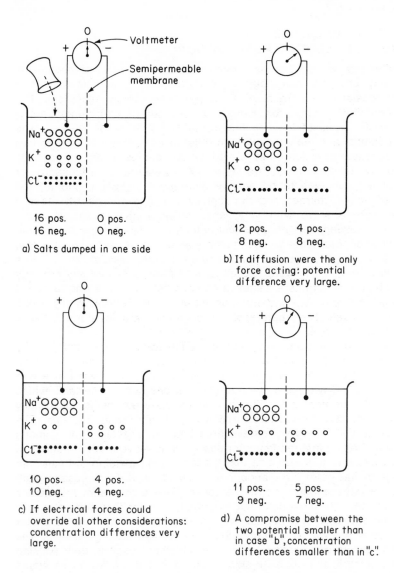

FIGURE 2-10—A simplified diagram of equilibrium or compromise between diffusional tendencies of particles and electrical attraction/repulsion.

The original side of the tank would have more positive ions than negative, while the opposite half would have a surplus of negative ions.

Our tank of water is actually a reasonable, though simplified, model of the neuron, with the "opposite half" of the tank corresponding to the protoplasm inside the neural membrane. The fluids inside and outside the cell contain many more ions than we can discuss here, but sodium, potassium, and chloride are by far the most numerous. The relation between the electrical potential across a membrane and ionic concentration differences is known and is expressed in the Nernst equation:

$$\text{potential (voltage)} = k \log_{10} \left[\frac{\text{concentration outside}}{\text{concentration inside}} \right]$$

The equation can be worked out for only one ion at a time. What it tells us is this: If a given ion is free to pass back and forth across the membrane and the voltage is a certain value, then the concentration difference across the membrane must be equal to the term to the right in the equation. If the relative concentrations are known, then the log of the outside/inside ratio must be equal to the measured potential difference across the membrane. But what if there is a difference? If we measure the potential and the concentration differences for a given ion type and the two halves of the equation are *not* equal, the ion is not "at rest" or at equilibrium. It has a net tendency to move into or out of the membrane in one direction or the other because the electrical and osmotic forces are not at a compromise state. Since we would have shown that equilibrium was *not* being reached and that the ions were *not* moving in the direction they supposedly tend to take, there must be a barrier to movement. This barrier could be a membrane which is not completely permeable to that ion, or it could be an energy-using chemical process which works in the direction opposite to the electrical or osmotic gradients. It is our job to find out what the barrier is, for the equation merely shows us whether it does or does not exist. For each of the three ions discussed here the concentrations and equilibrium potentials have been calculated and are presented in Table 2-1.

Ion	Concentration outside	m/M liter inside	Equilibrium potential
Na^+	150	15	+ 60
K^+	5.5	150	-90
Cl^-	125	9	-70

Table 2-1. Ionic concentration and predicted potentials
[From Eccles, *Physiology of Nerve Cells*]

The table shows that most of the sodium is outside the neuron, as is most of the chloride. Potassium, on the other hand, is in very high concentration inside the cell. Since the measured internal resting potential of the neuron (or at least motor horn cells) is known to be −70 mV., we can see in the column to the right that only chloride is at rest or equilibrium during the resting potential. Sodium would not be at its equlibrium unless the cell interior were at +60 mV. instead of −70. At −70 sodium is electrically attracted by the cell interior and also has a powerful osmotic tendency to move inward. The measurements show, however, that it is not doing so. The barrier to such movement is assumed to be the small size of the membrane pores during the resting potential. Potassium is also not quite at rest when the internal potential is −70 mV. This potential is not quite negative enough for potassium. Potassium should have a tendency to leak out of the neuron so that it is a little less concentrated inside.

The agreement between the equilibrium potential for chloride and the actual resting potential might lead one to suspect that this ion is responsible for the resting potential, but it is possible to demonstrate experimentally that this is not the case. When chloride ions are added or subtracted from the external fluids the resting potential does not change as it should according to the equation. So while chloride has no tendency to preferentially enter or leave the neuron at the resting potential level, it does not actually determine that potential level.

It is an entirely different story with potassium ions, however. Even though potassium is not entirely at rest at −70 mV., it appears to be free to enter the neural interior from the outside. When the concentration of potassium is varied experimentally, the size of the resting potential varies in the predicted direction, which indicates relatively free passage through the membrane and an active role in determining the resting potential. The discrepancy between the equilibrium potential of potassium (−90 mV.) and the resting potential of the cell might be due to a property of the pores such that they allow freer passage inward than outward. Another possibility is that an active metabolic process transports some potassium into the cell against its natural tendency to leak out. This will be discussed later.

The electrical potential and ionic concentrations given here represent resting conditions, not activity. In the active neuron there are changes in potential and sudden movements of ions. The significance of the barrier property of the neuron and ionic movements can best be appreciated when one considers the experiments of Eccles (1957). Eccles did not merely record with a glass tube electrode but also used micropipettes to preset the internal voltage. A double-barreled electrode served this purpose. One barrel was used for recording purposes. The other barrel was also filled with an ionic solution, but different ions could be ejected from the tube and injected into the cell when the solution was connected with the pole of a battery. Using this method he recorded from a motor horn cell and measured the EPSPs and IPSPs produced through stimulation of sensory fibers to that cell. If he first hyperpolarized the neuron so that it was more negative than usual inside, the IPSP became smaller in amplitude. When the internal potential was preset to −80 mV., the usual value found during a maximal IPSP, the IPSP did not occur at all. When the potential was set to be even more negative than −80 mV., the IPSPs produced by sensory nerve stimulation were in the opposite direction so that they actually depolarized the cell, as an EPSP normally does. The IPSP, in other words, seemed to be seeking a level of −80 mV. Even though this value is not the equilibrium point for potassium (−90 mV.), it is probably due to an outward movement of potassium. The mechanism may involve removal of the last little barrier to potassium outflow. As some potassium flows out, however, the cell interior becomes more negative and thus repels some chloride. The outward passage of chloride (which is a slightly smaller ion than potassium) prevents the cell from reaching the potassium equilibrium point of −90 mV. The IPSP might then correspond to the effects of a slight enlargement of the membrane pores.

The point at which the EPSP "flips over" is the point at which the cell is preset to zero potential. If the neural interior is made positive, the EPSP appears as a hyperpolarizing potential resembling a normal IPSP (a downward deflection). Thus, the EPSP seems to result from a process seeking equilibrium at zero potential, the suggestion being that the mechanism is an opening of the membrane pores so that *all* ions can freely pass. According to this line of evidence, the graded potentials can be explained as electrical manifestations of ion flows stimulated by removal of barriers to passage.

Keynes (1958) and others have used a similar technique for setting the internal voltage, but in this system the voltage was "clamped" by means of a negative feedback system so that it could not vary from a set value. Instead of measuring voltage (except as part of the clamp technique), Keynes examined the flow of current into and out of the neuron. In these experiments only the action potential was studied because measurement was carried out using the squid giant axon. This axon is so large (sometimes the diameter of a pencil lead) that electrodes can easily be inserted into a cut end. By means of electrical stimulation the interior of the axon could be made positive and held there while measurements of current flow were being carried out. The experiments showed that a sudden inrush of current coincided with the change from internal negativity to positivity, and this was followed shortly by a slower outflow of current. The inflowing current has been identified with a movement of sodium ions into the neuron, resulting in the peak of the spike. The falling phase of the spike corresponds to the subsequent outflow of potassium. The hyperpolarization after the spike is then somewhat like an IPSP, except that chloride does not appear to accompany the potassium, and the hyperpolarization following a spike can be greater than an IPSP in value.

INITIATION AND PROPAGATION
OF THE ACTION POTENTIAL

The action potential is generated when the sum total of all graded potentials reaches a threshold value of about 10 mV.; the cell interior being depolarized to −60 mV. This change must occur within a reasonably short time, however, because neurons apparently have the property of accommodation to very slow changes. If a neuron slowly accommodates to −60 mV., an effective EPSP must change it by 10 mV., or to −50 mV. EPSPs seem to trigger spikes by summating to a threshold value in the axon hillock region, where the spike is initiated. During the EPSP the barrier to ions is reduced, and if the resulting ionic flow is great enough, it removes the block to sodium inflow. Sodium, being far from equilibrium and having both electrical and osmotic gradients acting upon it, pours into the membrane at the hillock region, changing the internal potential to a positive value which does not quite reach the sodium equilibrium point of +60 mV. Once inside, these ions are attracted by the more negative regions of the interior, which are farther down the axon. But as sodium ions veer off and travel even a short distance toward the negativity of the axon interior, they change the potential across the membrane which they are under. As this piece of membrane is depolarized, it too loses its ability to exclude sodium, and sodium rushes in. Thus, an inward movement of sodium at one point causes a following inrush at an adjacent point. In this way a current inflow passes down the axon. Meanwhile, back at the first point, sodium has rushed in while the barrier was temporarily removed and made the interior of the cell positive. Now sodium has no great tendency to go in or out, but potassium is far from equilibrium. Even the resting potential of −70 mV. is not quite negative enough for potassium, but +40 is intolerable. Thus, it is largely potassium which rushes out immediately after the spike. The barrier to sodium is restored before sodium has a chance to get out again, and the neuron ends up with an excess of sodium and a shortage of potassium after each action potential. The actual number of exchanged ions is, however, very small compared to the total number present, and the cell can fire many hundreds of times in rapid succession before the ionic imbalance begins to have a deleterious effect. Usually a neuron does not fire rapidly enough for potassium depletion to occur, because the ionic balance is restored in a short time by a metabolic process in which sodium is excreted.

The full details of this process are not known, but the mechanism of sodium excretion is called the *sodium pump,* a metabolic process using ATP as fuel. ATP is produced by the mitochondria, which are usually located near the site where ATP is used. There are several experimental procedures by which the manufacture or use of ATP can be blocked or poisoned. One is the removal of oxygen. When the production or use of ATP is blocked, the sodium pump peters out. The cell loses its ability to expel sodium, and eventually all potential changes come to a halt. It is believed that the process of sodium expulsion involves a simultaneous intake of potassium ions on a one-for-one basis, but the potassium may restore itself partly by simple diffusion.

We have previously characterized the action potential as traveling by means of energy stored at each point along the axon. Mitochondria are located at intervals on the inside of the axon, but ATP does not appear to be involved in the stored energy we are speaking of. Metabolic poisons which almost immediately inactivate the sodium pump have little effect on the action potential until the resting potential has been changed to an impossible level by sodium pump malfunction. The stored energy perhaps consists of a change in the configuration of the molecules making up the membrane. With one geometric arrangement the membrane might have small pores; with another the pores might be larger. The small-pore arrangement might occur as a result of the electrical potential characteristic of the resting state, and when this is reduced to -60 mV. the molecules might arrange themselves into the large-pored state.

SYNAPTIC TRANSMISSION

The arrival of the spike at the end foot causes the release of chemicals which transmit the excitation (or inhibition) across the synapse to the next cell. These chemicals are called *transmitter substances,* or simply transmitters. Transmitter substances enter the 100 Å synaptic cleft and cross over to the subsynaptic membrane and initiate EPSPs or IPSPs, probably by changing the membrane permeability in the ways outlined earlier. After this activation, the transmitter is broken down by an enzyme and removed from the site of action so that the way is cleared for the transmission of another impulse across the synapse.

When the end feet are examined under an electron microscope, they are found to contain globules or vessicles about 300 Å in diameter and enclosed by a membrane. The packaging of transmitter substance into these vesicles is probably carried out by the Golgi apparatus in the cell body, and the vesicles are then transported down the axon to the end feet. Since the vesicles are at least three times as wide as the synaptic cleft, they are obviously not discharged bodily into the synaptic region. Instead, they probably fuse with the membrane of the end foot and then open up to the outside (the cleft) and discharge their contents. (Such a mechanism has been found in some gland cells.) The vesicles are all about the same size and probably contain about the same amount of transmitter, as evidenced by the studies of Fatt and Katz (1951). Investigating the electrical activity of the synapse between motor horn cell and skeletal muscle (the motor end plate), under very high amplification these authors found that small potential changes occurred at random intervals even when the neuron was not active. Apparently some vesicles are released spontaneously, though not in great numbers. The important observation was that these tiny potential changes were always exactly the same size. If a larger potential was found (as when the nerve was active), it was always a multiple of the smaller micropotential. At this synapse the transmitter is known with virtual certainty to be *acetylcholine (ACh)*. There is some evidence that ACh is also a transmitter in the parasympathetic nervous system and at some other synapses in the brain or peripheral nervous system. Some sympathetic nervous system synapses probably involve *noradrenalin* as the transmitter. *Serotonin* is another substance believed to act as a transmitter in some brain synapses although it is difficult to prove beyond all doubt that a given substance is the naturally used transmitter at any given synapse.

After crossing the synapse and acting on the next cell, the transmitter must be broken down or inactivated by an enzyme. Acetylcholine is broken down by *acetylcholine esterase (AChE)*. The necessity for the removal of the transmitter from its active site is obvious. Without the presence of AChE a *cholinergic* synapse (one using ACh as a transmitter) could send just one very long-lasting message containing just one bit of information. By analogy, one could not send much of a message by telegraph if the key were pushed down and held there indefinitely. Messages of a complex nature, or repeated simple messages, involve the making *and breaking* of contact. If the ACh were not removed, the subsynaptic cell would be permanently depolarized.

A number of drugs which have potent effects on behavior are now known to have specific actions at synaptic sites. Curare, for example, is a powerful paralytic agent which is lethal in high doses because it paralyzes the muscles of respiration in addition to those which move the skeleton. Curare acts by occupying the sites normally taken by ACh on the post-synaptic membrane. It is not, however, broken down by AChE, nor does it activate the muscle. The poisoned subject is therefore unable to move his limp muscles until the curare has worked itself free or spontaneously disintegrated. Strangely, drugs which are effective in interfering with transmission across one type of cholinergic synapse are often ineffective at other types of cholinergic synapses. Scopolamine, for instance, is also anticholinergic, but it largely affects synapses between parasympathetic nerves and the target organs. It blocks such activity but does not paralyze skeletal muscles. Another drug (strychnine) gives a false appearance of being an excitatory agent because it produces powerful muscle contractions and seizures. Actually, strychnine is inhibitory, but it inhibits the function of small neurons which are themselves inhibitory in their effects on other neurons. Strychnine poisoning is thus due to a release of motor neurons from inhibition. Finally, there are drugs which affect the esterase or breakdown substance rather than the transmitter. Eserine, for one, prevents AChE from breaking down ACh in parasympathetic synapses. In consequence, the parasympathetic nervous system "runs wild" as its organs behave as if they were being continuously stimulated by the nerves.

SUMMARY

In this chapter we have tried to communicate something of what is at present known about the form and function of cells in general and neurons in particular. Our bodies are composed of cells. Each cell is a tiny unit of life which must perform a variety of functions in order to exist, and these are carried out by means of organelles. The fate of the collection of cells as a whole is decided by the specialized cells making up the brain and its connections with the periphery. It is the neuron which sizes up the state of the inner and outer worlds of the body, and neural networks relate this state to past experiences and extrapolate into the future. Each neuron is played upon by graded excitatory and inhibitory forces (the graded potentials), which interact in such a way as to decide whether communication with the next cell will or will not occur. If the balance of excitation over inhibition is so great that a threshold for the initiation of an all-or-none action potential is reached, a decision has been made. The neuron fires, and the action potential is sent as a unit of communication down the axon to the end feet, which synapse with the next cell. It is then up to the receiving cell to decide whether the information has arrived at the appropriate time and place for further transmission to occur. Both the graded potentials and the action potential were shown to be due to concentrations of, and movements of, charged particles (ions) across the cell membrane. Transmission across a synaptic gap, however, involves the additional step of the secretion of a chemical transmitter substance into the cleft. When the transmitter substance has performed its function (probably changing pore size in the postsynaptic membrane), it is broken down and removed to clear the way for the next message. The effect of the transmitter on the postsynaptic neuron depends on a number of factors including the location of the end foot and the state of the postsynaptic cell when the secretion occurs.

Much of what has been presented in this chapter is a matter of intense controversy. Further research may well show that many current conceptions of neural functioning are quite incorrect. Most of the facts will, however, probably hold up over time, and they can be found in the books and articles in the following list. The *Scientific American* articles are more geared to the beginner, but the others can largely be grasped by a student who has mastered the chapter.

SUGGESTED READINGS

Corning, W. C., & John, E. R. Effect of ribonuclease on retention of conditioned response in regenerated planarians. *Science,* 1961, *134,* 1363–1364.

*Eccles, J. C. *The neurophysiological basis of mind.* New York: Oxford University Press, 1953.

*Eccles, J. C. *The physiology of nerve cells.* Baltimore: Johns Hopkins Press, 1957.

*Eccles, J. C. *The physiology of synapses.* New York: Academic Press, 1964.

Fatt, P., & Katz, B. An analysis of the end-plate potential recorded with an intra-cellular electrode. *Journal of Physiology,* 1951, *115,* 320–370.

Hydén, H. Satellite cells in the nervous system. *Scientific American,* December, 1961, pp. 62–70.

Katz, B. How cells communicate. *Scientific American,* September, 1961, pp. 3–12.

Keynes, R. D. The nerve impulse and the squid. *Scientific American,* December, 1958, pp. 2–9.

*Ochs, S. *Elements of neurophysiology.* New York: Wiley, 1965.

Robertson, J. D. The membrane of the living cell. *Scientific American,* April, 1962, pp. 45–52.

* Books for the more advanced student.

THE ANATOMY OF THE NERVOUS SYSTEM

CHAPTER 3

The brain is a complex collection of billions of interconnected nerve cells supported by perhaps 5 to 10 times as many glial cells. If these were scattered uniformly throughout a globular mass, there would be little need for this chapter. Unfortunately for the student, such is not the case. There are many distinctly different kinds of neurons, and many clusters of cells with entirely different connections and functions. Before we can begin to understand how the brain works, we must have some knowledge of neuroanatomy. Fortunately, it is possible to begin at a simple level and build a more detailed knowledge over years of study. If the student finds himself overwhelmed with names and details, he should realize that he is not expected to retain all this material from a single reading. Let him read the chapter through at a brisk pace in order to get an overall picture, however nebulous, then reread it for details in conjunction with later chapters. Few people can memorize material that does not appear relevant to their interests. Most physiological psychologists did not begin to understand neuroanatomy until they first became interested in the function of a particular part of the brain. At that point a knowledge of the relations between the region of interest and the rest of the brain became both necessary and fascinating.

SOME INTRODUCTORY TERMINOLOGY

The nervous system can be divided and subdivided in a seemingly endless number of ways, each part having its own specific name. It is possible, however, to make many distinctions by using only a small number of relative directional terms. These are illustrated in Figure 3-1, which is a schematic side view of a human brain. The direction toward the front end is *rostral.* Other terms sometimes used with almost the same meaning are *anterior, upper, higher,* and *cranial.* These, and the others that follow, are relative rather than absolute terms. That is, a structure may be to the rear of the brain but still be rostral *relative to* another structure even farther to the rear.

The direction toward the tail end is generally termed *caudal,* although *posterior* and *lower* are also sometimes used. The top of the brain and the back of the animal are said to be *dorsal* while the base of the brain and the animal's belly are *ventral.* In applying these terms to man, the reader should imagine himself on all fours. Since we do usually stand upright, the terms "anterior" and "posterior" have sometimes been used in place of "ventral" and "dorsal" in describing the spinal cord of man.

Finally, the direction from the middle out to the side is *lateral,* and its opposite is *medial.* Now if you hear a brain region described as ventral posterolateral thalamus, you immediately know that it is located toward the bottom, rear, and side of the thalamus. You still must know where the thalamus is.

The terms "superior" and "inferior" are also often used descriptively. No value judgment is intended. *Superior* means to be situated above and *inferior* to be situated below some reference structure. It is unfortunate that "above" is ambiguous and might mean either dorsal or rostral or both. The most consistent rule is to equate superior with rostral and inferior with caudal, because the structures designated "superior" are consistently rostral to their "inferior" mates.

Numerous anatomical terms originated at a time when the only known method of investigating the brain was by gross examination of its superficial features. Names were given to various cracks and bumps. Many brain regions, however, can be seen only after the brain has been thinly sliced (sectioned) and stained with chemicals to make the individual cells and fibers "stand out." Still others require the use of a microscope. When these procedures became widely used in the nineteenth century, discrete masses of nerve cells were found, often located right inside or underneath an already named bump or protrusion. These clusters were usually then named after the bump but with the term "nucleus" tagged on. For example, the lateral geniculate *body* is a bump. Its name is descriptive and refers to a knee-shaped (geniculate) lump located to the side of the thalamus. Underneath this body is the lateral geniculate *nucleus.* It is best to keep these terms straight because in some cases there is more than one nucleus under a single bump.

Often a cluster of neurons (nucleus) can be seen only after the brain is sliced and stained with a chemical which makes the almost-transparent cell bodies readily visible. The slice or section can be cut at any angle, and the resulting view of the brain is most difficult to interpret unless the angle at which the section was made is known. Fortunately, sections are usually made in one of three standard planes, and these are at right angles to one another. The most common plane of sectioning is the transverse or *coronal.* When you slice a loaf of bread, you are making coronal sections. That is, a coronal plane is perpendicular to the base of the brain and extends from side to side at right angles to the midline. The next most commonly used section is the *sagittal,* which is also perpendicular to the base of the brain but extends from front to rear. A hot dog bun held with the slit up has a sagittal section, hopefully not quite complete. The final plane is self-explanatory: the *horizontal.* It is parallel to the base of the brain. These planes are shown in Figure 3-1.

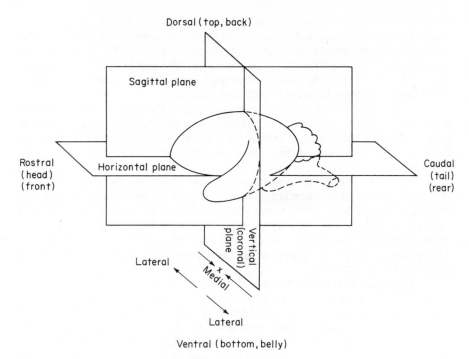

FIGURE 3-1–Schematic side view of a human brain.

MAJOR SUBDIVISIONS OF THE NERVOUS SYSTEM

As can be seen in Figure 3-2, the first major breakdown of the nervous system is into a *central nervous system* (*CNS*) and a *peripheral nervous system.* The CNS consists of the brain and spinal cord; the peripheral system, all neural tissue outside the CNS. The brain and spinal cord are wrapped in a continuous three-layer supportive membrane and enclosed by bone (i.e., the skull and vertebrae). The innermost of the three layers, the one which actually contacts the nervous tissue, is a tender sheet called the *pia.* The outermost is a very tough layer of connective tissue called the *dura mater.* Sandwiched between the two is a fibrous mass called the *arachnoid.* Cerebrospinal fluid, a liquid much like blood plasma in composition, circulates in the arachnoid layer between pia and dura and communicates with four interconnected pockets or *ventricles* within the brain itself and with a narrow cylindrical tube or canal which runs down the length of the spinal cord.

The peripheral nervous system includes bundles of axons arising from neurons. The bundles are called *nerves.* Clusters of cell bodies are called *ganglia* (singular: *ganglion*). A distinction in terminology is made between cell masses and fiber bundles depending on whether they are inside of or outside the central nervous system. That is, fiber bundles within the CNS are

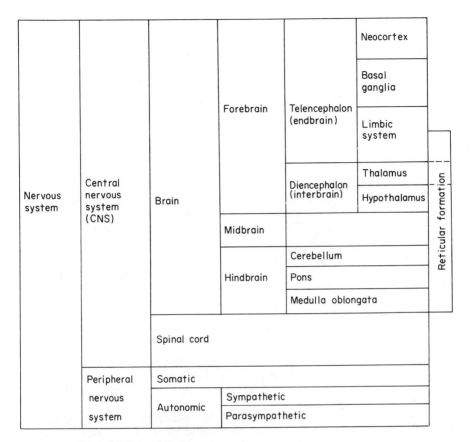

				Neocortex	
Nervous system	Central nervous system (CNS)	Brain	Forebrain	Telencephalon (endbrain)	Basal ganglia
					Limbic system
			Diencephalon (interbrain)	Thalamus	
				Hypothalamus	
			Midbrain		
			Hindbrain	Cerebellum	
				Pons	
				Medulla oblongata	
		Spinal cord			
	Peripheral nervous system	Somatic			
		Autonomic	Sympathetic		
			Parasympathetic		

(Reticular formation)

FIGURE 3-2–Subdivisions of the nervous system.

called *tracts* rather than nerves. Cell masses inside the CNS are *nuclei* rather than ganglia. Actually, there are physical differences between tracts and nerves, nuclei and ganglia, so the distinction in names is not completely artificial. The peripheral ganglia are encapsulated by tough connective tissue while nuclei are not. It is, in fact, often difficult to say where one nucleus leaves off and another begins.

The bundle of axons in a tract has no enclosing sheath (although each axon, of course, has its myelin sheath). A nerve, however, is protected by a tube of tough connective tissue which is much like the dura mater.

Peripheral nerves almost always include both *afferent* fibers, which conduct impulses into CNS, and *efferent* fibers, which conduct impulses from the CNS out to the periphery. There is, as far as we know, no physiological difference in the makeup of afferent and efferent nerve fibers. An axon will conduct indiscriminately in both directions if artificially stimulated in the middle portion. The direction in which impulses normally travel is determined by the site at which the depolarization of the membrane is normally generated. In a sensory neuron this will be near the receptor cell and in a motor neuron at the axon hillock. The terms "afferent" and "efferent" are also relative and are often used with reference to a particular part of the nervous system being discussed. Fibers carrying impulses into that region are said to be afferent, and those carrying impulses out are efferent. More often than not, however, "afferent" is synonymous with "sensory" and "efferent" with "motor."

THE PERIPHERAL NERVOUS SYSTEM

The peripheral nervous system has two basic divisions, the *somatic* and the *autonomic* nervous systems. The somatic system consists primarily of afferent fibers from the external sensory receptors and efferent (motor) fibers which innervate the striped or striated muscles that move the skeleton (and the animal) around. The autonomic system consists of various cell masses or ganglia and fibers which innervate the internal organs, glands, and smooth muscles. Smooth or visceral muscles lack the characteristic stripes of the skeletal muscles and respond much more slowly. Smooth muscles can contract in response to chemical substances in the bloodstream whereas skeletal muscles do not normally do so. The viscera are also provided with sensory nerve fibers but, strangely, these are not classed with the autonomic nervous system, which is considered only a motor system. Instead, they are said to be *visceral afferents*. We are seldom aware of activity in the visceral nerves, but visceral sensations probably add to the general level of activity of the central nervous system and contribute to feelings of well-being or malaise.

The autonomic system has, in turn, two subdivisions: the *sympathetic* and the *parasympathetic.* As a rule, any gland or smooth muscle is innervated by both systems, and the two have opposite effects. If the sympathetic nervous system stimulates an organ into activity, the parasympathetic system inhibits it, and vice versa. The sympathetic system is usually associated with energy expenditure and emergency reactions; the parasympathetic, with rest, digestion, and energy conservation.

THE CENTRAL NERVOUS SYSTEM

The CNS is composed of the brain and the spinal cord. The basic divisions of the brain are the *hindbrain,* the *midbrain,* and the *forebrain* (see Figure 3-3). The hindbrain is the small region immediately attached to the upper spinal cord and has three parts: the *medulla oblongata* (or simply medulla), the *pons,* and the *cerebellum.* The adjectives used to describe structures in these regions are: "bulbar," "pontine," and "cerebellar," respectively.

The medulla, pons, and midbrain form a continuous unit which we will refer to as the *brain stem.* On top of the middle portion of the brain stem is a shallow pocket of cerebrospinal fluid known as the *fourth ventricle.* In the

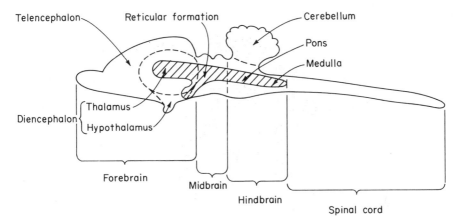

FIGURE 3-3—Highly schematic side view of brain of a rodentlike mammal.

caudal direction this ventricle gradually becomes a thin tube, the central canal, which runs down the middle of the spinal cord. In a forward or rostral direction it also becomes a tube, the *aqueduct,* which communicates with the ventricles of the forebrain. The aqueduct and fourth ventricle are surrounded by gray matter consisting primarily of very small cell bodies. This *central gray* matter (or periaqueductal gray) is, in turn, surrounded by a collection of nuclei which together are termed the *brain stem reticular formation.* The reticular formation extends all the way from the rear of the medulla up into the midbrain and even into a part of the forebrain known as the hypothalamus. Parts of the reticular formation are believed to function in governing the activity of the brain in general ways, such as increasing arousal and alertness.

The brain stem also contains many relay nuclei, regions where ascending and descending tracts make synaptic contacts with cells which have axons projecting farther along the central nervous system. The pons has a large number of fibers running to and from the cerebellum, which is situated directly above it.

The cerebellum, the part of the hindbrain not considered brain stem, is a large and highly convoluted (folded) structure which is well developed in all mammals but especially so in those capable of graceful and intricate movements such as cats and porpoises, as well as the primates. Integrated, coordinated sequences of movements are not possible with extensive cerebellar damage.

The two major divisions of the forebrain are the *diencephalon* and the *telencephalon.* The diencephalon consists of a *thalamus* and (located below it) a *hypothalamus.* The thalamus resembles a pair of footballs joined together at the midline at their thickest points. Much of the thalamus consists of what are termed *sensory relay nuclei.* These are places of synapse for axons of the sensory pathways from peripheral sensory receptors to the cortex. The thalamus in general can be divided into a dorsal thalamus (its

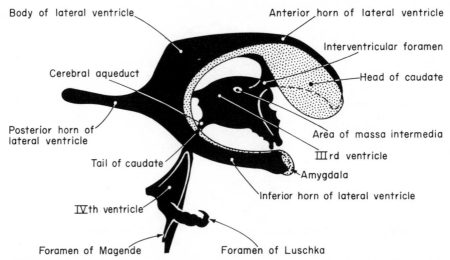

Body of lateral ventricle

Anterior horn of lateral ventricle

Interventricular foramen

Cerebral aqueduct

Head of caudate

Posterior horn of lateral ventricle

Area of massa intermedia

Tail of caudate

IIIrd ventricle

Amygdala

Inferior horn of lateral ventricle

IVth ventricle

Foramen of Magende

Foramen of Luschka

FIGURE 3-4–Drawing to illustrate the ventricular system and the relations of the caudate nucleus and amygdala to the lateral ventricle. (From E. C. Crosby, T. Humphrey, and E. W. Lauer. *Correlative Anatomy of the Nervous System.* New York: Macmillan, 1962.)

nuclear regions associated with the overlying neocortex) and a ventral thalamus (its nuclear regions associated with helping to govern motor activity). The dorsal thalamus is well developed only in those animals in which the neocortex has become well developed and differentiated.

The hypothalamus is a very small region ventral to the thalamus. Despite its tiny size, it is one of the more vital parts of the brain, because it is involved in regulation of the appetites, integration of the autonomic nervous system, and control of portions of the endocrine system. In addition, the brain stem reticular formation actually blends into the posterior portions of the hypothalamus and may in fact continue into some aspects of the thalamus. The hypothalamus is split in two along the midline by a slitlike ventricle (the third ventricle). As can be seen in Figure 3-4, a narrow passage connects this ventricle with the two lateral ventricles, which extend like wings into the forebrain.

The telencephalon is what the layman usually means by the term "brain." By weight it is by far the largest part of the brain of advanced mammals. When the human brain is viewed from the sides or top, nearly everything visible is *neocortex,* one of the three basic divisions of the telencephalon. Neocortex has a six-layered organization, and this is the basis for its identification. The remaining divisions of the telencephalon are the *limbic system* and the *basal ganglia.* This is one of the few cases in which a central nervous system structure is termed a "ganglion." The basal ganglia are located deep within the brain, usually rostral and lateral to the thalamus, and cannot be seen without cutting into the brain. Most of the limbic structures lie hidden in the brain. Some of them look superficially just like neocortex, but they have a different neural organization and number of layers.

The neocortical surface of the more advanced mammals is characterized by many bumps and cracks. A cortical bump is called either a *gyrus* or a *convolution.* A crack is usually termed a *fissure* or a *sulcus.* The human has roughly two and a half square feet of neocortical surface, but about two-thirds of it is buried in the fissures. Such a folded surface is said to be convoluted. Some small primitive mammals have essentially smooth brains with perhaps a dimple or two on the dorsal surface, but even these animals have a *rhinal fissure,* usually located on the ventral lateral surface. It separates neocortex above it from limbic system cortex below it. Two other common fissures are the *central* and the *lateral* (or *sylvian*). These, with the help of some dotted lines drawn by anatomists, are used to divide the brain of man into four lobes: *frontal, parietal, occipital,* and *temporal* (see Figure 3-5).

Both the limbic system and the basal ganglia are composed of many subdivisions, which will be discussed later. The limbic system has extensive connections with neocortex, hypothalamus, and brain stem reticular formation. Most limbic regions receive sensory input from a variety of sensory systems. Destruction of different parts of the limbic system results in characteristic changes in emotionality, learning, and memory.

The basal ganglia appear to be involved in the regulation of motor movements, since stimulation or destruction of these structures often results in tremor or limb jerking. Some motor pathways do seem to originate in the basal ganglia, but these regions also receive sensory input from a variety of sources.

THE SPINAL CORD AND PERIPHERAL NERVOUS SYSTEM

One of our remote ancestors may have been segmented like the earthworm of today. Evolution has blurred any fundamental segmental organization in mammals, but some evidence for it persists in the spinal cord. The spinal cord has between 30 and 32 segments, classed into five groups. From rostral to caudal these are cervical (8 segments), thoracic (12), lumbar (5), sacral (5), and coccygeal (between 0 and 2) (in some people no coccygeal segments are found). For most cord segments there is a corresponding ring of bone (vertebra) in the spinal *column.* Each cord segment has a pair of spinal nerves which pass to the periphery under the corresponding vertebra. In the course of evolution the neural spinal cord has become much shorter than the bony spinal column, but each cord segment has retained its affinity for its bony mate. As a consequence, the nerves descend from their place of attachment from the spinal cord down to the appropriate vertebra, where they exit to go into the periphery. The disparity in position becomes greater in the lower parts of the cord until the hole down the center of the vertebral column becomes filled with nothing but fiber bundles and is called the horse tail or cauda equina.

An idealized cross-sectional view of the spinal cord is shown in Figure 3-6. Actually, no two segments of the cord look exactly the same (see Figure

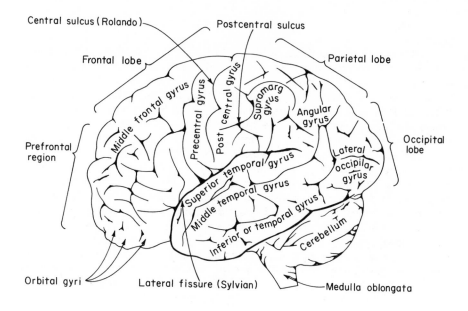

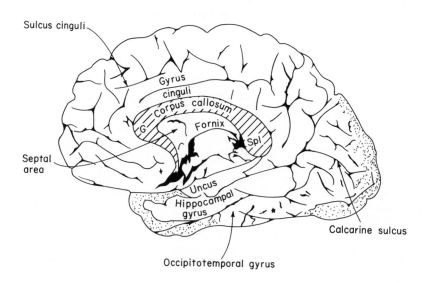

FIGURE 3-5—(Part 1) Lateral view of human brain with major lobes, fissures, and gyri labeled. **(Part 2)** Medial surface of right hemisphere of human brain. *g,* genu; *spl,* splenium of corpus callosum. **(Part 3)** Basal surface of human brain, with cranial nerves labeled. (From Truex. In Strong and Elwyn. *Human Neuroanatomy.* Baltimore: Williams & Wilkins, 1959.)

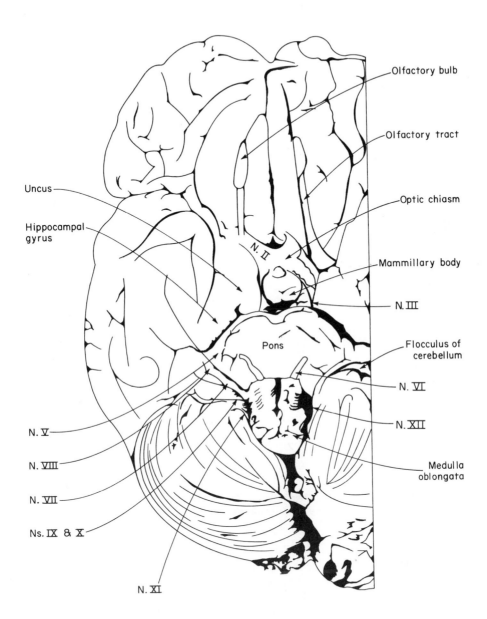

Olfactory bulb

Olfactory tract

Optic chiasm

Uncus

Hippocampal
gyrus

N. II

Mammillary body

N. III

Pons

Flocculus of
cerebellum

N. VI

N. V

N. XII

N. VIII

N. VII

Medulla
oblongata

Ns. IX & X

N. XI

3-7). The overall size and shape of the cross section differ characteristically
from one segmental group to the next, as do the size and shape of the
centrally located butterfly-shaped portion. The latter is called *gray matter*
and consists primarily of the cell bodies of neurons. The region peripheral to
this is called *white matter* and consists mainly of ascending and descending
myelinated fibers. The gray matter has three pairs of protrusions or "horns."
The ones on the top are the dorsal horns while the ones on the bottom are

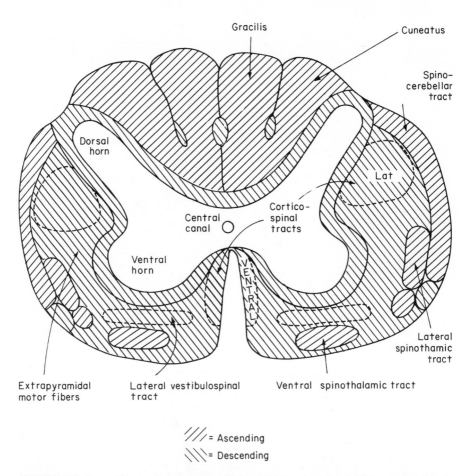

FIGURE 3-6–Ascending and descending fibers in the spinal cord. This section idealized, but more representative of cervical cord than any other region. Intermediate horn not shown.

the ventral horns. Those in between are known as the intermediate horns. In the very center of the cross section is the central canal, a tube filled with cerebrospinal fluid.

Each pair of horns has a different characteristic function. The dorsal horns contain cells related to the transmission of sensory information, the intermediate horns contain cell bodies whose processes control motor responses in the autonomic nervous system, while the ventral horns contain cells whose axons run out to terminate upon muscles of the somatic system. Incoming sensory fibers synapse upon neurons in the dorsal horn (in some cases), and the axons of the dorsal horn neurons then generally cross to the opposite side of the cord, passing just under the central canal. Motor neurons in the intermediate or ventral horns always exit to the same side of the body, never crossing to the other side.

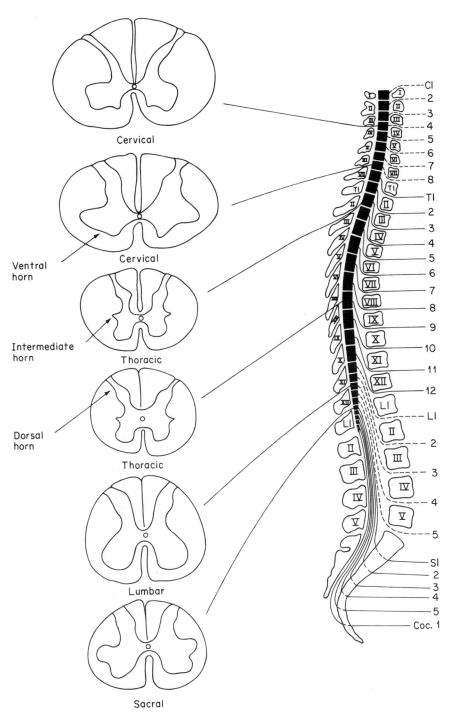

FIGURE 3-7–Segments of the spinal cord. (From Webb Haymaker and Barnes Woodhall. *Peripheral Nerve Injuries.* Philadelphia: Saunders, 1945.)

Descending and ascending tracts occupy different portions of the white matter, as shown in Figure 3-6. The dorsal white matter (between the two dorsal horns) consists almost exclusively of ascending (sensory) fibers. Pain and temperature sensations ascend over pathways found in the lateral white matter (lateral spinothalamic tract), and a crude touch and pressure sensory pathway is located ventrally in the cord. Another major ascending pathway is the spinocerebellar tract, situated at the extreme edges of the cord. Descending motor tracts are located in regions surrounding the ventral and intermediate horns.

At this time it should be pointed out, however, that sensory fibers play a role in reflexes mediated by cells in the cord, and also in projecting information to the brain. Stimulation of a sensory fiber, for example, might result in a reflexive response mediated by connections with motor cells in the cord. In addition, a branch of the same sensory fiber will ascend to the brain. Because of this dual role, many fibers branch profusely when they enter the cord, the different branches taking many different routes and serving many different functions.

SPINAL NERVES

Each cord segment has its pair of spinal nerves, as can be seen in Figure 3-8. Each spinal nerve has two branches which contact the cord, a *dorsal* and a *ventral root*. The roots fuse at some distance from the cord to form the complete spinal nerve. The ventral root, motor in function, contains axons of motor cells located in the ventral and intermediate horns. The axons of ventral horn motor cells are of two basic kinds, thick and thin. The thick axons, from large motor horn cells, synapse with striped muscle fibers and function to contract somatic muscles and move the organism. The muscles of the limbs are either extensors or flexors. The extensor muscles extend the limbs and, in the case of the legs, oppose the force of gravity. They are powerful and generally are in a state of tension or partial contraction. If they were not, we would fall to the ground. The flexor muscles draw the limbs toward the body. The thin axons in the ventral roots are the axons of small motoneurons, which are located in the ventral horn of the cord. Activation of the large motoneurons (alpha motoneurons) contracts the muscle. Activation of the small motoneurons (gamma motoneurons) regulates and modifies sensory receptors in the muscles themselves.

The dorsal root is unlike the ventral root in function and structure. It has a bulge midway between the spinal cord and the place of fusion with the ventral root. This is the *dorsal root ganglion,* consisting of the cell bodies of the axons which make up the dorsal root, and it includes fibers from the tactile, pain, temperature, pressure, and somatosensory systems. These cells have no true dendrites. Instead, they have a fiber which extends a short distance from the cell body and then splits into two parts or branches. One branch leads out to the area of the sensory receptors by way of the spinal nerve; the other, into the cord near the dorsal horn cells. The branch of the

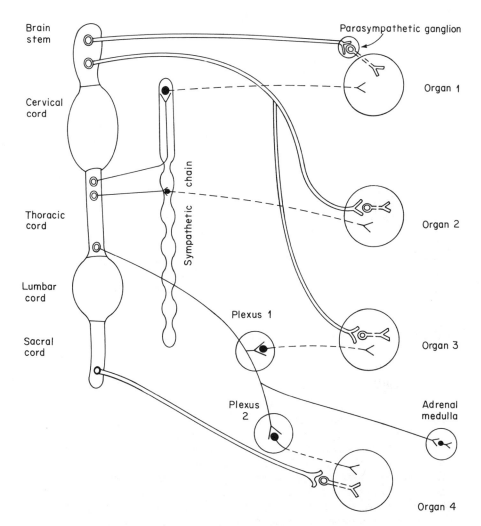

FIGURE 3-8–General principles of autonomic innervation. (Reprinted by permission. *Bailey's Textbook of Histology.* Baltimore: Williams & Wilkins, 1953.)

unipolar dorsal root ganglion cell which extends out to the receptors is sometimes called a functional dendrite because it conducts impulses *toward* the cell body, but it is constructed like a typical axon and conducts impulses like an axon. Impulses traveling toward the cord continue right past the branching point, and the cell body does not appear to be directly involved in their generation or conduction.

Since both sensory and motor innervation of the arms and legs is richer than that of the trunk of the body, the spinal nerves for the cervical and lumbar portions of the cord are relatively thick, and the cord itself bulges in these regions into what are known as the cervical and lumbar enlargements.

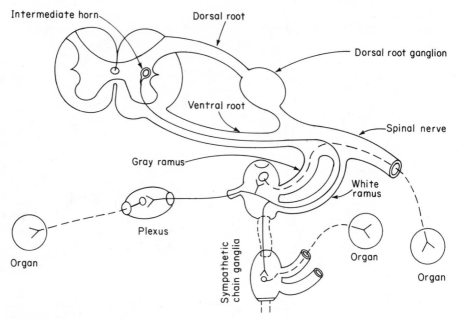

FIGURE 3-9—General principles of autonomic innervation.

AUTONOMIC PATHWAYS

The cells of the intermediate horn of the cord are also motor but related to the autonomic nervous system. In the thoracic portions of the cord these cells belong to the sympathetic branch of the autonomic system. Cells regulating the parasympathetic branch are located in the sacral portions of the cord and in some cranial nerves. The axons of autonomic neurons exit in the ventral or motor root of the spinal nerve, but they take a rather round-about path from that point onward (see Figures 3-8 and 3-9). That is, the sympathetic system axons enter the spinal nerve in the ventral root, then diverge from the nerve in a branch known as the *white ramus.* Fibers in the white ramus always synapse in a sympathetic ganglion, which is an important feature of the sympathetic system. Sympathetic ganglia run parallel to the cord in the cervical and thoracic regions: the *sympathetic chain,* a series of ganglia composed of cell bodies. Some sympathetic ganglia have migrated away from the chain to places closer to their ultimate target organ. These are called *plexuses.* An axon of the sympathetic system in the white ramus will *always* synapse with a neuron *either* in a chain ganglion *or* in a plexus. In some cases a sympathetic fiber synapses in the chain ganglion immediately at the point of exit from the white ramus and the axons of the postsynaptic ganglion cells reenter the spinal nerve by way of the *gray ramus.* In other cases the fiber will pass through that particular ganglion and ascend to another one before making synaptic contact with a new cell. In any event, there is one and only one synapse between the cord and the target organ in the autonomic system.

The sympathetic system has an unusual feature in that the adrenal medulla (the inside part of the adrenal gland) acts as if it were a nerve plexus, but its cells do not synapse with another target organ. Instead, they have become modified to secrete chemicals into the bloodstream. The secretory products (adrenalin, noradrenalin) are carried throughout the body by the bloodstream. These chemicals act to excite many organs in a fashion similar to that brought about by neural control. The parasympathetic system has no equivalent to the adrenal medulla.

The parasympathetic nervous system has a distinctly different anatomical picture in that it has no chain of ganglia and no general all-purpose chemical activator. Parasympathetic fibers stream toward their target organs in either the sacral spinal nerves or the cranial nerves and do not synapse until they reach a parasympathetic ganglion located near the target organ or even on it. The cells of the parasympathetic ganglia have very short axons which synapse on the organ.

THE CRANIAL NERVES

The brain stem is in many respects a rostral elaboration of the spinal cord. For example, sensory regions tend to be dorsal and motor regions ventral, as found in the cord. Similarly, the 10 pairs of cranial nerves which join the CNS at the brain stem are somewhat like modified spinal nerves. The main difference is that one spinal nerve is very much like another because they all serve the same sensory systems whereas most of the cranial nerves serve the specialized senses associated with the face and head. Some of the sensory systems located on the face and head contribute fibers to only one pair of cranial nerves; others contribute to several. Thus, the cranial nerves differ in size depending on the importance or degree of development of the particular sensory or motor system with which they are associated.

Another general rule about most cranial nerves is that they are mixed in function. This means that if a given cranial nerve contains motor fibers for a muscle it will also contain sensory fibers for the same muscle. Of the 12 pairs of cranial nerves, 2, the olfactory (smell) and optic (vision) nerves, differ from the rest in many respects. They are the least "mixed" of the cranial nerves, being almost entirely sensory in function. Cranial nerves are identified with Roman numerals, beginning at the rostral end and progressing in a rostral-caudal direction, as can be seen in Figure 3-5.

The first cranial nerve is the olfactory. *Unlike the other cranial nerves, the olfactory is not a discrete bundle. It is composed of a multitude of very short fibers joining the receptors (located in the olfactory epithelium of the nasal passages) with the olfactory bulbs. The olfactory bulb itself is part of the telencephalon, and pathways from the bulb to the rest of the brain are therefore called tracts, not nerves. The olfactory bulbs of man are said to be small, but only in comparison to the gigantic size of our brains. As far as the sense of smell is concerned, relative size means nothing. The absolute size of our bulbs (which is related to the number of neural elements it contains) is quite respectable, and our system is amazingly sensitive. Modern neuro-*

anatomists use fiber count as an index of sensory development rather than the outmoded and misleading relative size.

The second cranial nerve, the optic, is the only one which joins the CNS at the diencephalon (the thalamus). Most fibers in the optic nerve are the axons of ganglion cells located in the retina, which is actually part of the brain. This pathway is called a nerve until it reaches the optic chiasm near the anterior hypothalamus. At that point the fibers from the nasal portion of the retina (the half nearest the nose) cross over to the opposite side of the brain. Fibers from the nasal retina thus go to the contralateral part of the brain. Fibers that stay on the same side of the nervous system are called ipsilateral. Fibers from the temporal part of the retina do not cross at the optic chiasm and hence go to the ipsilateral half of the brain. Thus, if one considers the retina a reference point, the visual system is half crossed and half uncrossed. From the point of reference of what we see, however (the visual field), the system is almost completely crossed.

Movement of the eyeball is controlled by three cranial nerves: the oculomotor (III), the trochlear (IV), and the abducens (VI).

The fifth cranial nerve, the trigeminal, is typically very large in diameter in any animal. It consists mainly of sensory fibers from the head and face, including those mediating temperature, pain, touch, and pressure. Thus, it resembles a much enlarged dorsal root of a spinal nerve. Like the spinal nerve, the trigeminal has something which is like a dorsal root ganglion: the semilunar ganglion. Trigeminal fibers enter the brain stem and synapse in a very long nuclear region which extends well down into the spinal cord (in the dorsal horn region).

The seventh cranial nerve is the facial. Its motor fibers control movement of the face and scalp as well as two tiny muscles located in the middle ear. The seventh nerve also contains sensory fibers from the taste buds of the anterior two-thirds of the tongue.

The eighth cranial nerve was formerly known as the auditory but is now more commonly called the stato-acoustic. It serves two major sensory systems, the auditory and the vestibular. The auditory receptors are located in the cochlea, a structure resembling a snail shell. The vestibular system conveys information about the position of the head with respect to gravity (from the static organs, the utricle and saccule) and about the acceleration of head movements (from the semicircular canals). Fibers innervating these vestibular organs join together to make up the vestibular portion of the eighth nerve, and this portion then fuses with the auditory branch to make up the complete nerve.

The ninth, tenth, and eleventh cranial nerves have much in common. The glossopharyngeal (IX) and vagus (X) complete the sense of taste, with the former innervating the posterior third of the tongue and the latter the taste buds of the epiglottis. Both, with the addition of the eleventh or spinal accessory nerve, innervate the nontaste sensory receptors of various parts of the throat. The vagus and spinal accessory nerves are also important pathways for the parasympathetic nervous system, innervating the internal organs of the thorax and abdomen.

The twelfth and last cranial nerve is the hypoglossal. It contains motor fibers innervating the muscles of the tongue.

The nuclei serving (and served by) the cranial nerves are scattered throughout the brain stem but primarily in the pons and medulla. Their exact locations can be looked up, when needed, in any elementary neuroanatomy text.

THE BRAIN STEM

The brain stem is here defined as the medulla, pons, and midbrain. It is an elaboration of the spinal cord. The ventral portions of the brain stem are occupied by fiber bundles which are mainly descending motor pathways. The dorsal portions consist of either ascending sensory pathways or nuclear groups. Many of the nuclei are termed motor or sensory relay nuclei, as motor or sensory fibers synapse in these regions before continuing along their pathways. The term "relay" is highly misleading, however, as it seems to imply that these nuclei have no function other than to pass information along. Actually, all so-called relay nuclei contain a great many cells which play no part in simply relaying impulses from one cell to the next. Recent evidence indicates that the higher centers of the brain exert influences on incoming sensory information, and that this efferent control of sensory reception often involves a change in the signal as it passes through a "relay nucleus."

It is important to note that the different skin sensory systems begin to come together in the brain stem. For instance, in the caudal medulla the ascending somatosensory systems from the cord synapse in the dorsal medial regions (nuclei cuneatus and gracilis) while the fibers arising in the face coming in from the trigeminal nerve descend to synapse nearby. The axons of these cells of the relay nucleus then cross to the opposite side of the brain and ascend to the thalamus as a bundle called the medial lemniscus. Along the way the fibers are joined by those from other skin senses which had already crossed. By the time the thalamus is reached, all of the skin senses from the whole body are together as the fibers converge.

The core portion of most of the brain stem is collectively termed the *tegmentum*. Throughout the middle of the brain stem is the brain stem reticular formation, which extends from the lower medulla up through the midbrain and into the diencephalon. There may be over 100 separate nuclei in the brain stem reticular formation. Often the reticular formation is defined by exclusion—it is everything not identified as belonging to some other well-defined system. Some nuclei of the reticular formation contain giant cells with radi dendrites which are contacted by branches from ascending sensory fibers of various kinds. The axons of these cells split shortly after leaving the cell body, one major branch extending down into the spinal cord and the other extending rostrally into the forebrain. Since cells such as these are typically activated by stimulation in a variety of different sensory systems, the reticular formation as a whole is often said to be part of a *nonspecific sensory* system.

One area of the midbrain has no counterpart in either the pons or the medulla; this is its roof (*tectum*). The tectum contains two pairs of bumps. The rostral bumps are called the *superior colliculi* and the caudal bumps the *inferior colliculi.* The superior colliculi are associated with vision and are, in fact, the highest visual centers in many lower vertebrates like the fish. In mammals the cortex appears to override them in terms of complex pattern analysis, leaving the superior colliculus as an organizational center for visual reflexes.

The inferior colliculi function in the same way except that the relevant sense is hearing rather than sight. The inferior colliculus also lacks the typical layered structure of the superior. Both pairs of colliculi receive fibers from widespread regions of sensory and association cortex, as well as from the sensory receptors.

THE CEREBELLUM

The cerebellum is a large and highly convoluted structure located dorsally to the pons and fourth ventricle and connected to the brain stem by three pairs of peduncles (bundles of fibers). The cerebellum receives massive input from all of the sensory systems but primarily the somatosensory and vestibular systems. It also receives massive input from nearly every part of the forebrain. Stimulation or damage to just about any part of the cerebellum will have either a facilitative or an inhibitory effect on spinal reflexes and muscle tonus. The cerebellum tends to be large and well developed in graceful animals and those capable of precise movement. It is also one of the few brain regions closely related in size to the overall size of the animal. All animals become clumsy and uncoordinated after removal of the cerebellum.

The cerebellum probably began as an elaboration of the vestibular system, and its most ancient portions (including the nodulus and flocculus—see Figure 3-10) have to do with a sense of balance or equilibrium. The remainder of the cerebellum is usually divided into a central portion, along the midline, called the *vermis* or worm, and the lateral parts, termed *hemispheres.* The cerebellum has deeply placed nuclei which are generally places of synapse for outgoing or motor impulses. Sensory input comes in directly with no synaptic relay, but outgoing impulses do go by way of a synaptic relay.

The cerebellum has an amazingly simple cellular organization. There are three major types of cells, and most of the cerebellum seems to consist of an endless repetition of the same basic connections between them.

THE HYPOTHALAMUS

The hypothalamus is about the size of the tip of your little finger, but it has a host of important functions. It is shaped somewhat like a flattened funnel with the pituitary gland suspended like a ball from the bottom. Beginning rostrally near the optic chiasm, the hypothalamus extends caudally until it imperceptibly merges into the brain stem. It is continuous in a

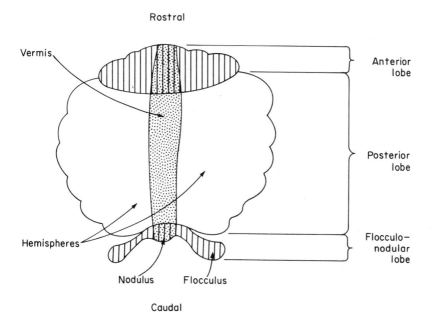

FIGURE 3-10–Highly schematic top (dorsal) view of cerebellum showing major subdivisions.

rostral direction with a small *preoptic region* rostral and dorsal to the optic chiasm. The preoptic region is functionally related to the hypothalamus and is, in fact, often considered part of it.

The hypothalamus is split in two by the third ventricle, and the cells lining this ventricle are similar to cells which surround the ventricles even down into the spinal cord.

Functionally, the hypothalamus can be regarded as having both an anterior-posterior axis and a medial-lateral dimension. The anterior hypothalamus (and the preoptic region) is basically parasympathetic in function while the posterior hypothalamus is sympathetic or excitatory.

A multisynaptic pathway, the *medial forebrain bundle,* extends from the most anterior regions of the brain all the way back and down into the brain stem. The name of this pathway is misleading because it occupies the *lateral* regions of the hypothalamus and is "medial" only with respect to the brain as a whole. The region of the medial forebrain bundle is always coextensive with the lateral hypothalamus.

The pituitary, suspended underneath the hypothalamus, is the master control gland of the endocrine system. The hypothalamus, in turn, largely controls the pituitary. The pituitary or hypophysis has two parts (see Figure 3-11). The posterior portion is actually part of the brain and receives axons of fibers originating in the hypothalamus. Nerve fibers with cell bodies above the chiasm or along the third ventricle send axons into the posterior pituitary, and these transport hormones (oxytocin, vasopressin) to the latter region.

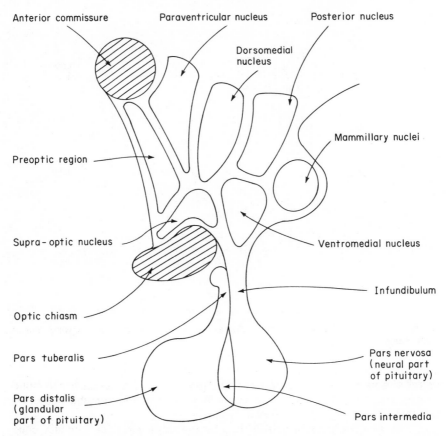

FIGURE 3-11–Lateral view of hypothalamus and pituitary (rostral is left, caudal right).

The posterior pituitary also contains substances which trigger the release of hormones from the anterior pituitary (a true gland), and they are carried to the anterior pituitary by way of blood vessels. The anterior pituitary secretes such hormones as ACTH, growth hormone, and hormones which stimulate the sex glands.

THE THALAMUS

The thalamus has two major divisions: dorsal and ventral. The dorsal thalamus is connected with the neocortex, with which it develops in close association. Since many of its nuclei project entirely to neocortical areas such as the specific sensory regions, they are often called relay nuclei. This term is no longer appropriate because these nuclei effect considerable modification of sensory input, and there is evidence suggesting that they have functions of their own quite aside from their role in transmitting impulses to the cortex.

The ventral thalamus is well developed in animals which have very poorly developed neocortex. It seems to be concerned with the coordination and regulation of motor activities.

The thalamus has been divided into numerous clusters of nuclei. Most obvious are the clusters containing the nuclei of the dorsal thalamus which project to the "sensory areas" of the neocortex. These include the lateral geniculate nucleus for vision, the medial geniculate nucleus for audition, and the ventral posterior group of nuclei for the somatosensory system. It should be emphasized that the ventral nuclei, concerned with the somatosensory system, refer to ventral nuclei of the dorsal thalamus. This is an unfortunate confusion in names since all the nuclei of the dorsal thalamus must be distinguished from those of the ventral thalamus. Fortunately, there is no ventral nucleus of the ventral thalamus. Therefore, when one talks about the ventral nucleus or the ventral nuclear group one is always referring to a cluster of cells in the dorsal thalamus.

Other nuclei can be distinguished in the thalamus. The thalamic reticular nucleus is a collection of small neurons located around the outer margin of the thalamus. It is probably related both functionally and anatomically with intralaminar nuclei, which are also small neurons spread out between layers of the thalamus. Certain nuclear groups of the midline region (not including the massa intermedia) are functionally related to the thalamic reticular nucleus and the intralaminar group. These nuclei are thought to project rather diffusely to neocortical and other forebrain areas and to participate in governing the overall excitability of the brain. In this respect these thalamic areas are functionally, if not anatomically, related to the brain stem reticular formation. Probably the arousing effects of the diffusely projecting thalamic nuclei are more limited in scope than those of the brain stem reticular formation.

Some thalamic nuclei of the dorsal division project to neocortical regions which are not part of specific sensory or motor systems as usually defined. They are sometimes called association nuclei since they project to neocortical areas called *association areas.* The dorsomedial nucleus and the pulvinar, for example, project to the prefrontal neocortical area and the parietal neocortical areas, respectively. Some thalamic nuclei only project to other nuclear groups within the thalamus.

Finally, the anterior group of nuclei of the dorsal thalamus project to the cortex of the limbic system, the cingulate gyrus. This is the cortex over the corpus callosum running from its most anterior to its most posterior extent. A diagram showing the major nuclear masses of the thalamus and its major projection systems are shown in Figure 3-12.

THE TELENCEPHALON

The *basal ganglia* are physically related to the ventral thalamus with respect to their position and function and are separated into two discontinuous masses, the *claustrum* and the *corpus striatum.* The claustrum is a thin sheet of gray matter of unknown function which runs parallel to, and just

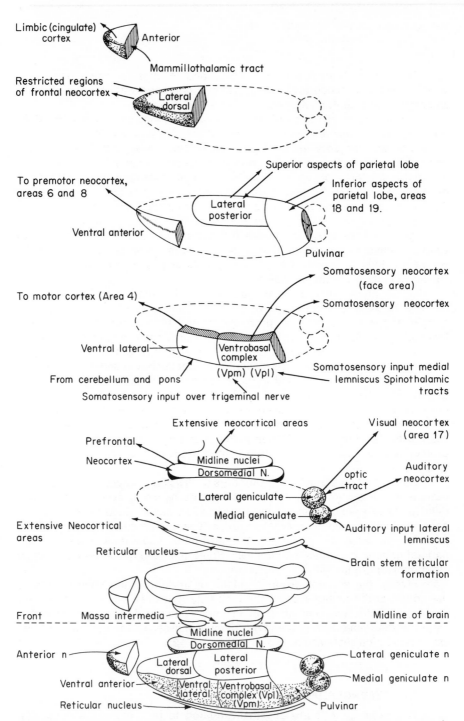

FIGURE 3-12–Schematic diagram of the major thalamic nuclei showing an approximation of a three-dimensional representation of the thalamic configuration. (From Truex. In Strong and Elwyn. *Human Neuroanatomy.* Baltimore: Williams & Wilkins, 1959.)

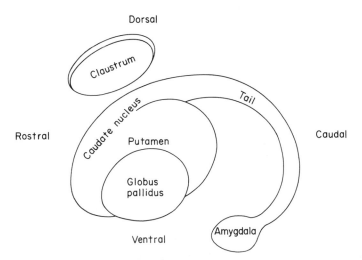

Dorsal

Claustrum

Tail

Caudate nucleus

Rostral   Caudal

Putamen

Globus
pallidus

Amygdala

Ventral

FIGURE 3-13–Basal ganglia. Side view looking from medial to lateral.

under, certain lateral neocortical areas. The corpus striatum or "striped body" consists of caudate nucleus, putamen, and globus pallidus. Since this large mass of tissue is difficult to visualize from sections, a three-dimensional view is shown in Figure 3-13. It can be seen that the largest area is the caudate nucleus, with its big head and long tail. The tail curves back and down until it ends in a region called the amygdala which is part of the limbic system. A portion of the amygdala should probably be considered part of the basal ganglia. One might easily mistake the long tail of the caudate for a fiber bundle, but it is actually composed of cell bodies with very short axons. Close by the tail of the caudate there is, however, a real fiber bundle known as the *stria terminalis*. This is a major limbic pathway connecting the amygdala with the septal area and the hypothalamus.

The basal ganglia are probably at least partly motor in function. They represent a chief ganglion for the extrapyramidal motor system, and diseases which afflict the basal ganglia often produce aberrations of movement or muscle tonus. Yet for the most part these structures do not contain large cells with the long axons necessary for action at a distance. The claustrum, which is a sheet of small cells detached from the corpus striatum, appears to be sensory in nature, perhaps duplicating or cooperating in the function of the neocortex immediately overlying it. The caudate nucleus and putamen also are composed largely of small cells, and these receive input from widespread regions of the cortex. Only the globus pallidus appears to be primarily efferent or motor in function. It sends axons downstream to synapse in such extrapyramidal relay nuclei as the red nucleus and the substantia nigra. The globus pallidus also exerts strong control over arousal or excitement. Electrical stimulation of this structure can arouse a subject from either natural or drugged (barbiturate) sleep.

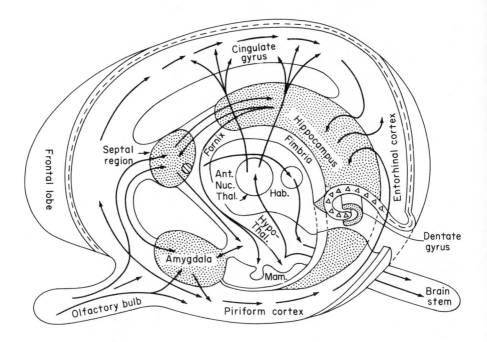

FIGURE 3-14–Some limbic system interconnections.

THE LIMBIC SYSTEM

Surrounding the diencephalon and beneath the neocortex is a roughly spherical system of structures called the limbic system. The structures share many functions and are closely interrelated by fiber systems. They also share one other important characteristic: All are tied in with mechanisms of the hypothalamus. Since the limbic structures tend to develop earlier in evolution than the neocortical mantle, some people believe they have lost their importance for the behavior of higher mammals. But, rather than being regressed or vestigial in higher animals, some parts of the limbic system reach their apex of development in man. The regressive idea may, however, have some validity when applied to parts of the system that approximate neocortex in their construction, like the cingulate gyrus and entorhinal cortex. These are said to be primitive cortex because they have fewer than the six well-defined layers which are used to define neocortex. Under the microscope the cingulate gyrus and entorhinal cortex, the limbic regions with two-dimensional organization, do appear to be relatively impoverished versions of neocortex, but it may be a serious mistake to think of neocortex as the ultimate in brain tissue design.

Some limbic regions like the amygdala and septal area are primarily nuclear in organization, as is the thalamus. The hippocampus, on the other hand, is structurally unique and not like any other part of the brain. As can be seen in Figure 3-14, the hippocampus is composed of two interlocking U-shaped sheets of tissue, one of which merges into entorhinal cortex, which merges into the neocortex of the temporal lobe. The other sheet, the dentate gyrus, is composed mainly of small granule cells resembling those found in sensory neocortex.

The sheet which is continuous with entorhinal cortex (by way of an intervening region called the subiculum) is sometimes called the hippocampus proper. Actually, the term "hippocampus" (sea horse) was originally intended to apply to the whole jelly roll structure plus the large fiber bundle known as the fornix. The hippocampus proper is characterized by densely packed large pyramidal cells much like those of motor areas of the neocortex although they do not produce motor responses. Many pyramidal cells of the hippocampus do not have long axons but instead contact hundreds of other pyramids through branching axons. These are called basket cells. Some are long-axon cells, however, and send their axons along the surface of the hippocampus where they eventually congregate into a huge fornix bundle which courses forward to the septal area, then turns ventrally and caudally so that it doubles back into the hypothalamus. Some fibers of the fornix synapse in the septal region and preoptic region while others are distributed throughout the hypothalamus. Still others, in the portion of the fornix located between hippocampus and septal area, take a reverse direction, or go into the hippocampus. Most of the input to the hippocampus, however, comes in "back way" through entorhinal cortex and subiculum. The dentate gyrus is the main receiving area for these fibers, as might be deduced from the type of cell it contains. This input probably includes sensory impulses from all the senses. In addition, recent evidence indicates that the dentate gyrus samples at least some types of hormones present in the bloodstream.

The pattern of fornix connections, with fibers distributed throughout the length of the hypothalamus, indicates that the hippocampus acts by influencing the hypothalamus. Many fornix fibers run all the way to the caudal end of the hypothalamus, where they synapse in the mammillary nuclei. A bundle of fibers from these cells (the mammillothalamic tract) then courses dorsally and rostrally to synapse in the anterior nuclear group of the thalamus. From here fibers radiate up to the entire length of the cingulate gyrus. Deep within the cingulate gyrus is a multisynaptic fiber pathway, the cingulum bundle, which runs in a rostral-caudal direction back to the rear end of the corpus callosum. Some of these fibers then enter the hippocampus by way of entorhinal cortex or subiculum, thus forming a path whereby impulses originating in the hippocampus wind up back where they started, after a long odyssey through the brain. This path is called Papez's circuit. It has many entrances and exits, however, and each leg of the journey is also a pathway for impulses which are not completing a circuit of any kind. The cingulum bundle, for example, is a pathway for impulses originating in medial frontal regions which travel to the cingulate gyrus, or even the hippocampus.

The amygdala, like the hippocampus and the limbic system in general, receives input from many sensory systems. At least some of its sensory input arrives from secondary sensory regions of the neocortex rather than directly from the receptors. The most ancient portion of the amygdala receives a wide band of fibers from the olfactory bulbs, the lateral olfactory tract. The amygdala has a number of efferent pathways to septal and preoptic regions and the hypothalamus. In a sense, the amygdala is the "reticular formation" of the limbic system. It also has two-way connections with the frontal lobes of the neocortex, even though the amygdala itself is located in the depths of the temporal lobe.

The septal region is a cluster of nuclei located on the midline and tending to be near the base of the brain. The medial septal nuclei send fibers into the hippocampus. The septal region receives input from the reticular formation of the brain stem, and it has connections with the amygdala, preoptic region, and hypothalamus.

The habenula is sometimes considered part of the limbic system, but it is also part of the diencephalon or epithalamus. The function of the habenula is almost completely unknown. Fibers reach the habenula from the hippocampus and septal area, while the main habenular outflow goes to a nucleus on the floor of the midbrain.

According to several theorists, the two large sheetlike regions of the limbic system, entorhinal cortex, and cingulate gyrus were regions of origin of primitive neocortex along their outer edges. This primitive ring of neocortex then gave rise to still another ring of slightly more advanced generalized six-layered cortex which became sensory "association" cortex. A diagram of the interconnections of the major portions of the limbic system is provided in Figure 3-14.

NEOCORTEX

The neocortex covers nearly the entire surface of the brain of the advanced mammals. As was mentioned earlier, it has a laminar organization consisting usually of six well-defined layers. There are, however, departures from this plan. The most specialized cortex is that of the motor and the sensory areas.

In all animals the brain is separated into two hemispheres by a longitudinal fissure. Many cross-connecting fiber bundles join the hemispheres. In the lower animals the anterior and hippocampal commissures are the main connecting bundles, but in placental mammals the largest commissural bundle by far is the *corpus callosum.*

In many mammals the neocortex is deeply fissured, but in others it is quite smooth. Even smooth-brained animals have a *rhinal fissure,* however. This can be seen in a side view of a smooth brain but is ventrally placed in man, where it lies under the expanding neocortex. It separates neocortex (above) from limbic cortex (below) and is a basic landmark of the brain. While different types of animals have very different fissural patterns, primates tend to have three fissures in addition to the rhinal: the *central* fissure, which separates frontal from parietal lobes, the *sylvian* fissure, and the *calcarine.* The sylvian fissure, sometimes called the lateral, is not really a fissure at all from numerous sources, including branches or collaterals of the fibers going from the relay nuclei to the specific projection areas.

In Figure 3-15 it can be seen that the primary visual projection area is in the occipital lobe, mostly on the medial surface in man, while the auditory region is in the temporal lobe, primarily on the lower lip of the sylvian fissure. The somatosensory region is just posterior to the central fissure, and at the lower end of this area is a newly discovered vestibular projection area. Visceral sensory fibers project to the buried insula, while the taste projection region is at the ventral forward tip of the insula.

Near the bottom of the motor areas is a region which is found only in man: Broca's area. Generally present only in the left hemisphere, it is the motor speech region and is concerned with speech and language. The problem of speech brings up another important difference between man and animals. In animals, by and large, each hemisphere duplicates the function of the other. In man there is a strong tendency for some functions to be localized on only one side. Most humans, for example, are right-handed, and this has been the case throughout all recorded history. Since motor systems are largely crossed, this means that the left hemisphere is frequently dominant for handedness—as for speech. We also tend to have a dominant eye and ear, as well as leg, and there is evidence that the sense of position and orientation in space (probably a higher manifestation of the vestibular and proprioceptive systems) is localized in the right parietal lobe. Humans with damage in this region are usually unable to find their way about, even by using maps.

When all motor and sensory regions have been mapped out on the neocortical surface, many large areas are left unaccounted for. Some of the space is filled with what are called supplementary motor and sensory regions, apparently crude duplications of the primary areas. There is, for example, a small motor homunculus on the medial surface of the frontal lobe in some animals and a secondary somatosensory area in the parietal lobe. Even when these are included, however, large areas of "silence" exist which often give neither a definite response to sensory stimulation nor a discrete movement when electrically stimulated, especially when the animal is under anesthesia. These regions have long been called *association cortex.* It was formerly believed that they received information from the various specific sensory association regions, and that it was in association cortex that complex multisensory concepts and ideas were formed. This is a different kind of multisensory interaction from that considered to occur in the reticular formation because in this case the sensory input has been previously "analyzed" or "processed" by the specific sensory regions.

EVOLUTION OF THE NERVOUS SYSTEM

CHAPTER 4

The ultimate goal of the physiological psychologist is to know the workings of the human brain. However, the human brain is not available for experimentation, and most research must be confined to the brain of lower animals such as the rat, cat and monkey, with an occasional exotic beast thrown in. Does this mean that what is learned about a lower-animal brain does not apply to humans, and vice versa? Not at all. The brains of placental mammals are amazingly alike in structure and, in many cases, function— especially the "lower parts" of the brain, the hypothalamus and brain stem. If one discounts the addition of passing fiber tracts, for example, the medullas of most mammals look much the same. Even the "higher" brain regions are similar, but one must be aware of shifts of position and size which have occurred in evolution before he can effectively "translate" from one brain to the next. By analogy, although German and English sound dissimilar to the man in the street, to the scholar who is aware of the sound changes that have taken place in each language over the centuries the two are highly related. There are also a few evolutionary trends which clearly indicate the relations between different types of brains (see Figures 4-1, 4-2, 4-3).

Unfortunately, little *direct* proof exists that what we will discuss are truly evolutionary trends because our phylogenetic ancestors are dead and gone. At best, we can get some general clues about the structure of their brains by examining the relatively rare fossil brain casts which have been found. A true study of evolutionary changes would require a time machine to take us back to prehistoric days. Lacking one, however, we still have a few courses of action open. While it is true that all present animals have had about the same length of time in which to evolve, not all seem to have taken advantage of the opportunity. Some contemporary animals still have their ancestral form, and these "living fossils" can serve in place of unobtainable subjects from the past. In many cases there is adequate supporting evidence that their brains, as well as bodies, are much the same as they were hundreds of millions of years ago. Whenever possible, the animal type chosen for such study is the most generalized or nonspecialized member of its group. The salamander, for example, is a better example of an archtype amphibian than the specialized frog. The most primitive mammals alive today, the platypus and the spiny anteater (or echidna), probably have

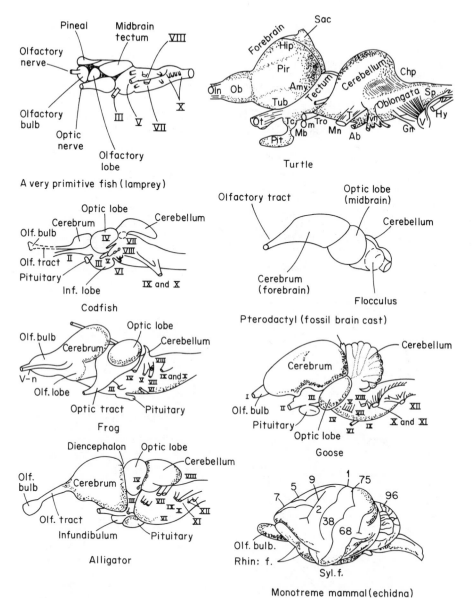

FIGURE 4-1–A comparison of the brains of a variety of animals.

managed to survive only because of their extreme specialization. If these are used as representative animals, their specialized features must be ignored. It is unlikely, for example, that any ancestor of ours was toothless like the echidna. Finally, it is possible to learn a lot about evolution from studying the development of the embryo, including aborted human fetuses. In many cases

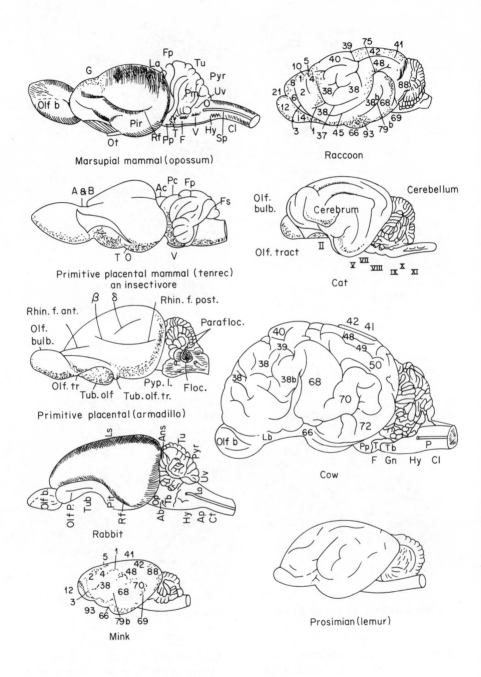

FIGURE 4-2–A comparison of the brains of a variety of animals.

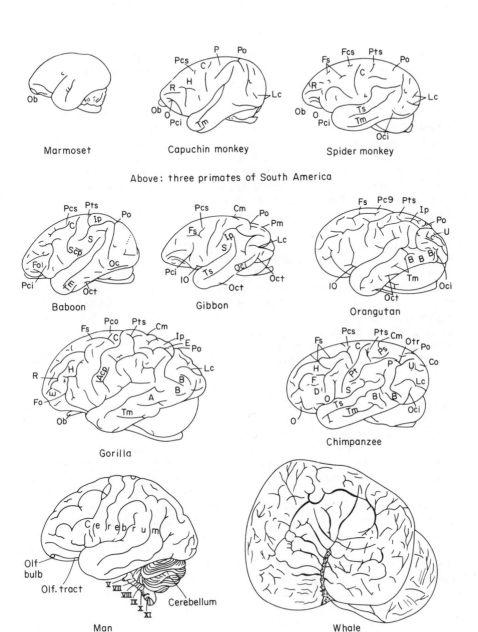

Marmoset

Capuchin monkey

Spider monkey

Above: three primates of South America

Baboon

Gibbon

Orangutan

Gorilla

Chimpanzee

Man

Whale

FIGURE 4-3—A comparison of the brains of a variety of animals. (Figures adapted from C. J. Connolly. *External Morphology of the Primate Brain.* Springfield, Ill.: Thomas, 1950. Raymond C. Truex and Malcolm B. Carpenter. *Human Neuroanatomy,* 5th ed. Baltimore: Williams & Wilkins, 1959. J. W. Papez. *Comparative Neurology.* New York: Crowell, 1929.)

ontogeny really does recapitulate phylogeny. The last parts of the brain to develop in evolution are also the last to develop in the individual, and the embryo of man passes through ancestral stages.

There are two main trends in evolution. The most obvious and most discussed is the tendency toward extreme dependence on the environment through specialization of certain functions; a formerly versatile body part is changed to a less versatile special-purpose tool. The horse, for example, has traded five toes for a hoof. A hoof is useful for running at high speed across a meadow and for kicking wolves but not for much else. Over the short haul such specialization gives a competitive edge in exploiting a particular environment to the fullest, and its survival value is obvious. But, it represents a gamble that things will always stay the same. The gamble is nearly always lost because, in the long run, things do change.

The second trend is toward the development of independence from the environment, or nonspecialization. Following this trend, changes occur which increase versatility. Until the advent of man (and really up to the last several thousand years) this "strategy" did not "pay off" in terms of the number of progeny produced. Our ancestors were probably never numerous. When highly specialized animals become extinct, they disappear quickly without issue or descendants. When generalized animals pass from the scene, it is often because they have given birth to an improved version of themselves.

Changes in the form of generalized animals tend to be such that they increase their independence from the environment. For example, the adoption of an upright posture in man, along with a modification of the feet, actually widened his scope of activity. The new, upright primate could walk with his feet and manipulate things or carry them with his hands. In addition, many of the changes which have occurred in generalized animals are true improvements and not merely changes. Over the course of time some members of a class developed new means of coping with the environment, and a number of more or less specialized forms developed from the basic generalized animal. Thus, there are many side branches in the progression of ancestors leading to man. At various points in evolution different groups of animals diverged from the generalized stock and took separate paths. Since most retained the brain structure characteristic of the stage of evolutionary development at the time of their divergence, one can often accurately judge the point at which a given group broke away from some more general line by examining its brain. Of course, one must take account of the fact that the specialization in behavior will be accompanied by parallel changes in particular parts of the brain. The bat brain, for example, is very much like that of its primitive insectivore ancestor but differs in that the auditory system has become elaborated in conjunction with the development of sonar navigation.

The brain cannot be understood in isolation from the physiology and structure of the body in general. The more complex the organization of a given brain structure, for instance, the greater the demand for an optimal temperature and a ready supply of oxygen to burn. The former is no problem to the fish, as water provides a conservative temperature externally. The fish is barred from possession of a truly complex brain by the fact that comparatively little oxygen can become dissolved in water, from which it must be extracted by the fish. When the fish crawled out of the water, he solved the oxygen problem but faced the new problem of internal control of temperature. Efficient internal temperature control was not achieved until the advent of higher mammals and birds.

FROM INDEPENDENT CELL TO COLONY

The evolutionary path up to the fish is much more conjectural than that onward from the fish because soft body parts rarely become fossilized. It seems logical, however, that life must have begun as one independent cell. The most important single advance was from the independent cell to the colony, for once this step was taken the subsequent ones probably were inevitable. At some point along the way cells developed an affinity for one another and existed as clusters or colonies. Slime mold (a type of ameba) of the present day actually continues to take and retake this step; the cells live for long periods as individuals, but at intervals they congregate into what looks like a slug. The "slug" then crawls as if it were an animal in its own right. It settles down presently and develops stalks which contain spores at the top, and these become the individuals of the next generation.

Once a group of cells exists as a colony, specialization of some of the cells for different purposes gives it a clear survival advantage. Some cells might specialize in the digestion of food, others might sharpen their sensory capacities, etc. In this way the whole colony would soon become more efficient than any of the parts, while each cell would become dependent on its fellows. The presence of differentiated cells demands a means of communication and coordination between them, and two different communication systems have evolved. The first is the secretion of chemical messages which travel to their destinations in an internal circulatory system. This is the hormone system. Hormones in higher animals are produced by the ductless or endocrine glands. A second system involves the transmission of information over long distances to discrete sites, beginning with efficient communication between receptors and effectors. The skin is the area of contact where the organism meets the world; and many sensory receptors, as well as all neurons, are derived from basically skin cells, and some may develop into specialized cells for long-range information transmission. Jellyfish have a primitive communication system which amounts to a network of nerve fibers over their surface that communicates excitation from receptor to effector, but these animals completely lack a central nervous system.

DEVELOPMENT OF THE CENTRAL NERVOUS SYSTEM

The presence of a central nervous system represents the next stage of complexity. Sensory cells differentiated so that they sampled various aspects of the environment. The integration of these was necessary for an optimal balance between flight, fight, eating, and reproduction, and the accomplishment of ever more successful integration of information from different sources had an obvious bearing on survival. Thus, the CNS was born as an integration center, carrying out the second main function of nerve cells. The flatworm (Platyhelminthes) is probably the lowest animal to possess a central nervous system, but it also retains the old nerve net, like that in the jellyfish, over its body surface. Its brain consists of a pair of ganglia in the head, with paired strands of fibers extending into the body. Frequent cross-connections between the two strands make the system resemble a ladder. In this animal most of the features which will be retained and enhanced in higher animals are already present. For example, the flatworm has bilateral symmetry and an apparent tendency toward segmentation in the "rungs" of the ladderlike nerve fibers, which are a crude analogy to the spinal cord.

The flatworm is elongated, with a front and hind end. The head end, habitually meeting the environment, develops special sensory capacities not needed at the rear, and the ganglion which coordinates sensory impulses becomes located in the head. The tendency for neural elaboration to occur at the head end of the nervous system is termed *encephalization.* In this general tendency the existing portions of the brain remain largely unchanged while a newer addition differentiates out of it, superimposed on the structure from which it grew. The next advance is usually an outgrowth from this newly developed part of the brain. From the spinal cord a medulla is differentiated, from the medulla a diencephalon, and so on, until in man the neocortex is so extensively developed that it overshadows the lower part of the brain.

Elaboration at the rostral end of the CNS is not so mysterious when one considers that the primary job of the lower centers was to govern vital reflexes. These cannot be lightly tampered with. The mechanism of respiration, for example, is already just about perfect. Any change in the respiratory reflexes of the medulla and pons is likely to be fatal. The neocortex, on the other hand, can be altered or damaged in a number of ways with no great effect on life. In fact, large regions of neocortex can be cut with a razor blade without demonstrably affecting behavior.

One exception to the encephalization rule is the cerebellum. It first appears at the "correct" evolutionary time as a primitive outgrowth of the pons, but it does not approach peak development until long after the telencephalon is developed. The flocculonodular lobe is the most ancient part of the cerebellum (see Figure 3-10 in the previous chapter) while the anterior lobe is next. The posterior lobe is the latest addition, often called the neocerebellum. Note that even here the newer additions are of progressively larger size.

Since our spinal cords have a definite segmental organization, it is suspected that one of our ancestors passed through a stage in which it resembled an annelid worm (the earthworm is an annelid). This segmented creature, after a series of modifications, developed into a fishlike form. The fish possesses all the major brain divisions, with the telencephalon represented as the olfactory lobes, swellings of the olfactory bulbs. The fish that later developed into an amphibian differed considerably, however, from the ray-finned bony fishes so successful and common now. The form of today's most highly advanced bony fish was a relatively late phyletic development. It is strange to consider that there were probably mammals before there were perch.

The fish ancestral to mammals had fleshy lobe fins capable of supporting the body on land and containing bones which could develop into the limb skeleton. It also had the ability to gulp air into a highly vascularized sac where oxygen exchange could occur, however inefficiently, as well as possessing gills. There is little doubt that these features imply life in a seasonally dry river, where they would facilitate movement from one puddle to the next. It must have been a river because amphibians, the descendants of this fish, have never been able to tolerate salt water.

THE AMPHIBIANS

Evolution, of course, is not a response to a consciously felt need. When a genetic change or mutation has survival value the mutants thrive and multiply. Evolution has tended to take place in bursts which occur in a relatively short time. As we can see today, life in a muddy river is slim pickings, and so the fish found it. In contrast, the land had become covered with vegetation and had been invaded by insects. For a variety of reasons insects have a severe reduction in efficiency if they grow beyond a certain small size. Thus, the land represented an unexploited niche for a large predator, and fish have always tended to be carnivorous. When the first fish crawled out onto the land, they found a bountiful food supply and conditions ripe for rapid evolution. Territory that is vacant or relatively unoccupied promises viability to a great many mutations. Practically any animal will survive if it can move its jaws. For this reason it is possible under such circumstances for animals to evolve into an efficient final form even when some of the intermediate stages are disadvantageous or even ridiculous. As the new environment becomes occupied, however, new carnivores evolve to eat nature's mistakes, and, even more serious, competition for the food supply develops. The kangaroo, for example, was hardly affected by the dog when the latter was introduced into Australia but has been wiped out of large areas by the more efficient and prolific rabbit, which eats all the grass. The process outlined above has been repeated countless times in the earth's history, with probably the last great episode taking place in Australia. One of the first occurrences of this situation was the emergence of the fish from the water in the Paleozoic era. Within a relatively short time at the end of this era fish moved onto the land and became amphibians, reptiles, and finally mammallike reptiles.

The fish brought with it from the water a sensory mechanism which was useless on land: the *lateral line system.* The lateral line system consists of rows of sensory "hair cells" located on the head and trunk, which are used to detect pressure waves in water, much like a sonar system. The lateral lines located on the sides, however, became elaborated at the anterior end. There the cells developed into a primitive version of the vestibular system. The latter, in turn, developed a bump which would become elongated and eventually curl into the cochlea. The receptors remained hair cells in form and can be found in the cochlea in primates. The cerebellum is also essentially an outgrowth of the vestibular system in its origins. Once on land, the amphibian lost its lateral line system, and development of the vestibular and auditory systems was accelerated.

The brain of the amphibian was also an advance over that of the fish. The olfactory bulbs began to enlarge and differentiate, as can be seen in the illustration of an amphibian brain in Figure 4-1. The lateral portions tend to receive many olfactory fibers. This portion is primitive paleocortex and in later animals became the more ancient part of the amygdala, the corticomedial division. The more medial portion, with relatively fewer olfactory fibers, is primitive archicortex, which would become hippocampus in more highly developed animals (see Figure 4-4).

The amphibian was never destined to dominate the earth, as it was not fully terrestrial. Amphibians have moist skins, lay eggs, and spend part of the life cycle in water competing with fish. Their bloodstreams mix oxygenated with stale blood, and legs which sprawl out to the side and are weak further contribute to fatigue. Their habitat is severely limited by an inability to regulate temperature internally.

THE REPTILES

Shortly after the appearance of amphibians, their descendants, the reptiles, came upon the scene. While not correcting all the faults of the amphibians, they did have more powerful and better placed limbs, a formidable array of teeth, and independence from the water life cycle. The reptilian brain was also an improvement. Paleocortex was still lateral and tending to move ventrally, and archicortex was dorsal and medial. Between the two was the beginning of what later became true neocortex.

In the sequence of development the region of the hippocampus apparently differentiated into what are termed entorhinal and cingulate cortex (juxtallocortex). It is from the latter that the neocortex arose, and it did so before the hippocampus had assumed anything like its present shape or development. The hippocampus in mammals is not merely a primitive remnant of a structure present in the reptile. It continued to elaborate until it reached a developmental peak in man. The same is true of the amygdala, another important component of the limbic system. The amygdala added a whole new part, the basolateral portion, associated more with the basal ganglia than the sense of smell.

Long before the reptiles evolved into the dinosaurs of the Mesozoic era, some of them had developed definite mammallike tendencies. One of the very first reptiles had differentiated teeth, for example. Reptiles are usually characterized by the same tooth form (cone shaped), which is endlessly repeated. In mammals the teeth become differentiated into snippers or biters (incisors), slashers (canines), and mashers or grinders (molars). Differentiation like this should not be mistaken for specialization. It is a form of generalization since it makes a more varied diet possible. Specialization occurs when one form of tooth becomes used and others neglected. Some

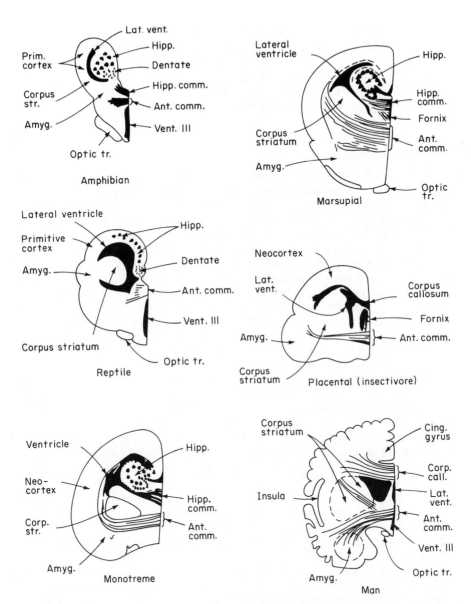

FIGURE 4-4—Cross (coronal) sections through the anterior commissure region from reptile to man. Only half of brain shown, with lateral to the left and medial to the right.

early reptiles also had mammalian limbs which directly opposed gravity, but we unfortunately can never know whether they had hair or milk glands. Thus, by the end of the first great era of life animals had progressed from the lowest beginnings to a distinctly mammallike form.

The next logical development should have been that the mammals took over the earth. It did not work out that way, however. In the next era, the Mesozoic, reptiles which were *not* approaches to mammalian forms radiated and took over the land, the sea, and the air. True mammals lived and evolved during this period but probably clung to life as small, furtive creatures of the night. They were typically insectivores. Apparently the dominant reptiles had not yet learned that they were inferior.

THE MAMMALS

Many different types of mammals developed during the Mesozoic period, but only three have survived. Although there are clearly three classes of advancement from primitive to advanced, they do not necessarily represent successive stages of evolution, with each the ancestor of the next. The highest type might well have evolved directly from a reptile. In any event, the most primitive mammal type alive today is the monotreme (one hole), which has a cloaca like a reptile's and lays eggs. Two species, the duck-billed platypus and the spiny anteater, still exist in the evolutionary backwaters of Australia and neighboring islands. Many features of their skeleton and physiology are decidedly reptilian, but their brains are strictly mammalian. They have other mammalian features, such as the secretion of milk and the presence of hair, and they care for their babies. The smooth platypus brain is perhaps the more primitive. The echidna brain has a few shallow indentations but no deep convolutions. In basic construction their brains are very much like that of the next highest form, the marsupial, and both are definitely unlike the brain of the highest form, the placental mammal. Strangely, however, some scientists interested in skeletal and dental factors insist on lumping marsupial and placental mammals together. If only the brains are considered, the marsupial and the monotreme are part of the same group, while each is separated by a vast chasm from the placental animals.

Marsupial Mammals

In marsupial and monotreme brains the cross-connections between the two hemispheres, including neocortex, pass primarily by way of the hippocampal and anterior commissures. Neither animal possesses even the beginnings of a corpus callosum, the distinctive feature of the placental brain (see Figure 4-4).

The marsupial gives birth to young which are almost embryonic because it lacks a placenta with which to nourish the young internally. The babies are born, however, with powerful front legs, which they use in migrating into the pouch and finding a nipple. The common opossum is a very primitive but highly successful marsupial while the kangaroo and koala are highly specialized and not so successful forms. For the most part marsupials are not very social, and in a crisis it is generally everyone for himself. Marsupials never develop a large amount of neocortex, but some have relatively and absolutely more neocortex than some of the most primitive placentals. In the more advanced marsupials the growth of neocortex has created what looks like the beginnings of a temporal lobe. The hippocampus occupies a medial position about where the corpus callosum would be if there were one, but it also bends down into the temporal lobe. It extends as far forward as the region occupied by the septal area in placentals, even ahead of the anterior commissure.

Placental Mammals

Placental mammals are the most advanced and numerous of the mammals. Because of the placenta, young can be nourished longer in the mother and born in a more advanced state than the marsupial young. Even so, in most placental mammals the young are relatively helpless at birth. Placental mammals tend to be good mothers—one example of their characteristic social interaction. Some present-day insectivores, among them the hedgehog, resemble the ancestral placental mammals in many respects. All present-day placental mammals are highly related and appear to have evolved from a small insectivore ancestor. In the insectivores, even the most primitive ones, there is a corpus callosum. This factor largely accounts for the great differences between the brains of placental mammals and those of the marsupials and monotremes. The corpus callosum is not just an expanded anterior commissure but develops in a distinctly different region dorsally to the anterior commissure. When the corpus callosum is very small, as it is in the more primitive insectivores, it does not force a drastic reorganization of the brain. As it grows with evolution, however (or in the individual during development), it expands backward.

The corpus callosum grows just in front and on top of the hippocampal commissure, a fiber bundle cross-connecting the two hippocampi. When it grows in size due to the number of fibers in it it must, of necessity, push against the hippocampal commissure. As it pushes against the hippocampal commissure, it forces the hippocampus to move backwards so that it no longer extends to the septal region-anterior commissure area (see Figure 4-6). As the corpus callosum assumes the form of a thick sheet, it forces the hippocampus back along its boomerang curve so that in such intermediate animals as the placental carnivores or herbivores the bottom part of the boomerang is pushed down into the temporal lobes (or areas analogous to temporal lobes) until the more vertical part of this curved structure is much larger than the dorsal, more horizontal, part. Finally, in animals with the greatest corpus callosum development (primates, porpoises) the hippocampus is pushed back so far that there is no longer any dorsal horizontal portion, as can be seen in Figures 4-4 and 4-6. Despite this extensive migration the hippocampus maintains its connections with septal region and hypothalamus (the fornix), but these fibers become greatly elongated. Most placental mammals left the evolutionary stream to become specialized at a point where the hippocampus had a boomerang shape, and this is the most common form today. Human embryos proceed through these stages in the same way as their ancestors, with the hippocampus beginning as the dorsal medial cerebral wall and then proceeding to invaginate, roll up, and go through the forced migration into the depths of the temporal lobe (see Figure 4-5).

While this is happening the cerebral hemispheres go through a great

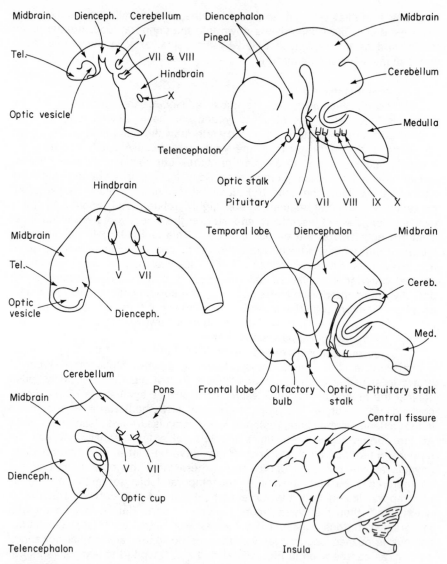

FIGURE 4-5–Development of the human brain from early fetus (upper left) to birth (lower right). (From Truex. In Strong and Elwyn. *Human Neuroanatomy*. Baltimore: Williams & Wilkins, 1959.)

expansion so that the hippocampus seems to be becoming smaller and smaller. Looks are deceiving in this case, because the hippocampus is actually growing at a remarkable rate. The hippocampus of man may have been pushed around, but it is still by far the largest and best developed hippocampus of any animal. We also possess a most remarkable amount of neocortex, which is partly why we have such a large corpus callosum, but actually the whale has us beat in this respect. A whale brain may weigh 7,000 grams, as compared to our 1,500, and the neocortex of the whale is highly convoluted. In some smaller whales (e.g., the porpoise) the brain may be exactly the same size as ours and appear to be in every way but one as well developed. The porpoise hippocampus is smaller than that of a sheep whose total brain size is comparatively tiny.

The amygdala has perhaps been less influenced by evolutionary changes than the hippocampus. The expansion of the neocortex has resulted in a rotation of the amygdala so that its two main parts have changed relative position. The more advanced portion of the amygdala, the basolateral complex, has increased in size relative to the ancient corticomedial complex.

The thalamus undergoes changes which occur in parallel to those of the neocortex over the course of evolution. The auditory and visual relay nuclei are rather recent developments, and the dorsomedial nucleus, which projects to frontal cortex, grows in relation to the increasing size of prefrontal cortex. Finally, there has been a vast increase in a polysensory nucleus (the pulvinar), which projects to temporal lobe neocortex (association cortex).

The relatively advanced brain of the placental mammal did not, apparently, lead to any immediate superiority. The entire Mesozoic era was dominated by reptiles, and before it ended they had evolved into very respectable forms. Some had the capacity for live birth, some had visual systems probably not equaled by many mammals, and some had reached perfection in self-defense perhaps far beyond anything found today. We can only speculate about reptilian physiology during this era, but some may well have developed a form of internal temperature control. At least one reptile today guards and cares for its young (the alligator), and fossil footprints suggest that some adult dinosaurs kept their young to the inside of the herd. The flying reptile (pterodactyl) had a brain much like that of present-day birds and was, in fact, probably lighter in weight for its wingspread (up to 25 feet) than modern birds. From fossil brain casts we know that the brains of most Mesozoic reptiles remained small to the end, yet in many cases a greatly enlarged lumbar region of the spinal cord may have performed some of the functions carried out by the brain in mammals. One thing is certain: Mammals never competed successfully with Mesozoic reptiles. The primitive mammals were few in number and small in size. They probably depended heavily on the sense of smell and kept out of sight in the daytime.

One of the biggest mysteries of science is what happened to the dinosaurs. They disappeared completely and within a very short time, from land, sea, and air. This sudden disappearance was not matched by a simultaneous increase in mammals. Instead, after a period in which apparently few animals were left alive, the mammals radiated to fill the vacancies left by the departed reptiles. In many cases the mammal almost exactly duplicated its reptilian predecessor in body form and behavior, as far as the latter can be deduced. Most of the more profound evolutionary changes occurred within a short period at the beginning of the Cenozoic era, as one would

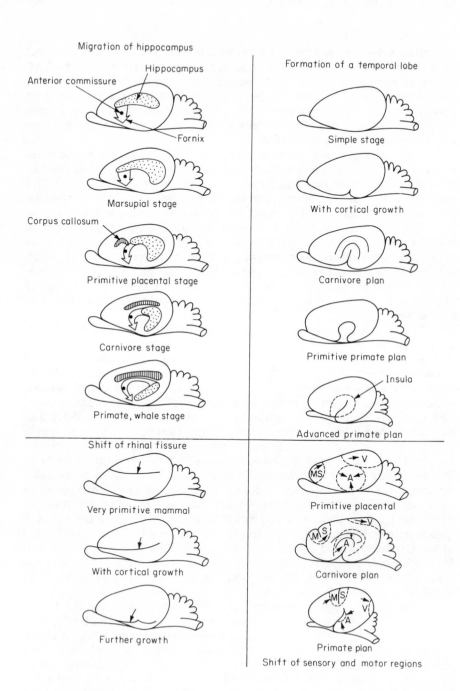

FIGURE 4-6–Examples of evolutionary changes and trends. M = motor cortex; S = somatosensory cortex; A = auditory cortex; V = visual cortex.

expect if the land were vacant. Three main classes of herbivores developed: the proboscideans such as the elephant, the perissodactyls (odd toed), and the artiodactyls (even toed). The latter class, including goats, sheep, cattle, and antelopes, is by far the most successful. With all of their meat food supplies available, carnivores developed from an original all-purpose form into the variety we see today, with one branch diverging into cats and dogs. Since carnivores are largely a response to preexisting prey, we would expect their brains to reflect a later divergence from the main line, with all trends further advanced than is the case with the herbivores.

Primates

Meanwhile, the primates were developing from an early version of the insectivore which took to the trees. It is very difficult to be an insectivore and not be exposed to fruit. As the insectivore became an omnivore, tending to eat more fruit, it found the sense of olfaction to be of little use in the trees, whereas vision (including color and stereoscopic vision) became highly relevant to survival. With pressure for the maintenance of an elaborate olfactory system absent, the mutations producing a smaller snout were not harmful, and since this resulted in a flat face, the eyes could look straight ahead. This allowed the simultaneous viewing of objects from two different angles. The eyes became coordinated into the primate form of binocular vision. This process was not quite completed, and we still retain a region sensitive to monocular visual input in our brain. The hands, and possibly the feet, became adapted for grasping but retained to an amazing degree features of the amphibian. It may have been at a very early point along this line of development that the ancestors of man departed from the other primates. Some of the most primitive primates (actually prosimians) are able to run on two feet on the ground. Although our similarity to the great apes (gorillas, chimps, orangs) cannot be denied, they are as much our descendants as we are theirs. All are highly specialized, pitiful creatures doomed to extinction, completely dependent upon tiny, vanishing environments. Their hind feet are like hands, whether they climb trees or live on the ground. One especially human characteristic is the grasping hand with the thumb opposing the fingertips. It is seldom mentioned that this feature is *regressed* in the ape, as compared to many monkeys.

While most primates are more carnivorous than is generally appreciated, only man and his ancestors progressed to the point of hunting big game. The first creatures which could be called "human" were socially organized weapon- and tool-using hunters. Once weapon and tool making progressed beyond the point of an idle pastime (as in the chimp), it was clear that a vicious circle would ensue. Each advance in creativity or intelligence would lead to an enhancement of survival probabilities. The earliest humans (Homo erectus) had physiques much like ours, although more robust, but their brains were very much smaller. In a relatively short time they evolved into large-brained Homo sapiens. The dental peculiarities of one version of Homo erectus (Sinanthropus) are virtually identical to those of the modern men who occupy the same territory in China. Actually, there may have been a slight reversal in the trend toward greater brain size, for Neanderthal man had a brain possibly larger than ours.

To sum up, the trend toward greater encephalization of neural control of behavior began with a small spot of reptilian "neocortex" which has expanded to the point where in man it represents the bulk of the brain. The cranium, however, was a little tardy in its expansion, and neocortical growth proceeded within the relatively limited space of the skull. As the neocortex expanded it pushed the paleocortex and archicortex so that they rotated, rolled up, and were tucked out of sight. Neocortical regions which were originally on the dorsolateral surface were pushed to the rear so that visual cortex is now on the medial surface and can hardly be seen on the exposed neocortical surface at all in man. Auditory cortex, originally on the lateral surface, is now pushed down into the sylvian fissure of the temporal lobe. One region which has become especially enlarged in primates is premotor or prefrontal cortex. In most subprimates motor and somatosensory cortex (sensorimotor cortex) are located very near the rostral tip of the brain. As prefrontal cortex expands, it pushes sensorimotor cortex back toward the center regions, where it downfolds into the central fissure. Parietal-temporal cortex has increased in size even more than prefrontal.

BRAIN SIZE

The overall trend toward increased brain size is found in a wide variety of animal types. In many cases, for example, a given ecological niche has been filled by a succession of different animal types, each having a larger brain than its successor. There was a herbivorous dinosaur (Triceratops) which greatly resembled the modern rhinoceros. Later a primitive mammal appeared in the role of robust herbivore (Titanotherium), and finally we have the rhinoceros, an advanced mammal. These animals were so similar that each had a long horn on the tip of its nose, yet each succeeding animal had a decidedly larger brain.

There is a powerful correlation between the total volume of brain tissue and the extent to which the brain surface is convoluted. While these may in part be two independent trends, folding of neocortex into convolutions appears to be partly a product of increased size. Neocortex is essentially a two-dimensional projection of an underlying three-dimensional organization of the dorsal thalamus. As the radius of a sphere increases, its volume increases faster than its surface. Thus, in order to maintain a constant relationship between a volume and a surface, the latter must increase at a faster rate than would the surface of a sphere. Since there is a definite relationship between a cell in the dorsal thalamus and one in the neocortex, an expanding brain must have folds in its surface (cortex). This development can be illustrated by the fact that many animal classes have both large and small species which appear to be equally intelligent and to behave similarly. Often in these cases the brain of the larger animal is both greater in volume and more convoluted than the brain of the smaller version.

FIBER BUNDLES

A final tendency in evolution has been a trend toward the highly discrete fiber bundles of the sensory and motor systems. The relatively diffuse ventral and lateral spinothalamic tracts are, for example, phylogenetically older than the extremely discrete dorsal systems. Similarly, the pyramidal tract is a later product of evolution than the primitive extrapyramidal system. The number of fibers in the pyramidal tract is, in fact, sometimes used as an index of evolutionary development.

EVOLUTION OF THE CEREBELLUM

The growth and development of the cerebellum has been neglected so far but in many ways parallels that of the neocortex. From observing the grace and coordination of an animal's movements one can accurately deduce the degree of cerebellar development. Studies of cell division in the cerebellum and other brain regions have recently suggested another possible rule of development. Animals which are relatively limited in movement or coordination (like the guinea pig) have little cell division in the cerebellum after birth. In a more coordinated animal, such as the cat, cell division in the cerebellum may continue for months. Cells in the neocortex are also somewhat retarded in cessation of cell division, requiring about a month of continued division after birth in the rat. It should be noted that dividing neurons cannot function as components of brain circuits. For the latter purpose they must grow dendrites and axons, which then make proper connections. Pending further research in this new field, it would appear that, in general, the later a brain region develops phylogenetically, the later it develops in the individual.

THE BIRDS

The bird is difficult to fit into this picture. In some ways birds have evolved features which parallel those of the mammals. They have, for example, a mammallike four-chambered heart, and they control their temperature internally. The bird brain is, however, notably reptilian in form. Avian neocortex is scant, and archicortex is in the dorsal medial position characteristic of the reptile. Nevertheless, the basal ganglia have become highly modified. The highest part of the bird brain may be the hyperstriatum, an elaboration of the corpus striatum. The hyperstriatum is not found in mammals.

BRAIN STRUCTURE AND BEHAVIOR

With these trends in mind, consider the animal and its life-style before examining the brain. You will find that species idiosyncrasies are paralleled by differences in brain structure and connections. A great deal can be inferred from the total behavioral characteristics and from the general level of brain development in animals. If, for example, the rhinal fissure is high up on the side of the brain and the animal has a long snout with large olfactory bulbs, there will be relatively few uncrossed fibers in the optic chiasm, sensorimotor cortex will be far anterior, visual cortex will be dorsomedial to dorsolateral, the dorsal part of the hippocampus will be large, and the corpus callosum will be small or even absent. If an animal does not manipulate with its forefeet, it will be difficult to find the sensory or motor representation of the forefeet. If the animal shows evidence of special sensory capacities or frequent use of a body part, the brain regions corresponding to these will be large and elaborate. Bats and porpoises, for example, have well-developed auditory systems in keeping with their special use of this system for sonar. This finding should not be surprising if one believes that behavior is determined by the sensory and motor capacities of the nervous system and the ability of the brain to put the two together appropriately. While behavior may be determined by the brain, we have seen that behavior has had more than a little to say about how the brain has evolved.

Chapter 5

SENSORY PROCESSES

CHAPTER 5

The story goes that a freshman in an introductory psychology course once asked whether a patient undergoing brain surgery could see a beam of light focused directly on the visual cortex. Whether the story is true is unimportant; it does illustrate rather dramatically that the brain exists in an isolated, "unreal" world. It is entirely dependent upon afferent nerves to bring it information about the external world. A beam of light focused directly on the visual cortex could not be seen.

The brain's hang-up is one of *transduction*. It cannot receive and process directly the many physical energies like light waves which exist in the outside world. These energies must first be converted or transduced into neural energy. The transduction process is performed by a *receptor cell*. In this chapter we will consider in detail how biological transducers (receptor cells) work, building upon this knowledge to increase our understanding of the physiological basis of sensation. A second concern will be *sensory coding*. Not only do receptor cells transform physical energies but they also give the brain some indication of the various physical characteristics of the energy. Receptor cells encode stimulus characteristics like magnitude, frequency, and duration at the same time the energy is being converted to neural energy.

RECEPTOR CELLS

A receptor cell possesses all the general properties listed for cells in Chapter 2. It is, however, especially sensitive to environmental changes and is able to transform environmental energies into a form that can be utilized by higher neural centers. Receptor cells detect many kinds of environmental changes, e.g., electromagnetic radiation of particular wavelengths, temperature, pressure, and concentrations of certain chemicals, but a single receptor cell is maximally sensitive to only one kind of environmental stimulus, which is called an *adequate stimulus* for that receptor. The degree to which an individual receptor cell is attuned to one kind of energy can be seen from the tremendous differences in the amount of energy required of an adequate and an "inadequate" stimulus.

The receptor cells of the visual system, for example, are maximally sensitive to light (the adequate stimulus) and will respond to quantities of

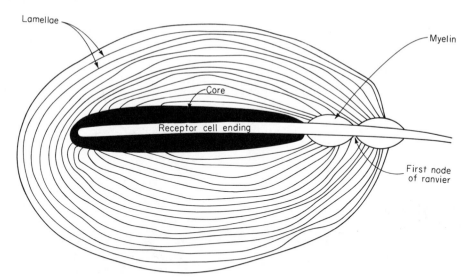

FIGURE 5-1–Diagrammatic view of an isolated pacinian corpuscle.

light as small as a few photons. Visual receptor cells will also respond to temperature and pressure changes, but they must be of far greater magnitude. The reader can readily demonstrate this fact to himself by applying gentle pressure to his eyeball when the eyelid is closed. The psychological experience will be one of light. This demonstration also illustrates what is sometimes called the *law of specific nerve energies:* A given receptor always gives rise to the same psychological experience regardless of the nature of the initiating stimulus.

There is perhaps no better way to introduce the general principles of receptor cell function than to study the workings of the *pacinian corpuscle.* Located throughout the body, pacinian corpuscles are concerned with touch-pressure sense. Figure 5-1 shows one of these structures in diagrammatic form.

The receptor cell is surrounded by a granular mass called the *core,* which in turn is surrounded by concentric layers (*lamellae*) of connective tissue like the coats of an onion. The spaces between these layers are filled with fluid. Pacinian corpuscles are relatively large, and it has been possible to isolate them from the cat's mesentery for study of receptor cell properties.

Employing a fine stylus, W. R. Loewenstein was able to stimulate an isolated corpuscle mechanically (Figure 5-2). At the same time, he inserted a recording electrode into the receptor cell. Before any mechanical stimulation occurred, there was a resting potential (see Chapter 2) of 200–300 mV. across the cell membrane. When mechanical stimulation was applied to the outer surface of the corpuscle, the membrane potential decreased, i.e., the inside of the cell became less negative with respect to the outside. This *depolarization* of the receptor cell is called a *generator potential.* It is fundamentally identical to an EPSP as described in Chapter 2. The main difference

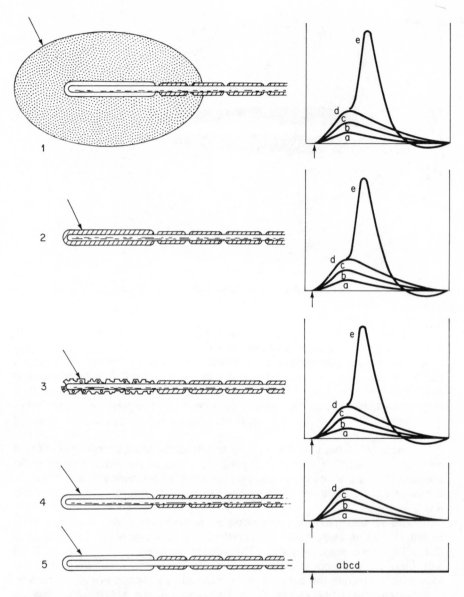

FIGURE 5-2–Dissection of corpuscle revealed the site of the transducer mechanism. Stimulation (*arrow*) of the corpuscle when intact (1), with outer layers removed (2), or after partial destruction of the core sheath (3) produced the same responses. A weak stimulus produced a weak generator current (*a*); progressively stronger stimuli produced correspondingly stronger generator current (*b* and *c*); the threshold stimulus (*d*) fired an all-or-none nerve impulse (*e*). When the first node of Ranvier was blocked (4), no all-or-none impulse could be induced. After degeneration of nerve ending (5), receptor did not respond at all to stimuli. (From W. R. Loewenstein. Biological transducers. *Scientific American, 203,* No. 2, 98–108. Copyright © 1960 by Scientific American, Inc. All rights reserved.)

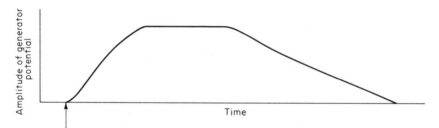

FIGURE 5-3—Arrow on left indicates the onset of a continuous stimulus of constant magnitude. The process of adaptation can be seen in that the magnitude of the generator potential becomes less and less over time.

centers around the fact that EPSPs are the result of chemical transmitter substances whereas the permeability changes underlying this generator potential were caused by the mechanical pressure produced by the stylus.

Loewenstein further found that an increased generator potential followed greater mechanical stimulation (see Figure 5-2). When the generator potential reached a critical magnitude (this value is called the *depolarization threshold*), an action potential was generated at the first node of Ranvier and was propagated down the receptor cell axon.

In this brief example the basic process of transduction can be seen. We have illustrated the mechanism by which a stimulus (pressure on the skin) is converted first into a generator potential and then into action potentials of single neurons. Such action potentials are carried by sensory nerves to the central nervous system, and after a number of synapses cortical neurons are activated. Activation of these cells is the neurophysiological basis for the psychological experience of pressure.

Before leaving the pacinian corpuscle, we must consider a few additional aspects of generator potentials. Figure 5-3 illustrates the process of *adaptation.* With application of a constant stimulus, the generator potential becomes smaller and smaller. Adaptation is the result of a physical characteristic of the receptor cell in question. In the pacinian corpuscle, for example, the onion-like structure surrounding the cell ending is probably intimately involved. The lamellae are resilient and, it is thought, with constant stimulation or depression they begin to push outward against the stylus, thus causing less pressure to be transmitted to the receptor cell proper. The outcome is, of course, a smaller and smaller generator potential.

The process of adaptation is often confused with that of *accommodation.* We mentioned earlier that the generator potential must reach a certain critical magnitude (the depolarization threshold) before action potentials occur. Accommodation refers to the fact that with constant stimulation the depolarization threshold shifts upward; that is, a greater and greater generator potential is needed before action potentials occur. Adaptation, then, involves the absolute size of the generator potential while accommodation refers to a changing threshold for the initiation of action potentials. Both processes can, of course, be occurring at the same time in a given receptor cell.

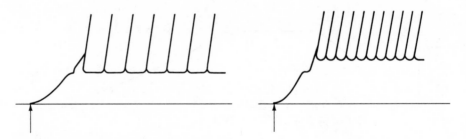

FIGURE 5-4–Stimulation (arrow) on the left is of smaller magnitude and results in fewer action potentials per unit of time.

As we saw in Chapter 2, the action potential is an all-or-none event and not graded like an EPSP. One can legitimately ask, therefore, how stimulus intensity is coded by receptor cells if the action potentials which ultimately reach the cortex are all of equal size. The basic answer is that *stimulus intensity* is coded in the number of action potentials reaching the cortex and not in their size. As a general rule, the more intense a stimulus, the greater the resultant generator potential. A greater generator potential causes action potentials to occur more frequently (see Figure 5-4). This fact—that stimulus intensity is coded in the number of action potentials and not in their size—is sometimes called the *law of stimulus intensity.*

Armed with these few principles of receptor cell function, we are now ready to consider the transduction process in greater detail in specific senses.

VISION

It is important at this time to distinguish between a receptor cell and a sense organ. We previously defined the receptor cell as that cell which performs the transduction process. The receptor cell plus any cells which "help" or are somehow involved in the transduction process make up a sense organ. In the visual system, for example, the entire eye is the sense organ while the *rods* and *cones* are the receptor cells.

The eye (Figure 5-5) has been compared to a camera in its structure and modus operandi. Like the camera, it has a lens that focuses light waves (electromagnetic radiations) on a photosensitive structure, the *retina.* The rods and cones are activated by entering light waves, and their axons travel toward the central nervous system. After a few synapses, activation of neurons in the visual cortex takes place and forms the neurophysiological basis of vision. In the following discussion we shall be concerned primarily with the visual system in man. Presumably, however, many of the principles illustrated can be applied to other animals as well. In fact, much of our understanding of man's visual system has come directly from experiments with animals.

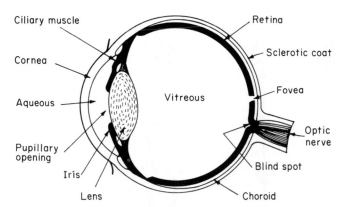

Ciliary muscle

Cornea

Aqueous

Pupillary
opening

Iris

Lens

Retina

Sclerotic coat

Vitreous

Fovea

Optic
nerve

Blind spot

Choroid

FIGURE 5-5–Simplified representation of the human eye. (From R. L. Isaacson, M. L. Hutt, and M. L. Blum. *Psychology: The Science of Behavior.* New York: Harper & Row, 1965.)

Anatomy of the Visual System

Although the retina is a complex structure, our purposes will be served if we are concerned only with *rods and cones, bipolar cells,* and *ganglion cells.* Basically, the retina can be regarded as a three-layered structure (Figure 5-6). As light waves enter the eye, they must first traverse the ganglion cell layer, then the bipolar cell layer, and they finally reach the layer containing the photosensitive rods and cones.

Rods and cones have synaptic connections with bipolar cells, which in turn synapse with ganglion cells. The axons of the ganglion cells form the fibers of the optic nerve, which course caudally along the base of the brain and enter the brain proper at the optic chiasm. Once these axons enter the brain they are referred to as the *optic tract.*

There are roughly four times as many rods as cones in the retina. The cones are thought to mediate color and very acute vision while the rods are most involved in sensing small quantities of light such as would exist in a dimly lit room. Rods are very numerous in the peripheral areas of the retina. The cones, on the other hand, are plentiful in the central (macula) retinal area. In fact, within the macula area there is a small area (the *fovea*) which consists entirely of cones, and it is upon this point that the visual image (the object one is looking at) is focused.

The fact that there are roughly 115 to 130 million rods and cones and approximately 1 million optic nerve fibers indicates the extensive *convergence* in the visual system, with many rods and cones converging on one bipolar cell and many bipolar cells converging on one ganglion cell. The visual system also illustrates the principle of *divergence,* for within the foveal area one cone may synapse with several bipolar cells (Figure 5-6).

We mentioned previously that the axons of the ganglion cells form the optic nerve and subsequently the optic tract. The point at which these axons

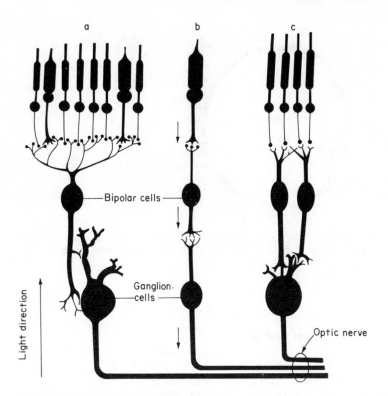

FIGURE 5-6–Three types of retinal connections. Association neurons have been omitted. (a) Mixed rod and cone system, both types synapsing with one bipolar cell and this in turn with a ganglion cell. (b) Single cone system, found only in the fovea. (c) Multiple rod system, several rods converging upon bipolars and these upon a ganglion cell. The optic nerve is formed by axons of the ganglion cells. (Modified after Polyak. From E. Gardner. *Fundamentals of Neurology,* 5th ed. Philadelphia: Saunders, 1968.)

leave the retina is called the *blind spot* or optic disk (Figure 5-5). Because there are no rods and cones at this point, images falling here cannot be seen. The reader can demonstrate this fact to himself by closing his left eye and focusing on some small object a few feet away. If the reader will move his gaze at the same level slowly to the left, he will find that the object disappears after about 15 degrees of rotation only to reappear as rotation to the left continues.

Two terms that are often confusing to the beginning student are *visual field* and *retinal field.* The visual field is simply the extent of the outside world which can be seen at any given moment without moving the eyeball. There is a visual field for left and right eyes with a region of overlap seen by both eyes. Because of the optical characteristics of the eye, the visual field is projected upon the retina upside down and reversed from what would be expected if straightforward projection were to take place. Those objects, for

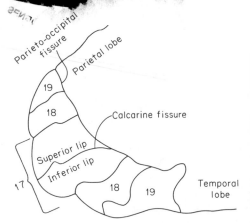

Parieto-occipital fissure

Parietal lobe

19

18

Calcarine fissure

Superior lip

Inferior lip

17

18   19

Temporal lobe

FIGURE 5-7–(Left) Diagramatic view of a medial section through the occipital lobe of the human cortex. **(Right)** Photomicrograph of the lateral geniculate nucleus showing the laminae. The numbers, 1 to 6, designate the cell laminae from the hilus to the dorsal surface of the nucleus. Cresyl violet stain. Magnified about 10 times. (From E. C. Crosby, T. Humphrey, and E. W. Lauer. *Correlative Anatomy of the Nervous System.* New York: Macmillan, 1962.)

example, in the right superior temporal quadrant of the right visual field are projected onto the right retina (the right retinal field) in the left inferior nasal quadrant. The importance of visual and retinal fields will become clearer as we follow the visual system centrally. Axons from a particular retinal area tend to remain in close proximity in the optic nerve and tract. This *retino-topic organization* continues all the way to the cortex.

Axons from the right and left retinal fields enter the brain at the optic chiasm. Fibers originating in the nasal half of each retinal field cross to the other side of the brain at the optic chiasm. Fibers from the temporal half continue on the same or ipsilateral side. Thus, if one were to destroy the right optic tract, images falling on the temporal half of the right retinal field and the nasal half of the left retinal field would not be seen. Because of the optics of the eye, of course, the unseen images would be those in the nasal half of the right visual field and the temporal half of the left visual field.

The first synapse made by the axons of the optic tract is in the thalamus at the *lateral geniculate nucleus* (LGN). There are approximately the same number of fibers in the optic tract as there are cells in the LGN. The nucleus consists of six rather discrete layers (Figure 5-7). Ipsilateral fibers end in three of these layers while crossed fibers end in the other three. Probably little or no cross communication of information originating from the two eyes takes place at this level. Retinotopic organization is also maintained at the LGN in that fibers from adjacent parts of the retina usually end in adjacent areas. There is almost a point-to-point projection of the retina upon the LGN; a similar situation exists within the striate cortex, described below.

Axons leaving the LGN travel directly to the cortex. Their pathway (called the *geniculocalcarine* tract or, alternatively, the *visual radiations*) ends in the occipital lobe along the superior and inferior lips of the *calcarine fissure* (Figure 5-7). This entire area is sometimes called the *striate cortex* because under a microscope clear striations formed by the various layers of cells and fibers can be seen. Surrounding the striate cortex is a visual association area, the *parastriate cortex* (Figure 5-7) (Brodmann's area 18). A second visual association area, the *peristriate cortex* (Figure 5-7) (Brodmann's area 19) surrounds area 18. These two visual association areas possess rich interconnections with each other and with their counterparts on the other side of the brain.

Bilateral and total destruction of the striate cortex in man results in the loss of most, if not all, vision. Lesions of the parastriate cortex, sparing the striate cortex, result in *visual agnosia.* The affected human patient will walk around an object placed in his path (indicating, of course, that he has seen it), yet be unable to name the object if it is a familiar one or give its function. The effects of lesions of the peristriate cortex are less clear, but there is some indication that following destructive lesions of this and related areas *visual hallucinations* and *perseverations* occur. A patient suffering from visual perseveration may, for example, see the plaid pattern of a companion's shirt as extending all over his face and arms (perseveration in space). A second type of visual perseveration (in time) occurs when a patient viewing a familiar road sees a child crossing it even though no child is present at this particular time.

Functions of the Retina

A primary question to be asked of any sensory system is how the transduction process takes place. In the visual system we want to consider how light waves (electromagnetic radiations) are converted into neural energy.

It has been possible to isolate from rods a purple pigment called *rhodopsin* or visual purple, which upon exposure to light is bleached and breaks down into the yellow-colored pigment *retinene* and a protein, *opsin.* After rhodopsin has been bleached, a considerable amount of time in the dark is necessary for it to resynthesize and regain its purple color. The hypothesis is that the bleaching or breakdown of this pigment is the instigating force enabling the rods to respond to light stimuli. The precise mechanism by which the breakdown of rhodopsin is able to cause a generator potential in rods remains largely unknown. It is thought that during normal daytime vision the rods' rhodopsin remains bleached and the rods are therefore relatively unresponsive to light. After the eyes have been kept in the dark for some time (*dark-adapted*), however, rhodopsin resynthesizes and the rods recover their sensitivity and begin to function.

Figure 5-8 shows a *dark-adaptation curve.* Such a curve is plotted by repeatedly determining the weakest flash of white light which is visible after the human subject has been in the dark for various amounts of time. The initial component or phase in this curve is due to the adaptation of cones. Only after 7–8 minutes of dark adaptation can the rod component be seen. It was mentioned above that isolated, bleached rhodopsin resynthesizes when

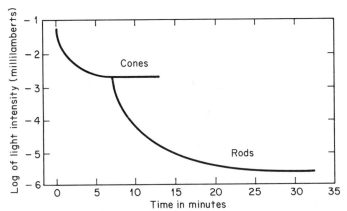

FIGURE 5-8–Adaptation of rods and cones to darkness. Change in light threshold is shown on a *logarithmic* scale. (From E. E. Selkurt. *Physiology.* Boston: Little, Brown, 1962.)

left in the dark. The resynthesis time-course and the time-course involved in the rod adaptation curve are close enough to support the notion that rhodopsin is, in fact, the photosensitive pigment in rods.

Isolated rhodopsin does not absorb (i.e., is not bleached) equally by light of every wavelength. The shorter wavelengths are more effective. Figure 5-9 shows the amount of light absorbed by rhodopsin plotted as a function of wavelength. When this absorption spectrum curve of rhodopsin is compared (Figure 5-9) with a human sensitivity curve for *scotopic* (rod) vision, the two curves are seen to be remarkably similar. The latter curve is determined in the following manner. The subject is first placed in a dark room and the eyes are allowed to become thoroughly dark-adapted. Only stimuli of low intensity (below the cone threshold) are employed, and the subject is required to match the relative intensity of these stimuli of various wavelengths to a standard, constant luminous spot. The close correspondence between the rhodopsin absorption spectrum curve and the human scotopic sensitivity curve is, of course, further support for identifying rhodopsin as the rod visual pigment.

Retinene has a chemical structure closely related to that of vitamin A. Clinical data have shown that vitamin A is a necessary component of man's diet to prevent *night blindness.* The affected patient has difficulty seeing under conditions of *low illumination,* and there is evidence that deprivation of vitamin A results in actual damage to the rods themselves.

Since rods exist in great quantity around the peripheral areas of the retina and the rods alone function in levels of very low illumination, it follows that night vision would be at its best when the visual image falls on the peripheral retinal areas. Lookouts scanning the horizon for lights of ships are directed, for example, not to look directly at the suspected target but slightly to one side of it.

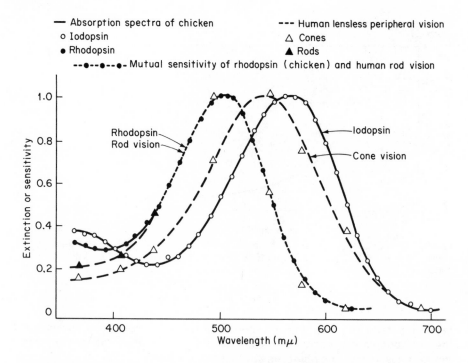

FIGURE 5-9–Absorption spectra of chicken rhodopsin and iodopsin compared with the spectral sensitivity of human rod and cone vision. (Adapted from G. Wald, P. K. Brown, and P. H. Smith. Synthesis and bleaching of rhodopsin. *Journal of General Physiology*, 1955, *38*, 677. By permission of The Rockefeller Institute Press. Adaptation from C. T. Morgan. *Physiological Psychology*. New York: McGraw-Hill, 1965.)

Color Vision

From the cones the visual pigment *iodopsin* has been isolated. When exposed to light, iodopsin breaks down into retinene and a protein called *photopsin*. Retinene, then, is a component of the visual pigment in both rods and cones; it is the protein that is different. The chemical reactions which occur as a response to light are quite similar in rods and cones.

We have described only two visual pigments, rhodopsin and iodopsin, but there are, in reality, many different kinds of visual pigments in verte-

FIGURE 5-10–Microspectrophotometer measures the absorption of light by a single cone. Monochromatic light, held to a constant flux by a feedback loop, is formed into two beams. A rotating chopper disk allows the "test" (A) and the "reference" (B) beams alternately to pass through the specimen to the photomultiplier tube. Depending on which beam is passing through, photodiodes switch the photomultiplier output into a test or a reference channel. The transmissivity of the specimen, A over B, is recorded and punched on tape. (From E. F. MacNichol. Three-pigment color vision. *Scientific American*, *211*, No. 6, 48–56. Copyright © 1964 by Scientific American, Inc. All rights reserved.)

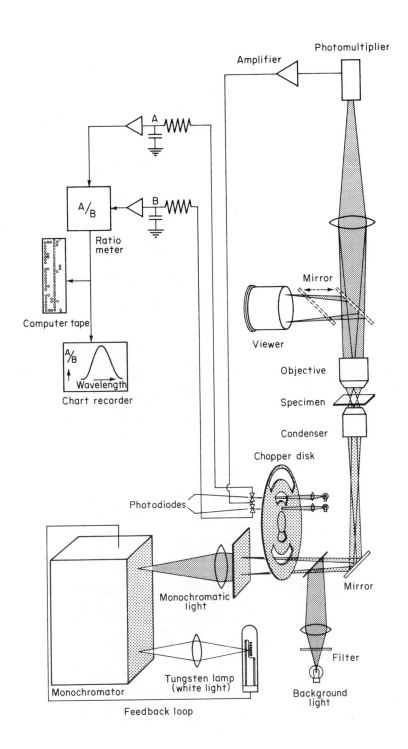

Photomultiplier

Amplifier

A

B

A/B

Ratio
meter

Computer tape

A/B
Wavelength

Chart recorder

Mirror

Viewer

Objective

Specimen

Condenser

Chopper disk

Photodiodes

Monochromatic
light

Mirror

Monochromator

Tungsten lamp
(white light)

Filter

Background
light

Feedback loop

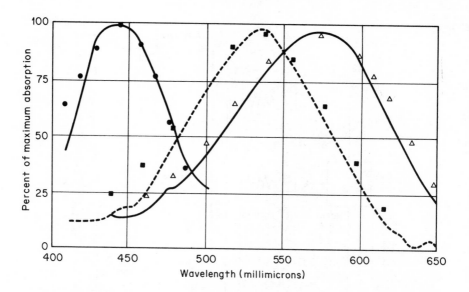

FIGURE 5-11–Color vision in primates is mediated by three cone pigments responsible for sensing light in the blue, green, and red portions of the spectrum. Their spectral-sensitivity curves are shown here; 447 millimicrons (blue-violet), 540 (green), and 577 (yellow). Although the "red" receptor peaks in the yellow, it extends far enough into the red to sense red well. Symbols accompanying curves trace shapes of hypothetical pigments with peaks at each wavelength. (From E. F. MacNichol. Three-pigment color vision. *Scientific American, 211,* No. 6, 48–56. Copyright © 1964 by Scientific American, Inc. All rights reserved.)

brates, depending upon the organism in question and whether we are considering rods or cones. In general, it is the opsin which differs from pigment to pigment, the retinene remaining a constant component.

In the case of man, three kinds of iodopsin are found in the cones. Each has a slightly different kind of opsin, with retinene common to all. These three cone pigments show differential sensitivity to light of various wavelengths; that is, they do not respond equally to the entire visual spectrum.

In an ingenious series of experiments E. F. MacNichol was able to demonstrate not only that three different kinds of cone pigments exist but also that within a given cone only one kind of pigment is present. He focused very narrow beams of colored lights on isolated cones in goldfish, monkey, and human retinas and measured the amount of light of various wavelengths transmitted through a given cone. Figure 5-10 shows a diagram of the experimental apparatus utilized. Though there was some variability from species to species and from cone to cone within a given preparation, Mac-Nichol and his colleagues found that one group of cones responded (absorbed maximally) at about 440 mμ (blue), another at 540 mμ (green), and a third at 600 mμ (red) (see Figure 5-11).

Evidence such as the above has led to greater and greater acceptance of the *trichromatic theory of color vision.* Beginning with three basic hues (blue, green, and red), one can mix colored lights to produce all spectral hues. It is conceivable, then, that the three populations of cones activated in various combinations by entering light waves are capable of mediating color vision. This possibility becomes even more plausible when one considers that both convergence and divergence exist within the visual system. With many different cones (presumably from all three populations of cones) converging upon a single bipolar cell and a given cone projecting to several or many bipolar cells (divergence), the possibilities for mediating or coding the many colors we are able to see become almost unlimited.

The cones not only mediate color vision but also function during conditions of high illumination. Figure 5-9 shows a human sensitivity curve for *photopic* (cone) vision. As can be seen, the curve has its peak at about 550 $m\mu$. This, of course, means that under conditions of high illumination humans are most sensitive to light of a yellow-green hue. With essentially three different kinds of cones operating during normal daytime vision, it is obvious that substantial pooling and coding of information must take place in the visual system. Possible mechanisms involved will be considered in the next section.

R. Granit was able to record the neural activity of single ganglion cells in the retina, with interesting results. Ganglion cells fell into two general groups. The first group, called *dominators,* were thought to mediate luminosity (light intensity). They showed sensitivity curves much like those for scotopic and photopic vision, depending upon light intensity. Because they function during conditions of both bright and dim illumination, such cells were thought to receive input from both rods and cones. The second group of ganglion cells were called *modulators* by Granit. Modulators fell into three rather distinct groups on the basis of their spectral sensitivity curves, the peaks of which were very close to the three found for cones. The fact that there are not only three types of cones but three types of ganglion modulators is, of course, further support for the trichromatic theory of color vision.

The trichromatic theory (originally proposed by Helmholtz) has not received total backing from electrophysiological studies. It has been possible, for example, to record a *chromaticity response* from the retinas of fish and frogs. The exact source within the retina of this graded response, which can be positive or negative depending upon the wavelength, remains unknown. Such a biphasic phenomenon originating from the retina could be taken as support for the *opponent process theory* of color vision proposed at the beginning of the twentieth century by Hering. Hering's basic theory was that there were three visual pigments—one mediating black-white vision, one for red-green vision, and one for yellow-blue vision. Hering's views are behaviorally supported in that extensive preexposure to a blue light, for example, causes a subsequent yellow light to appear more yellow than it normally would. Hering's theory would explain such color contrast phenomena by postulating that preexposure to the blue light caused the blue component of the yellow-blue system to be depleted or weakened. When the yellow light was shown, the yellow component was then free to function

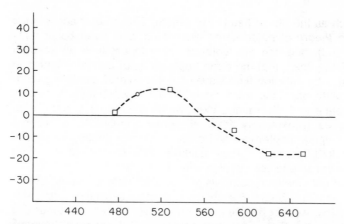

FIGURE 5-12—Plot of the responses of a cell in the lateral geniculate nucleus of a primate. The cell increased its rate of firing to green light and showed decreased firing to red light. Abscissa: wavelength in mμ; ordinate; number of spikes per second during the light with respect to the spontaneous rate. (Modified after R. L. DeValois. *Behavioral and Electrophysiological Studies of Primate Vision*. In W. D. Neff (ed.) *Contributions to Sensory Physiology*. London: Academic Press, 1965, 137–178.)

unimpeded by the normally antagonistic blue component, with the resultant enhancement of the perception of yellow.

The chromaticity response findings are certainly compatible with Hering's theory. To use the example of yellow and blue light again, a positive potential was found as a response to blue light and a negative potential to yellow light. When both yellow and blue lights were simultaneously shown on the retina, there was little or no chromaticity response. Finally, if the retina was extensively preexposed to blue light, a subsequent application of a test blue light resulted in a chromaticity response that was substantially depressed from normal; on the other hand, application of a test yellow light caused a response that was greater than normal.

Further support for the opponent process theory of color vision has come from the work of R. DeValois and his colleagues, who recorded the responses of cells in the lateral geniculate nucleus of primates to lights of various wavelengths. As mentioned previously, the LGN, consisting of six rather discrete layers in primates, is the thalamic relay nucleus for vision. In two of the six layers DeValois found cells which responded in a manner consistent with the opponent process theory. They increased their rates of firing to red light, for example, and showed decreased rates of firing to green light (Figure 5-12). Other cells in the same layers showed increased activity as a response to blue light and decreased activity when exposed to yellow light. It should also be mentioned that DeValois found cells in two other layers which behaved in a way compatible with Granit's modulators—that is, cells with peak spectral sensitivities in a rather well-defined area of the visual spectrum.

Obviously the question of whether color vision is coded in a three process or opponent process system must remain unanswered at this time. It is also possible, of course, that neither theory will prove to be totally correct. The alternative of a three process system coding at the receptor cell level and an opponent process mechanism operating at higher levels has been suggested.

Spatial Coding in the Visual System

We are, of course, able to see not only colors but a rich variety of shapes and forms as well. Possible mechanisms involved in such spatial coding will be the next topic of consideration. Before proceeding, however, we must introduce the concept of the *receptive field* of a *ganglion cell.* Recall that rods and cones synapse with bipolar cells, which in turn synapse with ganglion cells. An area of the retina (a few millimeters in diameter) in which changes of illumination will influence the activity of a given ganglion cell is said to comprise the receptive field of that cell. Ganglion cells (like all neural cells) should not be viewed as passive structures that remain inactive until light enters the eye. They show a base level of activity in the absence of any stimulation. This level of activity can be either increased or decreased when small spots of light are projected upon their receptive fields.

Receptive fields can be divided into two general types. In the center of one type is a small circular area (the "on" region), in which light increases activity. Surrounding this center is a larger area (the "off" region), which upon stimulation decreases activity (Figure 5-13). The second type has just the opposite arrangement, with a small "off" center in the middle surrounded by a larger "on" region.

If two spots of light are simultaneously focused on separate parts of a given cell's excitatory area, the response is more vigorous than either spot alone is able to produce. Simultaneous illumination of "on" and "off" areas produces little or no response; that is, the two effects tend to cancel each other. The most effective stimulus to a cell with an "on" area in the center is one which covers the entire "on" area, stimuli smaller or larger bringing less response. Diffuse lighting of the entire retina, in fact, is not nearly so effective in activating ganglion cells as small spots of light covering "on" areas. Apparently, then, the main spatial feature coded by the ganglion cells is the contrast in illumination falling on a given retinal area and on its surrounding areas.

Retinal ganglion cells vary tremendously in the size of their receptive fields. Cells serving the foveal area tend to have quite small fields; in some cases, the field may consist of a single cone. Cells in the periphery have much larger fields, receiving inputs from many receptor cells. Such cells are thought to function primarily in dimly lit environments, being able to sum small quantities of light falling on relatively wide areas of the retina.

Cells in the lateral geniculate nucleus of the cat have been found that share many of the properties or characteristics of the ganglion cells just described. They have receptive fields on the retina with either "on" or "off" centers surrounded by an opposing periphery. The main difference is that at the geniculate level the surrounding areas are far more effective in canceling out effects originating in the center. Cells of the LGN seem to be even more specialized in responding to spatial differences in retinal illumination rather

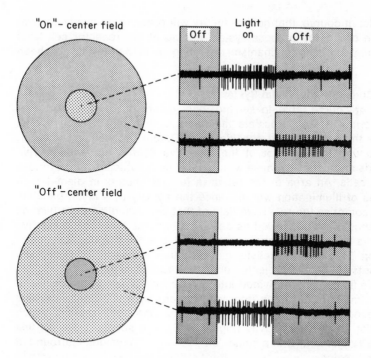

FIGURE 5-13—Concentric fields are characteristic of retinal ganglion cells and of geniculate cells. At top an oscilloscope recording shows strong firing by an "on"-center type of cell when a spot of light strikes the field center; if the spot hits an "off" area, the firing is suppressed until the light goes off. At bottom are responses of another cell of the "off"-center type. (From D. Hubel. The visual cortex of the brain. *Scientific American, 209,* No. 5, 54–62. Copyright © 1963 by Scientific American, Inc. All rights reserved.)

than to the illumination itself. In other words, the lateral geniculate body further increases the disparity already encoded by ganglion cells between responses to small, discrete spots of light and to diffuse light.

D. Hubel and T. Wiesel carried the analysis of spatial coding in the visual system a step farther by recording the activity of single cells in the cat's striate cortex (area 17). Again, cortical cells were found to have receptive fields on the retina; however, the fields were no longer of the concentric shape found at lower levels but of many different shapes and sizes. Nevertheless, the characteristic "on" and "off" areas continued to exist.

Hubel and Wiesel described two kinds of cells in area 17—"simple"

FIGURE 5-14—(Top) Response is weak when a circular spot of light is shone on receptive field of a simple cortical cell. Such spots get a vigorous response from retinal and geniculate cells. **(Bottom)** Importance of orientation to simple cortical cells is indicated by varying responses to a slit of light from a cell preferring a vertical orientation. Horizontal slit *(top)* produces no response, slight tilt a weak response, vertical slit a strong response. (From D. Hubel. The visual cortex of the brain. *Scientific American, 209,* No. 5, 54–62. Copyright © 1963 by Scientific American, Inc. All rights reserved.)

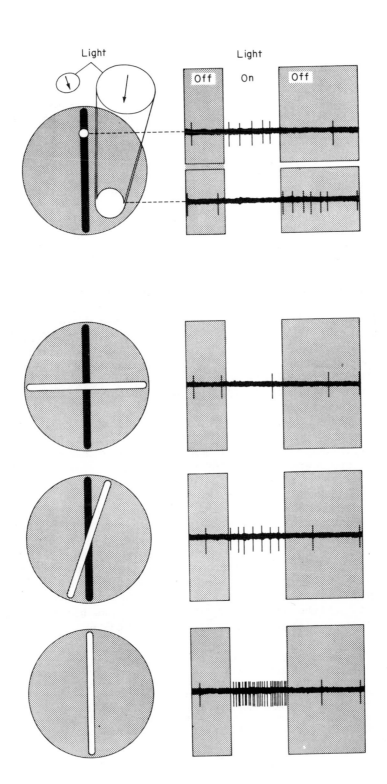

and "complex." *Simple cells* respond to line stimuli (bars of light, bars of darkness surrounded by light), and edges—straight-line boundaries between light and dark regions. Whether a given simple cell responds to a line stimulus depends upon the orientation of the stimulus and its position on the cell's receptive field (Figure 5-14). A bar of light, for example, may activate a particular cell if shown vertically but fail to activate the same cell if moved slightly from its vertical position. This does not mean that the nonvertical stimulus does not activate other simple cells having receptive fields with slightly different orientations.

Cells of the second kind found in striate cortex, called *complex cells*, are much like simple cells with two major exceptions. Simple cells respond only to line stimuli which are of the proper orientation and in a fixed part of the receptive field. Complex cells will respond to a line stimulus in any part of the receptive field provided it is in the proper orientation (Figure 5-15). Moreover, unlike simple cells, complex cells respond with sustained firing to moving lines. The implication is that complex cells receive their inputs from a large number of simple cells having a common orientation of their receptive fields.

Pushing their analysis a bit farther, Hubel and Wiesel recorded the activity of cells in the parastriate cortex (area 18), where they found *hypercomplex* cells. These cells seem to receive excitatory and inhibitory inputs from several complex cells. They respond to line stimuli at a particular orientation in their receptive fields, but only if the stimulus does not extend the entire length of the field. The line has to be contained within the receptive field at one or both ends.

Considering, then, the data as a whole, there is some evidence (at least in mammals) for the proposition that spatial coding is accomplished in a hierarchical manner. Higher centers seem to use or capitalize on the information coded at lower centers. This building up of the spatial properties of the visual stimulus presumably continues well beyond area 18. One would expect to find in other areas of the cortex cells which respond only to stimuli of even more specific and discrete shapes and sizes.

Our discussion to the present has been concerned primarily with spatial coding in mammals. One could legitimately ask how such coding is accomplished in less complex organisms lacking the large cortical areas possessed by mammals. When recordings are made of the activity of single optic nerve fibers in the frog, we find that much of the spatial coding which takes place in the cortex of mammals takes place in the retina of the frog. Five groups of optic nerve fibers can be described in the frog on the basis of the kinds of stimuli to which they respond (see Figure 5-16).

FIGURE 5-15–Single complex cell showed varying responses to an edge projected on the cell's receptive field in the retina. In group *a* the stimulus was presented in differing orientations. In group *b* all the edges were vertical and all but the last evoked responses regardless of where in the receptive field the light struck. When a large rectangle of light covered entire receptive field, however, as shown at bottom, cell failed to respond. (From D. Hubel. The visual cortex of the brain. *Scientific American, 209*, No. 5, 54–62. Copyright © 1963 by Scientific American, Inc. All rights reserved.)

Light

a

b

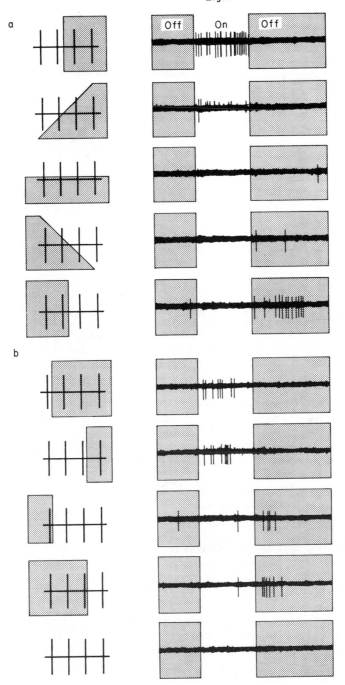

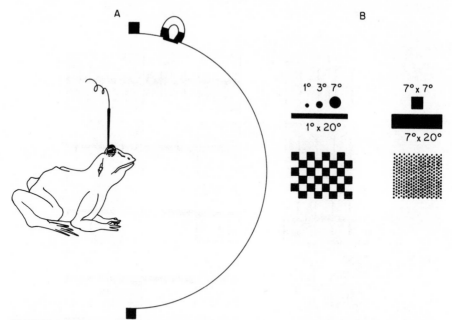

FIGURE 5-16–(a) Schematic drawing of the relations between the frog and the hemisphere that constitutes the experimental visual field. **(b)** Scale drawings of some of the objects used as stimuli. The degrees indicate their diameter when placed inside a hemisphere of the same radius as that represented in **(a)**. The actual hemisphere used was larger, 14 inches in diameter. (From H. R. Maturana, J. Y. Lettvin, W. S. McCulloch, and W. H. Pitts. Anatomy and Physiology of Vision in the Frog. *Journal of General Physiology,* 1960, *43,* 132.)

1. Boundary Detectors These fibers respond to any boundary between two grays in the receptive field, provided the boundary is sharp. Degree of contrast between two areas is less important than sharpness of the boundary. If there is no boundary present in the field, change of lighting, however sharp, is ineffective in producing a response. The cells continue to fire as long as the boundary is in the field.

2. Moving Boundary Detectors Fibers in this group respond best to sharp boundaries moving across a background. They fire only if the boundary is changing or moving, and cease to fire when the boundary remains stationary.

3. Complex Boundary Detectors These fibers also respond only to sharp boundaries between two grays; however, the boundary has to be curved, with the darker area being convex. In addition, this small dark area with sharp boundaries must be moving or must have moved into the receptive field. Complex boundary detectors are called "bug detectors" because they seem appropriate for detecting the presence of a fly (or some other insect upon which frogs feed) in the visual field.

4. Dimming Detectors These cells fire in response to a general diminution in illumination of the receptive field. The response is an enduring one which is maximal at the initial dimming but lessens as time progresses. Cells such as these conceivably have important survival value for the frog. Large animals which prey on frogs would cast shadows on the retina, and it is obviously important for the frog to be alerted to the fact that the animals are in the vicinity.

5. Dark Detectors These fibers are not so common as the other groups. They fire at a frequency which is inversely related to the intensity of the averaged illumination. When there are changes in illumination, the frequency of firing slowly changes to a new level.

The research to date on spatial visual coding mechanisms has indicated clearly that individual cells in the visual system are tuned to respond specifically to a given spatial configuration and only to that configuration. Further research will, no doubt, greatly increase the number of known spatial configurations for which there are specific cells. The interesting possibility exists, of course, that complex configurations exist in the external world for which man has no neural mechanisms for encoding. Presumably such configurations go undetected by man, and there is at least some question of just how aware man is of the world around him.

Visual Reflexes
It will be recalled that the first synapse made by axons in the optic tract is at the lateral geniculate nucleus. A number of axons, however, leave the optic tract before reaching the LGN and travel to the *superior colliculus* of the tectum. This small area on the dorsal part of the midbrain is a center mediating various kinds of visual reflexes. It has connections with the motor centers in the midbrain reticular formation and the spinal cord which control head and eye movements. In addition, it receives inputs from those cortical areas controlling voluntary eye movements and is presumably involved in such activities also.

AUDITION
Transduction in the auditory sense is intricate and complex. We are just now beginning to understand the necessity for the complexity, for while it is probably true that man's most important sense is vision, audition is undoubtedly a close second. Auditory stimuli play an important role in guiding and controlling all of man's behavior.

Anatomy of the Auditory System
The ear is traditionally divided into three parts—the external, middle, and inner ears. The *external ear* consists of the pinna (outer ear), the external auditory meatus, and the tympanic membrane (Figure 5-17). The *pinna* collects sound waves from the environment and funnels them into the *external auditory meatus.* The meatus provides a passage for sound waves to enter the middle ear and prevents large insects and other foreign bodies from entering and damaging the paper-thin *tympanic membrane* (the eardrum) at the end of the meatus. The tympanic membrane is conical in shape and marks the inner boundary of the external ear.

The *middle ear* is air filled and contains the three auditory ossicles

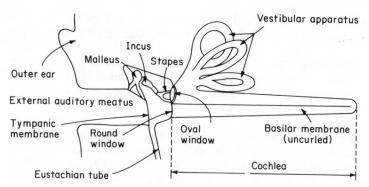

FIGURE 5-17–Diagram of the peripheral mechanisms of audition. The cochlea, straightened here, is naturally twisted about three and a half times—rather like a seashell. (From R. L. Isaacson, M. L. Hutt, and M. L. Blum. *Psychology: The Science of Behavior.* New York: Harper & Row, 1965.)

(Figure 5-17). The *malleus* (hammer) is attached to the tympanic membrane; the *incus* (anvil) is attached to the malleus and to the *stapes* (stirrup). Because body fluids absorb gases, air pressure inside the middle ear would be about 60 mm. below atmospheric pressure if it were not for the *Eustachian tube.* This tube connects the middle ear with the mouth cavity and allows air which equalizes the pressure to enter the middle ear when an individual yawns or swallows. A sleeping person on a descending airplane may suffer rupture of the tympanic membrane due to the increased external pressure if he does not swallow.

The *inner ear* is fluid filled and consists of a convoluted tubular structure called the *cochlea* (Figure 5-17), which resembles a snail in appearance, being coiled (two and one-half turns) on itself. At one end of this coiled tube is the *oval window,* to which is attached the stapes of the middle ear.

Before further consideration of the anatomy of the inner ear, it might be well to consider transduction up to this point. Sound waves enter the external auditory meatus and impinge upon the tympanic membrane, putting it into motion. The tympanic membrane transfers this movement to the auditory ossicles, which in turn transfer it to the oval window of the inner ear. The obvious question is why the necessity for the auditory ossicles at all. Why are sound waves not transferred directly to the inner ear from the external environment?

The tympanic membrane in man has an area of about 0.7 sq. cm. while the oval window is only about 0.03 sq. cm. in area. Although there is a relatively small amount of pressure on each unit area of the tympanic membrane, by funneling the pressure changes on the much smaller oval window the auditory ossicles make it possible to effectively move the highly resistant fluid of the inner ear. An analogy might be holding open the door of a moving automobile with one finger; all the air pressure on the large outer area of the door is transferred to the small area on the tip of the finger. The auditory ossicles, then, transform the high-amplitude but low-force move-

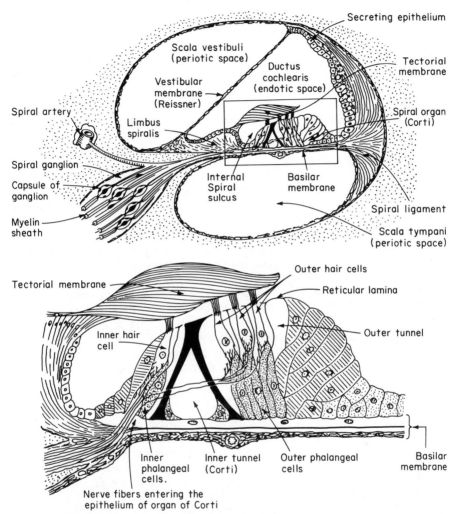

FIGURE 5-18–(Upper) Cross section of the human cochlea showing the spiral organ of Corti and the three ducts of the inner ear. **(Lower)** Basilar membrane with organ of Corti at higher magnification. The periotic spaces are filled with perilymph and the endotic space with endolymph. (After Rasmussen, 1943. Adaptation from E. E. Selkurt. *Physiology.* Boston: Little, Brown, 1962.)

ments of the tympanic membrane into high-force, low-amplitude movements by the stapes upon the oval window.

The cochlea (Figure 5-18) is not a completely hollow tube but is divided into three separate compartments by two thin membranes which extend almost its entire length. Resting upon and running the length of one of these membranes (*the basilar membrane)* is the *organ of Corti,* which contains the *hair cells,* the receptor cells of the auditory system. Pressure waves caused by movement of the stapes upon the oval window are set up in the fluid medium of the inner ear and cause the basilar membrane to move up and down. Suspended immediately above the organ of Corti and touching the tops of hair cells is the rather rigid and massive *tectorial membrane.* The up-and-down movement of the basilar membrane causes the hair cells on the basilar membrane to push into or brush against the overhanging tectorial membrane. This brushing (called *shearing*) somehow produces a generator potential in the hair cells. Individual axons of the auditory (the VIIIth) cranial nerve branch and surround individual hair cells, and a generator potential in a hair cell is able to cause an action potential in its surrounding axon.

Positioned immediately below the oval window is the *round window.* This thin elastic membrane can be viewed as an "escape valve" in that the pressure waves, after traveling through the fluid medium of the cochlea, cause the round window to expand outward. Once the wave has passed, the round window returns to its original position.

The pathways of the auditory system from the periphery to the auditory cortex are most complex and quite variable, as Figure 5-19 shows to some extent in diagrammatic form. As can be seen, there is extensive crossing of fibers from one side of the brain to the other.

All fibers on their way to the auditory cortex do, however, synapse at the *medial geniculate nucleus* in the thalamus. From here a tract called the *auditory radiations* goes directly to the superior gyrus of the temporal lobe (areas 41 and 42). Area 41 extends into the lateral fissure surface. Surrounding these primary sensory areas is a prime hearing association area (area 22) which is also part of the superior temporal gyrus.

Physiology of the Cochlea

In a classic physiological experiment, E. Wever and C. Bray in 1930 utilized a gross electrode to record the electrical activity of the auditory nerve in an anesthetized cat. They presented various kinds of sound stimuli to the cat's ear and recorded an electrical response which they called a *cochlear microphonic.* Interestingly enough, when the cochlear microphonic was amplified and fed into a speaker, the output from the speaker sounded very much like the sound being presented to the cat's ear. This was the case even with complex stimuli, such as symphonies.

The cochlear microphonic was initially thought to reflect the firing of axons in the auditory nerve. The current view is that the cochlear microphonic is produced by the hair cells of the organ of Corti. It is thought to be a reflection of a generator potential in these cells.

Coding of Pitch

Sound waves vary along two basic dimensions—frequency and amplitude. *Frequency* is measured in *cycles per second* and is the physical (stimulus) correlate of perceived *pitch;* sounds of high frequency are perceived to be of higher pitch than sounds of low frequency. How the ear is able to encode pitch has been the subject of extensive research. There are two theories—volley theory and place theory.

The *volley theory* holds that sound frequency is encoded by the rate of firing of the axons of the auditory nerve. Thus, a sound of 50 cps. would

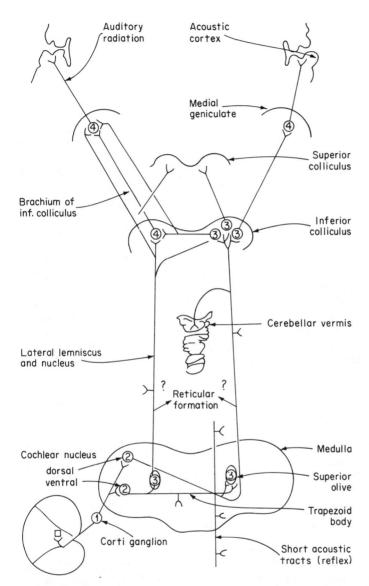

FIGURE 5-19–Schematic diagram of the auditory pathway. Numbers indicate the order of the neuron, starting with the sensory neuron as number 1. (Modified after H. Davis. Psychophysiology of Hearing and Deafness. In S. S. Stevens (ed.) *Handbook of Experimental Psychology.* New York: Wiley, 1951. Adaptation from R. F. Thompson. *Foundations of Physiological Psychology.* New York: Harper & Row, 1967.)

cause the axons of the auditory nerve to fire 50 times per second. In this simple form, volley theory is not totally correct, since in man the range of auditory sensibility is from 16 to 20,000 cps. During childhood, some humans can hear even higher sounds. Our knowledge of neuronal physiology, however, indicates that axons of the size found in the auditory nerve cannot fire faster than approximately 1000 times per second because of their absolute refractory periods.

In 1961 G. Von Bekesy won the Nobel Prize in medicine for his work on the auditory system. His special area of interest was neural coding of the sensation of pitch, and his work has provided strong support for a *place theory* of pitch encoding. Since the peripheral auditory apparatus continues to function for some time after death, Von Bekesy was able to observe the response of the basilar membrane to sounds of various frequencies in a number of animals, including man. Up to 60 cps., the volley theory appeared to be operating in that the entire basilar membrane moved or vibrated at a frequency corresponding to the frequency of the sound stimulus. Above 60 cps., however, an entirely new phenomenon occurred. The basilar membrane began to vibrate unequally over its area. The point or place of maximum deflection was dependent upon the frequency of the sound stimulus. The basilar membrane is not of uniform thickness. The stapes end is thin, stiff, and resistant to movement while the apical end (the end at the top of the two and one-half turns) is wide and flexible. High-frequency stimuli displace the membrane maximally at the stapes end, medium-frequency stimuli maximally displace in the middle parts, and low-frequency stimuli have their maximum effect at the apical end. The basilar membrane, then, acts as a mechanical frequency analyzer and is thus able to encode sound frequency. The area of the basilar membrane maximally displaced is the area where the hair cells are maximally distorted (sheared); hence this area has the greatest activation of auditory nerve axons.

There is electrophysiological evidence, however, that the volley mechanism may be operating at frequencies much higher than Von Bekesy's observations would indicate. While recording from the auditory nerve, Wever observed following up to 4000 cps.; that is, a tone of 4000 cps. produced 4000 evoked responses per second. At first glance, data such as these seem incompatible with our knowledge of axons and their absolute refractory periods. As mentioned above, no single axon in the auditory nerve can fire more than 1000 times per second. Wever explained this apparent contradiction by hypothesizing that different sets of fibers alternatively fire in volleys. The net effect is that no fiber discharges more than 1000 times per second, yet repetitive evoked potentials can travel in the auditory nerve 4000 times a second.

In summary, then, pitch seems to be encoded by the cochlea in two basic ways. For tones of lower frequency (up to 4000 cps.), volley theory appears to be operating. For tones of higher frequency, place of maximum distortion on the basilar membrane becomes the important consideration.

An interesting question is how the pitch-encoding process, initiated at the receptor level, fares on its way to the cortex. This question becomes even more meaningful when one considers that man's ability to discriminate between tones of two pitches is really quite remarkable. At some frequencies, for example, we can discriminate differences as small as 2 to 4 cps. While the basilar membrane shows differential distortion to sounds of various frequencies, a given tone activates a large area on the membrane, the peak point of distortion being rather flat. It is not likely that such a mechanism can totally explain the very fine pitch discriminations of which man is capable.

The central auditory pathways are organized in *tonotopic* fashion; axons originating from adjacent parts of the basilar membrane tend to remain in close proximity in the auditory nerve. Tonotopic organization continues to exist in the various nuclei and tracts which form the auditory pathway leading to the cortex. A number of investigators have looked at the frequency response characteristics of single cells in various auditory relay stations such as the inferior colliculus, trapezoid body, and medial geniculate nucleus (see Figure 5-19), and a clear trend has emerged. Cells in the higher stations tend to become more and more selective in terms of the tonal frequencies to which they will respond. An axon in the auditory nerve, for example, may respond to a wide range of frequencies whereas it is impossible to find any cells in the inferior colliculus with such a response range. Cells at higher levels have very narrow response ranges and are selective in their responses. Surprisingly, this "sharpening" of the range of frequencies which can affect auditory neurons does not seem to continue beyond the medial geniculate nucleus. Microelectrode studies of cells in the auditory cortex reveal that cells here have much broader response ranges than cells in the medial geniculate or inferior colliculus. Evidence such as this indicates that the auditory cortex, even though tonotopically organized, is not entirely critical for frequency analysis. This view is certainly compatible with the finding that destruction of the auditory cortex in cats does not substantially impair the animals' ability to make frequency discriminations. The auditory cortex does, however, have an important role to play in audition, which we will discuss in a later section.

Intensity Coding

Sounds vary not only in pitch but also in intensity or perceived loudness. The physical correlate of intensity is *stimulus amplitude.* Sound waves of greater amplitude (more energy) are perceived as being more intense (louder) than those of less amplitude. The processes by which the cochlear membranes encode sound intensity are even less well understood than the mechanisms involved in pitch encoding. Several possible explanations have been offered but remain little more than hypotheses at this point.

The hair cells are divided into two groups, sometimes called the *internal* and *external columns* (see Figure 5-18). The inner hair cells are situated in a single row close to the bony center around which the cochlea curls. There has been speculation that an intense sound activates not only the outer hair cells but the inner ones as well. The net effect would be quite compatible with the law of stimulus intensity; that is, a more intense stimulus would cause more action potentials ultimately to reach the cortex.

Microelectrode studies of auditory nerve fibers have also contributed to our understanding of intensity coding. In general, it has been found that a more intense sound results in (1) decreased latency of response, (2) greater probability of response, and (3) increased number of spikes per second. While this pattern occurs in a great number of fibers, other auditory nerve fibers react quite differently to more intense stimuli, showing increased latency and a decreased probability of responding. Other fibers respond maximally to a given intensity and are less affected by stimuli of lower and higher intensities. Findings such as these present the interesting possibility that inhibitory, as well as excitatory, mechanisms are intimately involved in intensity coding.

Microelectrode studies of auditory nerve fibers have shown further that a given fiber which is maximally sensitive to a very narrow band of frequencies will respond to a wider and wider band of frequencies as stimulus intensity is increased. In other words, it may be that more intense tones of a given frequency activate more auditory nerve fibers than would be the case with less intensity.

Unlike frequency coding, intensity coding seems to become less and less sharp or distinctive in the central auditory pathways. Cells at lower levels—in the cochlear nucleus (Figure 5-19), for example—are quite sensitive in their responses to relatively small changes in intensity. They show substantial increases in firing rate to increases in intensity. Almost the reverse situation exists at higher levels, with cells showing substantially smaller increases in firing rate to changes in intensity. Cortical cells do not respond to intensity changes at all. This seeming lack of cortical involvement in intensity discrimination is further supported by the finding that cats with auditory cortex destruction are not substantially impaired in their ability to discriminate intensity changes.

Summarizing the data dealing with intensity coding in the auditory system is most difficult. Basically, it appears that a more intense sound results in more action potentials in the auditory nerve. Then the picture becomes less clear, with possibly both excitatory and inhibitory influences coming into play at higher centers.

Localization of Sound Source

The several mechanisms for locating sound sources in the environment are worth considering. If the sound source is on the right, the right ear will be stimulated first, the sound wave impinging on the left ear a short time afterward. This *temporal delay* in time of arrival at the two ears is a prime mechanism of sound localization. Research has indicated that if the temporal delay is greater than 2 msec. the normal human perceives the stimulus as two separate sounds rather than a single sound originating on either left or right.

A second localization mechanism involves *intensity differences* between the two ears. Since the head itself tends to partially absorb sound waves, a sound originating on the right impinges on the left ear with less amplitude than it does on the right ear. The human subject can detect intensity differences and utilizes them to locate the origin of sounds. High-frequency sound waves are absorbed to a substantially greater degree than low-frequency sounds, and consequently localization is better with high-frequency sounds. Appreciation of stereophonic sound is heavily dependent upon the differences in intensity of high-frequency sounds between the two ears.

Complex Coding in the Auditory System

So far, we have been concerned with the simpler coding functions of the auditory system—coding of frequency and intensity. But man is able not only to discriminate between tones of different pitch and loudness but to hear a rich variety of tonal patterns and combinations as well. The mechanisms of such higher-order coding will be the subject of this section.

A number of investigators have reported finding units above the level of the auditory nerve which (1) increase their firing rate at tone onset, (2) decrease their firing rate at tone onset, (3) or fire continuously as long as the tone is on. The auditory nerve itself has units which spontaneously fire in the absence of any stimulation and may not react at all to the presentation of tone stimuli. Cells in the cochlear nucleus, the first relay station on the way to the cortex, have been found which substantially reduce their spontaneous neural activity as a response to tone stimuli.

Some cells in the auditory cortex react minimally to single tone stimuli but respond substantially to two beating tones with closely related frequencies. Such cells also respond strongly to more complex tones having harmonically related component frequencies.

Although the above data dealing with complex auditory coding are not nearly so complete or explanatory as the data derived from the visual system, they do give some indication that the auditory system is also organized in a hierarchical fashion, with higher centers utilizing the information already encoded at lower levels.

There is additional evidence that the auditory cortex is considerably involved in the perception of tonal patterns. Cats with bilateral destruction of the auditory cortex have been found to be deficient in their ability to discriminate between temporal patterns of tones. Human patients with damage to the right temporal lobe are severely impaired in their ability to discriminate between two tonal sequences and also between two chords of different timbre. Frequency discrimination—that is, the ability to distinguish between two tones varying along a frequency dimension—is, however, not significantly impaired. Human patients sustaining removal of the left temporal lobe do not show the tonal pattern deficits just mentioned but are impaired in their ability to understand spoken language, a deficit attributed to their inability to understand and discriminate between *phonemes,* the complex tonal sequences which compose spoken words.

Deafness

There are basically two kinds of deafness: *conduction deafness* and *nerve deafness.* The former term refers primarily to a malfunction of the middle ear. When the auditory ossicles are deficient or unable to transfer the movements of the tympanic membrane to the oval window, the affected patient's hearing is, of course, impaired. A common type of conduction deafness is *otosclerosis,* characterized by a stapes which is less mobile than normal. Because in cases of conduction deafness the inner ear remains unaffected, it is possible to stimulate the inner ear directly and overcome the deficit through the use of a hearing aid which causes the bone of the head to vibrate.

Nerve deafness involves damage to the inner ear caused by various kinds of infections or trauma. Sustained exposure to sounds of very high intensity, for example, can injure the organ of Corti. When the sound is a pure tone, the damage can be traced histologically to a localized area along the basilar membrane. The maximum loss in hearing is at a frequency which is approximately one-half octave above that of the tone originally causing the damage. A person suffering from nerve deafness will not, of course, profit from the use of a hearing aid.

There is a third type of deafness, called *central deafness,* which occurs much less frequently than the others. This is a malfunction of the auditory cortex itself. Again, a hearing aid has no beneficial effects for a person suffering from central deafness.

THE CHEMICAL SENSES—TASTE AND OLFACTION

Taste and olfaction are often considered jointly for several reasons. Their transduction processes have a basic similarity—both taste and olfactory receptor cells respond to molecules of substances in a dissolved state. Both senses are intimately involved in an organism's feeding behavior; one cannot tell, for example, whether an apple or an onion has been placed in his mouth when the nose is kept shut. The fact that food loses much of its taste when one is suffering from a severe cold is a similar phenomenon.

TASTE

Anatomy of the Gustatory System

The taste sense organ is called a *taste bud.* Taste buds are found on the top and sides of the tongue and throughout the oral cavity. On the surface and edges of the tongue, ridges of tissue called *papillae* can be seen, and many taste buds exist throughout the length of each papilla.

Figure 5-20 shows a cross section of a taste bud. As can be seen, each bud contains several receptor cells. The *supporting cells* are thought to be degenerating receptor cells which are no longer innervated. Taste receptor cells, unlike those in the other senses, are thought to function for only a matter of days and are constantly being replaced in some unknown fashion.

Each receptor cell sends a number of fine hairlike projections called *microvilli* through an opening (called a *gustatory pore)* which leads to the surface of the tongue. The microvilli are believed to be intimately involved in transduction, probably broadening the effective sensory area. Fibers from three cranial nerves (VII, IX, and X) enter the taste buds and give off branches which then surround individual receptor cells. A given receptor cell may receive branches from several different nerve fibers, and a given nerve fiber may branch to several different receptor cells. Cells in the anterior two-thirds of the tongue are supplied by the VIIth cranial nerve while the posterior third of the tongue is supplied by the IXth cranial nerve. Receptor cells in the larynx and pharynx are innervated by the Xth cranial nerve. The fibers

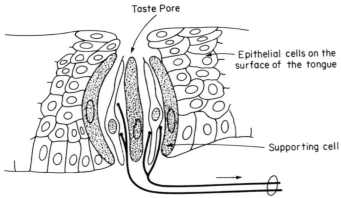

Taste Pore

Epithelial cells on the surface of the tongue

Supporting cell

FIGURE 5-20–Schematic representation of taste-sensitive cells in mucous membrane of the tongue. These and the supporting cells comprise a taste bud. Nerve fibers ending around the receptive cells are peripheral processes of unipolar neurons. (From E. Gardner. *Fundamentals of Neurology,* 5th ed. Philadelphia: Saunders, 1968.)

from all three cranial nerves join the *tractus solitarius* in the medulla (see Chapter 3) and synapse in the nucleus of the tractus solitarius. From here, gustatory fibers may or may not cross to the other side, then join the medial lemniscal system, traveling through the upper parts of the brain stem and synapsing again in the thalamus at the nucleus ventralis. From the thalamus, taste fibers travel directly to the cortex, ending up in the "sensory strip" just posterior to the central sulcus. Within the sensory strip they are positioned in close proximity to those cortical areas mediating tactile sensation from the tongue. It must also be mentioned that some taste fibers end in the adjacent insular cortex.

Stimulation of Taste Receptors (Transduction)

Molecules of substances in solution diffuse over the tongue and stimulate the microvilli. Such substances also enter the gustatory pore and directly activate the receptor cells, but by precisely what mechanisms remains unknown. There is some evidence, however, that the reaction is physical, at a submicroscopic level, rather than chemical. The stimulating particles are thought to produce changes in the molecular structure of the receptor cell wall such that "holes" form in the cell wall which substantially alter the cell's permeability characteristics. The change in permeability results in a generator potential in the receptor cells.

In less complex animals the depolarization (generator potential) is thought to spread electrotonically to a site on the receptor cell, where action potentials are generated. In the case of mammals, however, the data suggest that the site of spike initiation is not part of the receptor cell itself. The depolarization seems to spread by either chemical or electrical means to the nerve fibers which surround the receptor cells, and a spike is first initiated in these surrounding fibers.

As in the mixing of colors, there are basic tastes which if properly mixed result in the whole variety of taste sensations experienced by man. These are *salt, sweet, sour,* and *bitter.* Although chemical structure and perceived taste have certain general relationships, the relationships are not entirely specified or understood. Acidity, for example, is related to sour taste, yet some acids, such as the amino acids, taste sweet. Bitterness is produced by many chemical substances which have no obvious similarities. Substances with a salty taste are, however, water-soluble salts.

The tongue itself exhibits differential sensitivity to tastes. The tip of the tongue is most sensitive to sweets, the sides to sour, the back to bitter, the remaining parts to salty tastes. Presumably this localization is based upon a preponderance of given types of taste buds in certain areas. The strength of the differentiation can be seen from the fact that many substances (such as saccharin) taste sweet when placed on the tip of the tongue and bitter if placed on the back of the tongue. Such a finding supports the law of specific nerve energies: A given receptor cell always gives rise to the same psychological experience regardless of the nature of the initiating stimulus. On the tip of the tongue, saccharin supposedly activates a group of receptor cells the majority of which give rise to the sensation of "sweetness." In addition, saccharin must be able to activate receptor cells mediating "bitterness," for it causes this sensation when placed on the back of the tongue.

Electrophysiology of Taste

A basic problem in recording with a macroelectrode from a cranial taste nerve has been that no synchronous evoked responses can be easily observed because of the nature of the adequate stimulus: Diffusion of chemicals over the surface of the tongue causes asynchronous responses from gustatory nerve fibers. This is in contrast, for example, with the visual system where light waves activate all the receptor cells involved at approximately the same time, resulting in a synchronous evoked response. Gustatory nerve fibers are activated at different times as the chemical diffuses slowly over the surface of the tongue.

Studies of single nerve cells have added considerably to our knowledge. Microelectrodes introduced into taste receptor cells of rats and hamsters recorded what were presumably receptor potentials as a response to various taste solutions. These slow, graded potentials increased as the strength of solution was increased. Given that there are four basic taste sensations, one might reasonably expect there to be four distinct kinds of taste receptor cells. Such was not the case. Taste receptor cells were found to be differentially sensitive to a variety of substances, with maximum sensitivity to a single substance. No cells were found which responded to one substance exclusively.

Other investigators have recorded from single cranial nerve fibers in the rat. Recall that a single nerve fiber receives input from several or many receptor cells. Fibers were found which were maximally sensitive to a given substance, e.g., sweet or salty, but did respond to other substances as well. Some fibers, however, showed little differential sensitivity, responding almost equally to all the substances tested (see Figure 5-21).

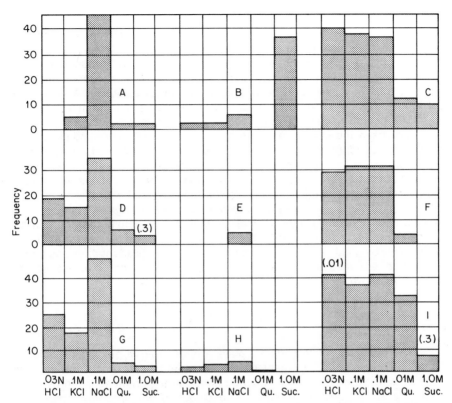

FIGURE 5-21–The frequency of response of nine different single-fiber preparations to five standard taste solutions. For elements D and I, the sucrose concentration was 0.3 molar; otherwise it was 1.0 M. (Adapted from C. Pfaffmann. Gustatory nerve impulses in rat, cat, and rabbit. *Journal of Neurophysiology*, 1955, *18*, 429–440. Adaptation from C. T. Morgan. *Physiological Psychology*. New York: McGraw-Hill, 1965.)

This general pattern—differential sensitivity to various taste solutions—has also been discovered in units in the nucleus of the tractus solitarius. A complete explanation of how the four basic taste qualities are encoded is not possible at this time, but it does not seem unreasonable to postulate patterns of discharge in many fibers rather than responses by single fibers or receptor cells exclusively to a certain taste.

A number of studies have probed the effects of destroying various central taste structures on an organism's eating behavior. This work has been done primarily in the rat. Removal of the thalamic areas involved in taste causes a marked reduction in various taste preferences. For example, rats with such lesions no longer prefer solutions with sweet or salty tastes. Rats with destruction of cortical taste areas show substantial impairment in making taste discriminations. Stimulation of cortical taste areas in humans has been found to elicit taste sensations.

Adaptation

Continuous application of a given taste solution results in adaptation in that the psychological experience of taste decreases over time. Adaptation to one taste can greatly influence the taste sensation of a subsequent solution, a phenomenon called *cross adaptation.* A sour solution tastes much stronger if the tongue has been previously adapted to sweet solutions. A very salty substance does not taste nearly so salty with previous salt adaptation.

The neural mechanisms involved in both adaptation and cross adaptation have been the subject of some research. The data have indicated that psychological adaptation (experiencing less and less taste sensation) cannot be explained on the basis of peripheral physiological adaptation. Peripheral neural structures show virtually no adaptation to some solutions and a very slow adaptation to others—much slower than would be predicted from a behavioral analysis. The peripheral events involved in cross adaptation have yielded similar results. Physiological adaptation to calcium chloride can be complete, yet subsequent application of sodium chloride causes an undiminished physiological response. Presumably, then, both adaptation and cross adaptation are mediated to a great extent at more central levels of the gustatory pathway.

OLFACTION

The olfactory sense certainly plays a larger role in guiding behavior in some of the less complex organisms than in more complex mammals such as man. This does not mean that olfaction is not an important sense in humans. Olfactory stimuli are important in food selection and in some cases give strong impetus to man to keep his environment clean and livable.

Anatomy of the Olfactory System

The olfactory sense organ is, of course, the nose. Olfactory receptor cells are located in the upper and posterior portions of the nasal cavity. Figure 5-22 is a schematic drawing of *olfactory mucosa,* which consists of *sustentacular cells* (supporting cells) and the receptor cells themselves. Olfactory mucosa occupies an area of approximately 2.5 sq. cm. in each nostril. The adequate stimuli for olfactory receptor cells are airborne molecules of volatile substances. Air currents carrying odoriferous substances reach the olfactory mucosa, located in a hidden part of the nasal cavity, not directly but by eddying. Sniffing (which increases inspiration) increases the eddying and brings the molecules into very close contact with the receptor cells, raising olfactory sensitivity.

As can be seen in Figure 5-22, olfactory receptor cells give off tiny hairlike projections into the nasal cavity. Each receptor cell narrows at its base and forms an axon which travels directly to the *olfactory bulb.* The axons compose the *olfactory nerve (cranial nerve I).* In the olfactory bulb, which is part of the central nervous system, the axons of the receptor cells end in a *glomerulus.* Glomeruli consist of groups of dendrites which branch and end in a spherical configuration. The dendrites are extensions of neurons called *mitral cells* and *tufted cells.* The olfactory system shows

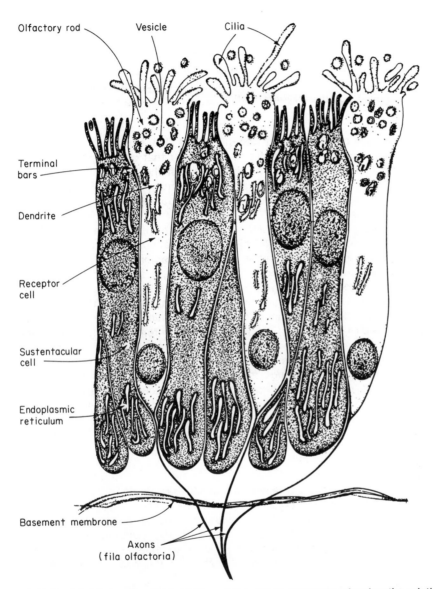

Olfactory rod   Vesicle   Cilia

Terminal bars

Dendrite

Receptor cell

Sustentacular cell

Endoplasmic reticulum

Basement membrone

Axons (fila olfactoria)

FIGURE 5-22–Schematic representation of the olfactory mucosa showing the relationships of the various cell types. (From A. J. D. de Lorenzo. Studies on the Ultrastructure and Histophysiology of Cell Membranes, Nerve Fibers and Synaptic Junctions in Chemoreceptors. In X. Zotterman (Ed.) *Olfaction and Taste.* Elmsford, N.Y.: Pergamon Press, 1963.)

extensive convergence in that many receptor cell axons enter a single glomerulus—in the rabbit, for example, as many as 26,000.

Axons of mitral cells form the *lateral olfactory tract* while tufted cell axons join a tract called the *anterior commissure* and travel to the olfactory bulb on the other side of the brain. The lateral olfactory tract terminates in the ipsilateral olfactory tubercle, in those portions of the prepyriform cortex immediately adjacent to the olfactory tract, and the cortical and medial groups of the amygdaloid nucleus (see Chapter 3). Strictly speaking, only the areas receiving direct input from the lateral olfactory tract can be called olfactory; however, olfactory information is spread throughout the brain from these primary areas.

Stimulation of the Olfactory Receptor Cells (Transduction)

It should come as no surprise to the reader that olfactory transduction is not completely understood. One theory is that the stimulating molecules adhere to the receptor surface, causing a generator potential. Substances of lower vapor pressure are believed to adhere (be adsorbed) more readily than those of higher pressure.

The adsorption of molecules is thought to produce a permeability change in the receptor cell wall. This results in depolarization (a generator potential), which spreads electrotonically to the region of the cell where an action potential can be generated.

Macroelectrode recordings from a group of olfactory receptor cells in the frog revealed that a long-lasting, slowly changing electrical potential could be observed as a response to olfactory stimuli. This graded response (called an electro-olfactogram) increased as the intensity of the stimulating odor was increased. It was thought to represent the sum of generator potentials in the receptor cells.

Macroelectrode recordings from the olfactory bulb itself have shown that substantial high-frequency, irregular activity occurs during the absence of any olfactory stimulation. Presentation of olfactory stimulants results in low-frequency, regular activity in the olfactory bulb. There is evidence from both unit and gross electrode studies that olfactory bulb areas show differential sensitivity to various types of odors.

Olfactory Coding

There is much less agreement about the basic categories of olfactory experience than there is about taste sensations. One investigator has proposed *seven basic odors:* camphoraceous (mothballs), musky (heavy putrid oil), floral (roses), pepperminty, putrid (rotten eggs), pungent (vinegar), and ethereal (dry-cleaning fluid). Whether one postulates more or less basic odors, the question remains as to the nature of the basic coding mechanisms.

One group of workers has advanced a *structural theory* of olfactory coding. This position postulates that each category of odor has some specific structural or chemical feature which interacts with the receptor cells in a given way. One of the more prominent structural theories is the *stereochemical theory,* which states that there are differently shaped holes in the receptor cell wall, each hole being receptive to odoriferous molecules of only a certain shape and size. According to the theory, five of the seven "basic" odors are differentiated on the basis of shape and size; the remaining two are dependent upon the electrical charge of the molecule. This theory, which is relatively new, has received some empirical confirmation in that it has been possible to predict the odor characteristics of several new compounds on the basis of their size and shape.

Another approach to olfactory coding at the receptor level is the *radiation theory.* It holds that stimulating particles differentially absorb and radiate heat or light energy depending upon their molecular structure, and this characteristic is responsible for olfactory quality. That radiation theory is not entirely correct can be seen from a recent study showing that olfactory receptors cannot be activated by odoriferous substances when a thin membrane which transmits light and heat energy is placed over them.

Before leaving the general topic of olfactory coding, we should mention that recordings from individual receptor cells have shown their selectivity to groups of odors. The situation is similar to that found in taste, with an individual cell responding strongly to some odors, moderately to others, and to some not at all. After a whole series of studies, it was possible on the basis of sensitivity to divide receptor cells into eight general categories somewhat similar to the postulated seven basic odors mentioned earlier.

Adaptation
Olfactory adaptation is rapid and almost complete to a large variety of odors. The neural mechanisms involved have been the subject of some research.

Interestingly enough, macroelectrode recordings from the olfactory mucosa indicate that little physiological adaptation takes place to a prolonged stimulus. After an initial decline in activity, further decrease is negligible. This is in seeming contradiction to the rapid behavioral adaptation which takes place.

Macroelectrode recordings from the olfactory bulb reveal almost the opposite picture, with rapid decreases in electrical activity taking place with a prolonged stimulus. If one severs the efferent pathways to the olfactory bulb (the pathways originating in other parts of the brain concerned with olfaction), virtually no electrophysiological adaptation takes place to a stimulus of long duration. This finding has led to the conclusion that olfactory adaptation is due to central neural regulation of olfactory bulb activity. Central brain areas, in simplest terms, shut off or inhibit the olfactory bulb (and, therefore, olfactory inputs) to produce adaptation.

Secondary Olfactory Areas
It was remarked previously that olfactory inputs are spread beyond the primary sensory areas. The *hippocampus* and *septum,* parts of the limbic system, and the *pyriform lobes* receive direct inputs from the primary sensory areas, and there has been some effort to determine the extent of involvement of these structures in olfaction. In the dog, destruction of the prefrontal cortex, including the olfactory bulb, for example, produced severe deficits in olfactory discrimination. Dogs with the same lesions were not impaired on discriminations involving auditory, cutaneous, and visual cues. Destruction of the hippocampus in the dog, on the other hand, has not been found to interfere with olfactory discriminations. An investigator working with

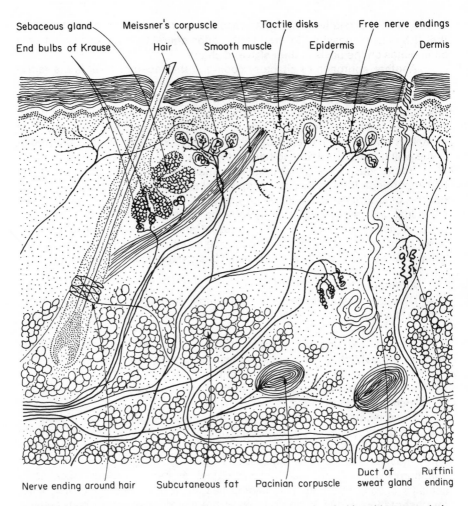

Sebaceous gland   Meissner's corpuscle   Tactile disks   Free nerve endings

End bulbs of Krause   Hair   Smooth muscle   Epidermis   Dermis

Nerve ending around hair   Subcutaneous fat   Pacinian corpuscle   Duct of sweat gland   Ruffini ending

FIGURE 5-23–Schematic representation of the nerve supply of skin with sparse hair. Not all the endings shown are to be found in any one skin area. The heavy lines are myelinated fibers; the light lines, nonmyelinated fibers. (Modified after Woollard et al., *Journal of Anatomy,* Vol. 74. Adaptation from E. Gardner. *Fundamentals of Neurology,* 5th ed. Philadelphia: Saunders, 1968.)

rats has reported that lesions of the septum, amygdaloid complex, and pyriform lobes do not interfere with olfactory discrimination.

The rather limited data available at present certainly minimize the importance of structures other than the olfactory bulb in olfactory function, but it is possible that structures such as the hippocampus and septum have an important, as yet unknown, role to play in olfaction. Perhaps more extensive and sophisticated behavioral testing techniques will clarify the issue.

SOMATOSENSORY SYSTEMS

We began this chapter with an example of a somatosensory receptor—the pacinian corpuscle, a pressure (touch) receptor. There are four kinds of somatosensory sensations traditionally thought to be mediated by four distinct types of receptors: pain, by *free nerve endings;* cold, by *Krause end bulbs;* warmth, by *Ruffini endings;* and touch, by *pacinian* and *Meissner's corpuscles* (see Figure 5-23). Recent evidence has indicated, however, that the situation is more complex. All four sensations, for example, can be evoked from the cornea, a structure which possesses only free nerve endings. A number of hairy regions of the human body do not have pacinian or Meissner's corpuscles, yet the sense of touch is quite distinct in these areas.

Various explanations have been offered for the current dilemma. One rather extreme view holds that the anatomical differences among receptor cells have nothing to do with mediating different types of sensation but are the result of small injuries which occur to free nerve endings during the course of an organism's life. A less extreme view is that individual receptor cells do not mediate specific cutaneous senses; instead, cutaneous quality is accounted for by a pattern of excitation in a whole group of receptors.

One should not, however, get the impression that every receptor cell responds equally to every kind of environmental stimulus. The pacinian corpuscle, for example, is exquisitely sensitive to small displacements of its onionlike outer components but will not respond to thermal changes. Other receptors respond almost exclusively to thermal stimuli. Cells have also been found showing no specificity whatsoever, responding equally to all kinds of somatosensory inputs.

An alternative system of classification of cutaneous experience was proposed by a psychologist, Henry Head. This system bypasses the problem of receptor specificity and divides sensory experience into two general categories on the basis of anatomical localization within the central nervous system. Head divided cutaneous experience into *epicritic sensation* (very fine, discrete touch, pressure, and proprioception [position of the body part in space]) and *protopathic sensation* (pain, temperature, and primitive, relatively unlocalized touch). Head's epicritic sense is thought to be mediated by the *lemniscal system* while protopathic sense is mediated by the *spinothalamic system.*

The Lemniscal System

Meissner's corpuscles in the outer layers of the skin and deeper-lying pacinian corpuscles as well as muscle spindle organs and Golgi tendon organs (see Chapter 6) are believed to be the receptor cells of the lemniscal system. Axons from these receptor cells in the body trunk and limbs enter the spinal cord through the dorsal roots. Their cell bodies are collected together at the dorsal root ganglion (Figure 5-24). The axons, which are large and myelinated, do not synapse at the spinal cord level but ascend directly in the dorsal columns to the base of the brain stem, where they terminate in the *nucleus gracilis* and the *nucleus cuneatus* (Figure 5-24). Axons originating from the legs and lower part of the body trunk terminate in gracilis while axons from the arms and upper part of the body trunk end in cuneatus.

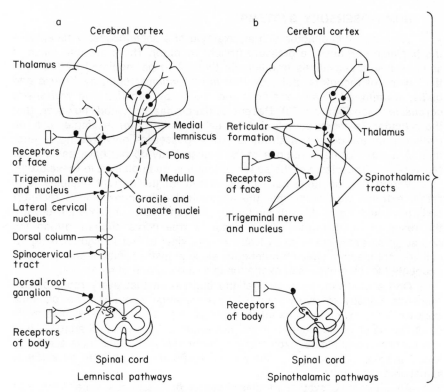

FIGURE 5-24—Schematic diagrams of the lemniscal and spinothalamic pathways of the somatosensory system. (From R. F. Thompson. *Foundations of Physiological Psychology.* New York: Harper & Row, 1967.)

Axons leave gracilis and cuneatus and immediately cross to the other side of the brain stem to join the *medial lemniscus,* which ascends to the thalamus terminating in its ventrobasal complex. From the thalamus, axons travel directly to the cortex ending in the *postcentral gyrus.*

There is also a facial component of the lemniscal system. Receptor cells located in the head and neck areas send axons into the brain stem in the *trigeminal nerve* (the *Vth cranial nerve).* After a synapse at the nucleus of the Vth cranial nerve, axons cross to the other side of the brain stem and join the medial lemniscus. This facial component also synapses at the thalamus (ventrobasal complex) and ascends to the sensory strip.

Figure 5-25 shows the *sensory homunculus* which exists within the postcentral gyrus. As can be seen, those areas of the body in which man has the greatest sensitivity have the greatest spatial representation in the cortex. Because the lemniscal system is a "crossed" system, the postcentral gyrus on the right side of the brain mediates sensations originating from the left side of the body. Recall that in the brain stem axons cross the midline before joining the medial lemniscus.

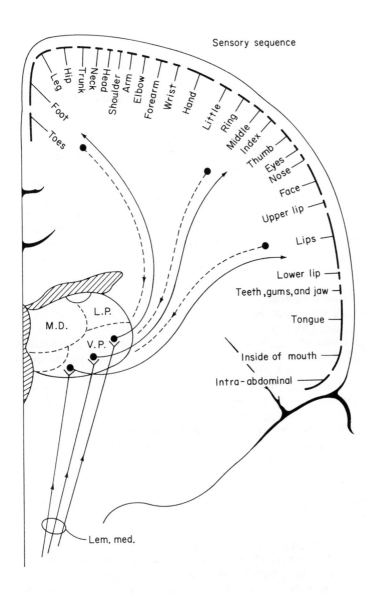

Sensory sequence

Hip
Leg
Trunk
Neck
Head
Shoulder
Arm
Elbow
Forearm
Wrist
Hand
Foot
Toes
Little
Ring
Middle
Index
Thumb
Eyes
Nose
Face
Upper lip
Lips
Lower lip
Teeth, gums, and jaw
Tongue
Inside of mouth
Intra-abdominal

M.D.
L.P.
V.P.

Lem. med.

FIGURE 5-25–Somatic sensation. Cross section of the left hemisphere along the plane of the postcentral gyrus. The afferent pathway for discriminative somatic sensation is indicated by the unbroken lines coming up, through the medial lemniscus, to the transmitting strip on the postcentral gyrus, and from there on by the broken lines into the centrencephalic circuits of integration. (From W. Penfield and H. H. Jasper. *Epilepsy and the Functional Anatomy of the Human Brain.* Boston: Little, Brown, 1954.)

Transduction in the Lemniscal System

The transduction process discussed at the beginning of this chapter utilizing the pacinian corpuscle as an example is a fair description of the process in all the receptor cells of the lemniscal system. Mechanical displacement of some part of the receptor cell results in a generator potential, which causes an action potential in single neurons.

Electrophysiological data have indicated that the entire lemniscal system is organized in a somatotopic fashion; that is, axons subserving adjacent areas of the body remain in close proximity at all levels of the system. In the ventrobasal complex of the thalamus, cells have been been found which respond only to mechanical displacement in a very small area of the body surface. In the monkey, for example, cells have been reported which respond only to stimuli in a region of 0.2 sq. cm. on the finger surface. Receptive fields located in less sensitive areas of the body (the back, for example) tend to be much larger, sometimes reaching a size of 20 sq. cm. Somatotopic organization is perhaps most obvious at the cortical surface with the appearance of the sensory homunculus described above.

The Spinothalamic System

The spinothalamic system is primarily concerned with the mediation of pain, temperature, and gross tactile sense. Axons of receptor cells which will feed into the spinothalamic system are smaller than those of the lemniscal system and mostly unmyelinated. They enter the dorsal root and synapse in the dorsal horn gray (Figure 5-24). Axons leave dorsal horn gray matter and cross to the other side of the spinal cord before joining the ascending *spinothalamic tract,* which travels directly to the thalamus without a synapse. It terminates in the ventrobasal complex. The cortical termination of the spinothalamic system remains largely unknown. There is some evidence, however, that axons in this system leave the thalamus and terminate in what has been called a secondary somatosensory area (Figure 5-24). In reality, very little is known about the facial component of the spinothalamic system, but the assumption is that such a component does exist. Presumably, it too terminates in the ventrobasal complex of the thalamus. A detailed description of its path through the brain stem is not possible at this time.

Transduction in the Spinothalamic System

Temperature As mentioned previously, some receptor cells seem to respond almost exclusively to temperature changes. The nature of the transduction process remains uncertain, though there is some speculation that thermoreceptors are activated by some chemical process.

Electrophysiological research has indicated that there are basically two kinds of thermoreceptors: *"cold" receptors* and *"heat" receptors.* Axons of thermoreceptor cells in the tongue of a cat have been isolated for study. "Cold fibers" were found to exhibit a steady rate of discharge when the temperature of the tongue was kept constant. Individual cells studied had maximum rates of discharge at particular temperatures, the range being from 20° to 34° C. Temperatures on either side of the temperature to which a given cell was maximally sensitive resulted in a rate of discharge proportionally less. Below 10° and above 50° C. no cold receptors were found that responded with steady discharge. A sudden drop of temperature on the tongue caused a burst of high-frequency discharge by cold receptors followed by a steady rate of discharge appropriate to the new temperature. The quicker the temperature dropped, the greater the initial burst of activity. Rapid warming of the tongue caused a brief cessation of activity followed by a rate of discharge consonant with the new temperature. The quicker the temperature increase, the longer the period of no activity.

Axons of "warmth" receptors in the tongue also showed a steady rate of discharge at constant temperatures. Once again, individual cells had maximum rates of discharge at particular temperatures, the range being 37.5° to 40° C. Warmth receptors responded with steady discharge to temperatures in a range from 40° to 20° C. A rapid rise in temperature brought a brief high-frequency burst of activity followed by a steady rate appropriate to the new temperature. A rapid decline of temperature (8° to 15°) also resulted in a high-frequency burst of activity before a new steady state was reached.

Pain   The adequate stimulus for pain sensation arising from the skin seems to be either potential or actual tissue destruction. Extreme environmental stimuli of all sorts result in pain sensation—needle prick, pinching, extreme heat and cold, application of strong chemicals, etc. One theory is that such strong stimuli cause a chemical to be released by the skin which, in turn, activates pain receptor cells. Whether one or many chemical substances are involved in pain sensation remains unknown.

One of the prime candidates for a pain-mediating chemical is *histamine*. Injection of a very small quantity of this substance into the skin causes pain sensation. That a histamine-like substance is present in those areas of the skin where tissue destruction has occurred has also been shown. Other substances—*acetylcholine* and *serotonin*—having chemical structures unlike histamine also cause pain when applied to an area exposed after the removal of blistered skin.

Gross Tactile Sense   To make the picture complete, the transduction process in the gross tactile sense component of the spinothalamic system should be considered. Unfortunately, little is known about the anatomical structure of the receptor cells or about the nature of the adequate stimulus. Presumably, however, the receptor cells of this system respond to mechanical displacement of some sort. Any further speculation, given our present knowledge, would not be meaningful.

Central Spinothalamic Mechanisms

Unlike the lemniscal system, the receptive fields of spinothalamic cells are quite large and they may cover parts of both sides of the body. Moreover, cells have been found, unlike those in the lemniscal system, which continue to respond for some time after the termination of stimulation. Evidence such as the above, of course, indicates that the spinothalamic system mediates somatosensory sensations of a relatively crude and unlocalized nature.

Localization of a central "pain center" would certainly be of substantial practical value. Conceivably, human patients suffering from intractable pain could have such a center removed with beneficial results. Unfortunately, there is evidence that no such localized area exists in the brain. Many cortical and subcortical areas have been implicated in pain perception. Stimulation of the somatosensory cortex in man, for example, has on some occasions been found to produce pain. There have also been reports in the literature of loss of pain perception following lesions in the parietal lobe. Prefrontal lobotomy (cutting the tracts which connect the prefrontal cortex with subcortical areas) has been found to lessen the aversive qualities of pain in human patients experiencing constant and severe pain. Research with animals has implicated subcortical structures as well. Stimulation of brain stem and diencephalic areas in animals causes behavior patterns typical of those seen in painful situations.

Phantom Limb Experience   In a number of cases a patient has reported receiving sensations from a limb that has been amputated. Such a phenomenon is called the phantom limb experience. While the patient may experience a wide variety of somatosensory sensations from the amputated limb, one of the most frequent and certainly most annoying is pain. A possible explanation lies in the irritation of severed nerve roots at the site of amputation. Another possible explanation is that the cortical areas mediating sensation from the amputated limb, because they are now devoid of normal afferent bombardment, act independently and so produce the conscious sensations. Support for this second hypothesis comes from the fact that young children who sustain amputation of a limb do not develop the phantom limb syndrome, presumably because they have not yet completely developed the necessary associational patterns in the appropriate cortical areas subserving the limb.

SENSATION—FINAL CONSIDERATIONS

Centrifugal (Efferent) Influences

In considering the five senses we have concentrated on the *afferent* (toward the central nervous system) aspects of sensation. There are certainly *efferent* (*centrifugal*) influences as well. To a great extent, the brain can control the type and extent of sensory stimulation it receives from the periphery.

In the auditory system, for example, there is an efferent tract (the *olivocochlear bundle*) arising in the brain stem which travels to the contralateral cochlea. Stimulation of this tract results in substantial reduction of evoked responses in the auditory nerve. Section of the olivocochlear bundle below the point of stimulation abolishes the suppression effects. A second centrifugal tract in the auditory system arises from the insular cortex and appears to have a suppressive effect on activity in the cochlear nucleus.

It was known for many years that very small efferent fibers existed in the optic nerve. More recently it was discovered that stimulation of the midbrain reticular formation resulted in modulation of the activity of ganglion cells in the retina. Some individual cells increased their rates of responding while others showed decreases. There is some speculation that these modulating influences are mediated by the small fibers just mentioned. Centrifugal influences have also been reported in the somatosensory system. Electrical stimulation of the reticular formation or somatosensory cortex causes suppression of activity in the nucleus gracilis and nucleus cuneatus. There is also evidence that stimulation of several areas of the brain causes suppression of activity in the spinothalamic system.

The existence of fibers which originate in central olfactory areas and travel to the olfactory bulb has been verified. Stimulation of these same central areas causes decreased activity in the olfactory bulbs. Centrifugal influences in the taste system have not been investigated to date, but they will undoubtedly be uncovered with future research.

The Reticular Formation

There is both anatomical and physiological evidence that all sensory systems are intimately involved with the *reticular arousal system* (RAS). As discussed in Chapter 3, the reticular formation is an arousal system existing in the core of the brain stem. The spinothalamic system is particularly illustrative of these relationships. As its axons travel through the brain stem toward the thalamus, they give off collateral fibers which synapse in the RAS. These collateral fibers are able to "activate" the reticular system, which in turn activates large areas of the cortex. Much of the "arousal value" of all different kinds of sensory stimulation, therefore, comes from this ability to interact with and activate the RAS.

The reticular system is also intimately involved with sleep. While the exact role of the RAS is not yet understood, it seems safe to state that a dormant or "quiet" RAS is conducive to sleep onset. Sensory stimulation, because of its activation influence on the RAS, is certainly not conducive to sleep. There is substantial behavioral support for this notion. Almost everyone has experienced difficulty "falling asleep" because of disturbing environmental stimuli—a dripping faucet, a roommate is typing, etc. It is common knowledge that sleep onset is most rapid in the absence of disturbing stimuli from the external or internal environment. The normal person prefers to sleep in a dark, quiet room and finds sleep difficult when he has an upset stomach or muscle pain.

MOTOR SYSTEMS

CHAPTER 6

In the preceding chapter we discussed the neural mechanisms involved in the reception and processing of stimuli. The present chapter will be concerned with the output or *efferent* side of behavior rather than the afferent or input side. Consideration will be directed toward understanding the neural processes enabling an organism to *respond* to a stimulus once it has been received.

There are three kinds of muscle tissue in the body, each with a different structure (see Figure 6-1). *Striated* or *skeletal* muscles are sometimes said to be under "voluntary" control while *smooth* and *cardiac* muscle reactions are sometimes called "involuntary." Although this basic distinction is valid in a sense, there are certainly exceptions. Bladder control, for example, seems to be under voluntary control to a great extent and it is mediated by smooth muscles. Recent evidence indicates that heart rate can to some degree be placed under voluntary control and such activity is mediated by cardiac muscle. Certain postural adjustments occur automatically and do not seem to require volition on the part of the organism, yet these are controlled by the skeletal muscle system. Perhaps, after studying in detail both reflex and voluntary movements the reader will be in a better position to evaluate the distinction between voluntary and involuntary movements and decide for himself whether it is meaningful.

SKELETAL MUSCLES

Skeletal muscles are the most familiar of the three types of muscle. They include the muscles of the arms and legs, the muscles which control tongue and eye movements, etc. When the psychologist talks about observing the "behaving organism," he is usually referring to observations of skeletal muscle activity. Skeletal muscles do one of two things: either contract or relax. This does not mean, however, that a given muscle or group of muscles cannot be in a state of partial contraction; in fact, this is probably the most common state for the majority of skeletal muscles. Muscles which upon contraction result in the extension or straightening of a limb are called *extensors* while those which pull or bend the limb toward the body trunk are referred to as *flexors*. *Antagonistic muscles* act to produce opposite body

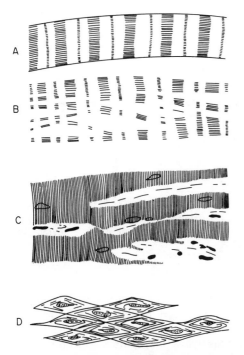

FIGURE 6-1–Types of muscle cells. A and B are striated muscle fibers; C shows the muscle fibers of the heart; and D is a sketch of some smooth muscle fibers. (Adapted from M. F. Guyer, *Animal Biology,* 3rd ed. New York: Harper & Row, 1941, p. 405. By permission of the publishers.)

movements. *Synergistic muscles* "cooperate" in producing the same body movement. (See Figure 6-2.)

Whenever an organism performs a motor response, two sets of muscles are involved. One set contracts while the antagonistic set relaxes. This integrative action is made possible by the *reciprocal innervation* of opposing muscle groups and will be the subject of a later section in this chapter. Muscle activation actually resulting in movement is termed *isotonic* muscle action. Not all muscle activity results in movement, however. A muscle can substantially alter its degree of tension without causing movement, and the outcome is *isometric* muscle activity. If two antagonistic groups of muscles contract equally, for example, no actual movement takes place, yet there is substantial muscular activity.

THE REFLEX ARC

A typical skeletal reflex arc is shown in diagrammatic form in Figure 6-3. If a painful stimulus is applied to the arm, such a stimulus (after its transduction) will activate axons which travel toward the spinal cord, synaps-

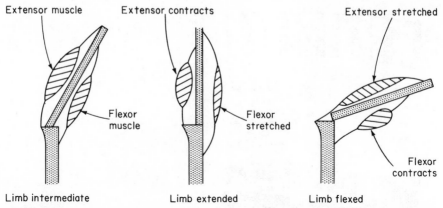

Extensor muscle   Extensor contracts   Extensor stretched

Flexor muscle   Flexor stretched   Flexor contracts

Limb intermediate   Limb extended   Limb flexed

FIGURE 6-2—Reciprocal actions of flexor and extensor muscles. When the limb is extended, the flexor is stretched and the extensor contracted. During flexion the flexor contracts and the extensor is stretched. (From R. F. Thompson. *Foundations of Physiological Psychology*. New York: Harper & Row, 1967.)

ing in the dorsal horn gray matter. From here, a second group of axons (*internuncial neurons*) travel to the ventral horn of the spinal cord and synapse on rather large neurons called *alpha motor neurons* or *ventral horn cells.* The axons of the ventral horn cells leave the spinal cord and travel directly to the muscles of the arm, causing them to contract so as to pull the arm away from the source of the painful stimulus.

Not all reflex arcs are, of course, as simple as the one in our example. A more intensely painful stimulus may result in not only arm withdrawal but a response involving the entire organism—jumping back and possibly vocalizing ("Ouch"). The neural structures engaged in such complex reflexes are obviously important for consideration by the behavioral scientist. A behavior

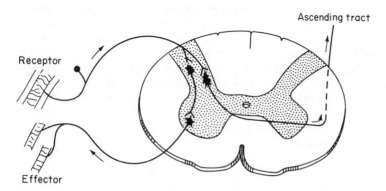

Ascending tract

Receptor

Effector

FIGURE 6-3—Diagram illustrating how impulses from a cutaneous receptor reach an effector (skeletal muscle), by a three-neuron arc at the level of entrance. Impulses also reach the cerebral hemisphere by way of an ascending tract. Arrows indicate direction of conduction. (From E. Gardner. *Fundamentals of Neurology*, 5th ed. Philadelphia: Saunders, 1963.)

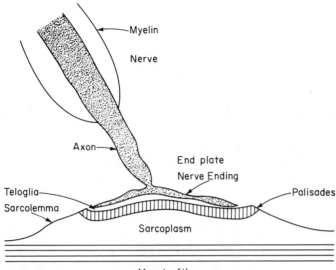

FIGURE 6-4–Diagram of end plate region. (Adapted by Couteaux from G. Acheson, *Federation Proceedings,* 1948, *7,* 447. Adaptation from J. Deutsch and D. Deutsch. *Physiological Psychology.* Homewood, Ill.: Dorsey Press, 1966.)

pattern such as "jumping" requires substantial coordination among the various muscles of the arms and legs. Recall from Chapter 3 that the spinal cord is a segmented structure with each segment serving a particular area of the body. When a reflex involves several or many spinal cord segments, it is referred to as an *intersegmental reflex arc.* Internuncial neurons spread the incoming information to the appropriate ventral horn cells in the segments on both the same and opposite (contralateral) sides of the cord, making coordinated, complex reflex movements possible. When a reflex involves the brain ("Ouch") as well as the spinal cord, it is called *supraspinal.*

Now that we have some general notions about what comprises a reflex arc, it is appropriate to consider certain particular aspects in more detail.

The Neuromuscular Junction

Axons of the ventral horn cells leave the spinal cord and travel directly to skeletal muscle cells. A single axon may branch into several or many fibers and activate a whole group of muscle cells, forming, with the muscle cells, a *motor unit.* Axon fibers terminate just short of the actual muscle cell. The small space between the end of the axon and the muscle cell is called the *neuromuscular junction.* Since the situation here is quite analogous to a synapse between two neurons, the neuromuscular junction is sometimes called a neuromuscular synapse. An action potential in the motor axon causes a chemical transmitter substance to be released from the end of the axon which diffuses across the neuromuscular junction and acts upon the membrane of the muscle cell. At a neuromuscular junction the muscle cell shows a pronounced structural modification in the form of an elevation (see Figure 6-4) called an *end plate.* It has been possible to record the electrical response of a muscle cell end plate to the chemical transmitter substance. Before the transmitter reaches the end plate, a resting potential (see Chapter 2) of approximately 88 mV. exists across the muscle cell membrane. As the transmitter begins to arrive at the membrane, the muscle cell begins to depolarize; that is, the inside of the cell becomes less negative with respect to the outside. The depolarization recorded from a muscle cell is called an *end plate potential* (EPP), and it is similar to an excitatory postsynaptic potential (EPSP) in a neuron and a generator potential in a receptor cell. Like these potentials discussed in earlier chapters, the EPP is a graded, nonpropagated potential. When it reaches a certain critical threshold (about 40–50 mV. of depolarization), an action potential is excited in the surrounding muscle membrane. By some as yet unknown mechanism the presence of an action potential in the muscle cell membrane causes mechanical contraction of the muscle cell itself. One possible explanation centers around the fact that muscle cells contain a protein substance known as actomyosin which is contractile and, in fact, contracts when electrically stimulated. It is thought that activation of the actomyosin chain molecules is to a large extent responsible for the mechanical contraction.

Substantial research has been devoted to identifying neural transmitters at the neuromuscular junction. In the case of skeletal muscles, there is good evidence that the transmitter is acetylcholine.

Sensory Receptors in Skeletal Muscles

The importance of sensory receptors in skeletal muscles cannot be overstressed. As will become clear shortly, they make smooth, coordinated muscle movements possible. Before considering directly the various types of receptors found in muscles, it will be necessary, however, to consider in some detail the anatomical structure of skeletal muscles (Figure 6-5). A given muscle is composed of two kinds of muscle bundles attached at each end to bone by *tendons,* which are very strong connective tissue. One type of muscle bundle consists of the cells in the muscle which contract and cause the actual motor movements—the *extrafusal fibers.* The second type of muscle bundle, called a *spindle organ,* consists primarily of *intrafusal fibers,* which, being muscle cells, do contract when activated, but only very weakly, and their contraction adds nothing to the total muscle movement. Spindle organs are "connected in parallel" with the extrafusal muscle bundles. They attach both to tendons and to extrafusal bundles. Intrafusal fibers are activated by small motor neurons (called *gamma neurons*) which have their cell bodies of origin in the ventral horn of the spinal cord. As mentioned previously, the larger motor neurons which activate extrafusal fibers are called *alpha motor neurons.*

Figure 6-6 shows a spindle organ in diagrammatic form. The intrafusal fibers together with their activating gamma motor neurons can be seen, as well as the sensory fibers surrounding and infiltrating the central, enlarged part of the muscle spindle. There are two kinds of sensory endings; the *annulospiral endings* cluster in the inner core of the muscle spindle while *flower-spray endings* terminate more peripherally around the sides of the spindle. The annulospiral endings send axons into the spinal cord through

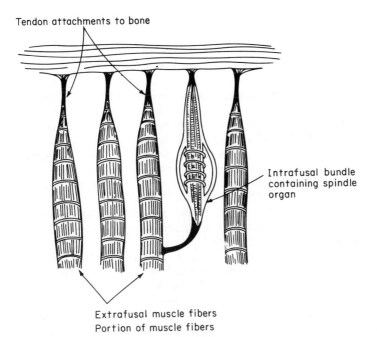

Tendon attachments to bone

Intrafusal bundle
containing spindle
organ

Extrafusal muscle fibers
Portion of muscle fibers

FIGURE 6-5–Anatomical arrangement of extrafusal (contractile) muscle fibers and an intrafusal muscle bundle containing a spindle organ. (From R. F. Thompson. *Foundations of Physiological Psychology.* New York: Harper & Row, 1967.)

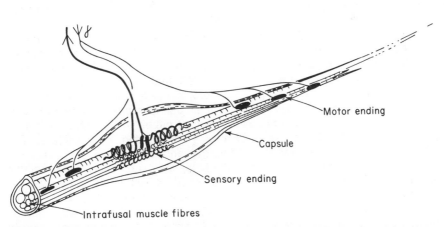

Motor ending

Capsule

Sensory ending

Intrafusal muscle fibres

FIGURE 6-6–Enlarged view of the muscle spindle organ showing the motor nerve end plates on the intrafusal fibers and the sensory endings leading to the sensory nerve fiber (*heavy line*). (From D. Barker. The Structure and Distribution of Muscle Receptors. In D. Barker (Ed.) *Symposium on Muscle Receptors.* Hong Kong: Hong Kong University Press, 1962.)

the dorsal root. These axons synapse directly on cell bodies of alpha motor neurons in the ventral horn of the spinal cord. The flower-spray endings also send their axons into the dorsal root of the spinal cord, to terminate on internuncial neurons which, in turn, synapse on alpha motor neurons.

A sudden stretch of a muscle causes both types of sensory endings in the muscle spindle to be activated. In the case of annulospiral endings, the axons have a direct excitatory influence on alpha motor neurons. The axons of flower-spray endings excite internuncial neurons, which then exert an inhibitory influence on a different, but related, set of alpha motor neurons.

Perhaps a familiar example will help to make things clear. When a muscle or its tendon is sharply tapped as is the case when eliciting the *knee-jerk response,* the tapping causes a sudden stretch of the muscle and the muscle spindle (recall that the two are connected in parallel fashion). This, of course, activates the sensory fibers in the muscle spindle. Axons of annulospiral endings activate alpha motor neurons, which cause the muscle to contract and the knee to lift upward (jerk).

Muscles always work in pairs; that is, when one set of muscles is contracting, opposing (antagonistic) muscles must be relaxing. In the case of the knee-jerk reflex, internuncial neurons (activated by axons from flower-spray endings) inhibit the opposing set of muscles and cause them to relax. This coordination between opposing muscles (one group relaxing while another group is contracting) is called reciprocal innervation, as was mentioned previously.

The knee-jerk reflex is an example of a *stretch reflex.* All stretch reflexes function in a similar way, literally keeping the body upright and preventing it from collapsing. The force of gravity stretches the extensor muscles of the legs and, of course, ultimately keeps them contracting to a sufficient degree so that the legs do not buckle.

Earlier in this section it was mentioned that small motor neurons (gamma neurons) leave the spinal cord and travel to the intrafusal fibers of the muscle spindle. The central portion of each intrafusal fiber is enlarged and noncontractile. Recall that it is in the central portion of the fiber that the sensory endings originate. The slender ends of intrafusal fibers, which attach either to a tendon or to an extrafusal muscle bundle, are contractile and it is to these slender ends that the gamma motor neurons come. When activated, the *gamma efferents,* as they are sometimes called, cause the ends of intrafusal fibers to contract, and this shortening of either end of the fiber makes the central portion stretch. As a result of the stretching, the muscle spindle afferents increase their rate of discharge and can cause the extrafusal muscle fibers to contract. Gamma efferents, then, are able to control the sensitivity of the muscle spindle and to some extent reflex contraction of muscle. If it were not for them, a given muscle would only reflexly contract when it was stretched and would never contract when it was already shortened because of partial contraction. Gamma efferents give the organism a measure of control over reflex muscle contraction. Many postural adjustments are heavily dependent upon them and, in fact, would be impossible without them.

The second type of sensory receptor associated with skeletal muscles is the *Golgi tendon organ*. This receptor is nothing but a sensory neuron which has several receptive branches located in a tendon. Golgi tendon organs are connected "in series" with muscles. When a muscle contracts, it produces pull or increased tension on its tendons; the stretching of a tendon results in the activation of its Golgi tendon organs. Tendon organs can also be activated by a second mechanism: If a muscle is stretched passively, as occurs when an antagonistic muscle is contracting, the tendon organs can also be activated. The passive stretch must be rapid and of substantial magnitude, however, to be effective. Such moderate stretching as occurs when a muscle is at rest does not bring any great increase in the rate of discharge of Golgi tendon organs. Golgi tendon organs send their axons into the dorsal roots of the spinal cord. The axons end upon internuncial neurons which (1) have inhibitory synapses on the alpha motor neurons activating the very muscle that contains the particular Golgi tendons and (2) have excitatory synapses on alpha motor neurons activating antagonistic muscles. Thus, the tendon organ system is an inhibitory one (or a negative feedback loop). When a given muscle contracts sharply, the Golgi system slows down or retards subsequent uncontrolled contractions of that muscle. Furthermore, if a given muscle is stretched sharply, as when a person lifts a heavy weight, the Golgi system prevents it from contracting against this great force and possibly damaging itself in the process.

To summarize, then, we have seen that there are basically two feedback loops operating within the skeletal muscle system. They effectively monitor the state of contraction or relaxation of skeletal muscles and prevent undue harm. The spindle organ system causes increased activation once activation has occurred and is analogous to a positive feedback loop. It promotes strong and continued muscle contraction. Operating as a counterinfluence to this excitatory system are the Golgi tendon organs, which exert an inhibitory influence on muscle contraction once contraction has begun and as such are analogous to a negative feedback loop. They, in other words, act as a damper on muscle contraction and prevent uncontrolled, prolonged activation. Finally, we have seen that the gamma efferent system can increase the sensitivity of the muscle spindle system. Presumably this gamma system is under voluntary control to some extent and it is in this way that an organism can prepare its muscles to respond quickly and strongly to the appropriate environmental stimulus. It is not inconceivable that the athlete has achieved greater voluntary control over his gamma system than the average person.

VOLUNTARY MOVEMENT

The organism not only reflexively responds to environmental stimuli but can initiate voluntary movements as well. As the reader will expect, voluntary movements certainly involve many neural structures beyond the spinal cord. Voluntary movements are primarily cortical phenomenon; yet, as we shall soon see, the spinal cord and alpha motor neurons are substantially involved.

The Pyramidal System

The *pyramidal system* controls fine voluntary movements such as those involved in writing, typing, and playing a piano. Its cell bodies of origin are located primarily in the *precentral gyrus* (area 4) of the frontal lobe (Figure 6-7). Single axons leave this cortex and travel directly to the spinal cord where they synapse either on alpha motor neurons or on internuncial neurons which synapse on alpha motor neurons. Recall that alpha motor neurons are the same cells that send their axons out to skeletal muscle cells and mediate the efferent side of reflex arcs. Because these same motor cells ultimately mediate all motor movements in the body trunk, they are sometimes called the *final common pathway.*

Experiments with patients undergoing brain surgery have added considerably to our understanding of the organization of the precentral gyrus. A mild electrical current applied to this region elicits very fine, precise movements—for example, a twitch of a single finger. After extensive research with this technique, it has been possible to map out in the precentral gyrus the anatomical loci where various body regions are represented. Such a map is called a *motor homunculus* (see Figure 6-8). As can be seen in Figure 6-8, those areas of the body over which man has the greatest motor control (the fingers, for instance) have the greatest proportional area of the

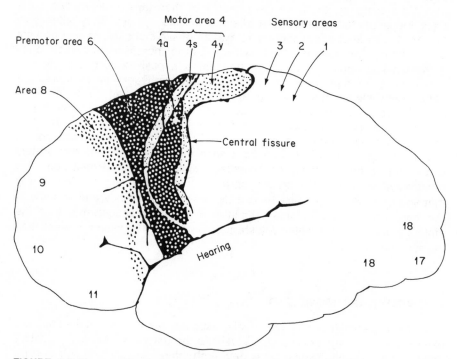

FIGURE 6-7–Diagram showing location of some of the main motor and sensory areas. (After von Bonin, in Bucy. *The Precentral Motor Cortex.* Philadelphia: Saunders; from Gardner, *Fundamentals of Neurology.* Philadelphia: Saunders.)

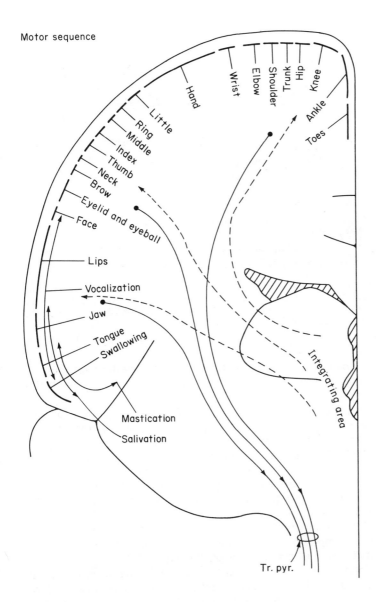

Motor sequence

Hand
Wrist
Elbow
Shoulder
Trunk
Hip
Knee
Ankle
Toes

Little
Ring
Middle
Index
Thumb
Neck
Brow
Eyelid and eyeball
Face

Lips

Vocalization

Jaw

Tongue
Swallowing

Mastication

Salivation

Integrating area

Tr. pyr.

FIGURE 6-8–Cross section through right hemisphere along the plane of the precentral gyrus. The sequence of responses to electrical stimulation on the surface of the cortex (from above down, along the motor strip from toes through arm and face to swallowing) is unvaried from one individual to another. (From W. Penfield and H. H. Jasper. *Epilepsy and the Functional Anatomy of the Human Brain.* Boston: Little, Brown, 1954.)

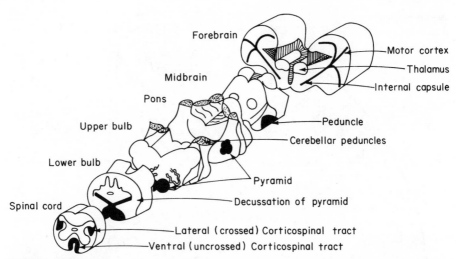

Forebrain
Motor cortex
Thalamus
Midbrain
Internal capsule
Pons
Upper bulb
Peduncle
Cerebellar peduncles
Lower bulb
Spinal cord
Pyramid
Decussation of pyramid
Lateral (crossed) Corticospinal tract
Ventral (uncrossed) Corticospinal tract

FIGURE 6-9–Diagrammatic representation of the pyramidal pathways. (Adapted from H. C. Elliot, *Textbook of Neuroanatomy,* 1963; courtesy of Pitman Medical Publishing Co., London. Adaptation from J. A. Deutsch and D. Deutsch. *Physiological Psychology.* Homewood, Ill.: Dorsey Press, 1966.)

motor homunculus devoted to them. A part of the body, like the back, subject to little motor control has proportionally less area devoted to it in the motor homunculus.

It would certainly be incorrect to give the impression that all axons traveling in the pyramidal system have their cell bodies of origin in the pre-central gyrus. There is both anatomical evidence and evidence from the human stimulation studies that axons from many cortical areas join the pyramidal system and mediate voluntary movements. An area of the cortex (Figure 6-7), for example, which contributes to the pyramidal system is just anterior to the precentral gyrus (Brodmann's area 6). It is called the premotor area, and we will discuss its functions in a later section.

The path of the axons that form the pyramidal system from the cortex to the spinal cord is complex, yet it is important to stress that there are no synapses along the way. A single axon travels the entire route.

Figure 6-9 shows the pyramidal system in diagrammatic form. As can be seen, the axons come from many cortical areas, join together (the *pyramidal tract*), and travel to the lower part of the brain stem. At an area called the *motor decussation* (Figure 6-9), approximately 80 percent of the fibers in the pyramidal tract cross to the other side of the brain. Once these axons reach the other side, they are referred to as the *lateral corticospinal tract* of the pyramidal system. Lateral corticospinal tract fibers continue on down into the spinal cord and, at their ultimate destination, turn out to synapse upon the appropriate alpha motor or internuncial neurons.

The 20 percent of the fibers in the pyramidal system which do not cross to the other side of the brain at the motor decussation continue on down to the spinal cord on the same side as their point of origin. They are located in a ventromedial position in the cord and are referred to as the *ventral cortico-spinal tract* of the pyramidal system. At their ultimate destination, they cross to the other side of the spinal cord and synapse with alpha motor or inter-nuncial neurons.

Ultimately, then, the pyramidal system is a totally crossed system; that is, all axons originating in the left half of the cortex end up activating motor neurons (and, therefore, muscles) on the right side of the body. It must, however, be remembered that not all axons in this system cross at the same point; one group crosses in the lower part of the brain stem while the other "waits" to cross at the actual point where muscle activation will take place.

It was mentioned earlier that stimulation studies of the human motor cortex have proved invaluable in increasing our knowledge of pyramidal system function, as have stimulation studies with animals. The exact nature of the motor movements resulting from electrical stimulation of motor cortex depends largely upon the intensity and duration of the stimulating current. An intense stimulus of long duration results in an organized, integrated movement such as flexion of an arm or finger. A stimulus just above threshold value applied for a relatively short time (1 or 2 seconds) can cause the contraction of a single muscle. In the past, researchers concerned with the pyramidal system debated whether muscles or entire movements were programmed or located in the motor cortex. Evidently *both* are, and whether one sees movement of a single muscle or a coordinated movement depends to a great extent upon the intensity and duration of the stimulating current. More intense current of long duration activates a wider area of the cortex, and thus coordinated movements occur.

Reports in the literature that different kinds of movements result from repeated stimulation of the same point in motor cortex have led to specula-tion that the motor cortex shows some "plasticity" of representation. While a final, definitive answer is not possible at this time, motor plasticity does not seem likely. The reports of plasticity presumably can be explained by one or several of the following possibilities. As mentioned above, varying the inten-sity and duration of the electrical stimulus can produce different kinds of movement. Moreover, the elicited movement depends heavily upon the posi-tion of the limb in question when the current is initiated. Regardless of initial position, however, the activated limb always ends up in the same final posi-tion. Careful and precise investigation of the effects of motor cortex stimula-tion upon the activity of single alpha motor neurons has revealed that a given cortical area can influence the activity of several or many different alpha motor neurons. Similarly, a given alpha motor neuron receives inputs from large areas of the motor cortex. Apparently, then, a given alpha cell fires or is activated when it receives the appropriate excitatory inputs from a wide area of the motor cortex.

Supplementary Motor Area   Research has indicated that in both man and lower animals there is a second area of the cortex devoted to voluntary movements. Referred to as the *supplementary motor area* and located primarily on the medial wall of the cerebral hemisphere, it lies just dorsal and anterior to the precentral gyrus (area 4, Figure 6-7). Within the supplementary motor area is a complete second motor homunculus representing the various muscles of the body trunk and limbs. Stimulation of the supplementary motor area produces movements which are different in character from those following stimulation of the precentral gyrus. They are slower in execution and resemble postural adjustments in that a limb will move slowly and hold its final position for many seconds after the stimulating current is turned off. In many cases the response is bilateral; that is, stimulation of the supplementary area on one side of the brain produces movements on both sides of the body. The primary output of the supplementary motor area goes to the precentral gyrus on the same and opposite sides of the brain. There is, however, both anatomical and physiological evidence that this area can mediate movements through areas other than the primary motor cortex. If, for example, one completely destroys the precentral gyrus, stimulation of the supplementary motor cortex produces basically the same pattern of movements as when the precentral gyrus is intact. It is thought that they are mediated by the extrapyramidal motor system, to be discussed in a later section.

The Premotor Area (Area 6)   The *premotor area* (area 6) of the cortex lies just anterior to the precentral gyrus (Figure 6-7). Early studies utilizing electrical stimulation of the premotor area revealed movements that appeared to be more complex than those resulting from precentral stimulation. Subsequent research, however, has indicated that the two areas do not give rise to essentially different types of movements. The early results can be explained by the fact that different muscle groups seem to be represented in the two areas, area 4 being primarily concerned with fine movements as in the fingers and face and area 6 controlling muscles closer to the body trunk such as those of the upper arm and leg. Thus, stimulation of area 6 tends to produce grosser and in a sense more coordinated movements. This is a function of the musculature represented here, and no indication that area 6 is somehow a center for higher, coordinated movements.

The Frontal Eyefields (Area 8)   Just anterior to area 6 in the cortex is a region of the brain called the *frontal eyefields* (area 8) (Figure 6-7), which upon stimulation results in eye movements.

In considering the pyramidal system up to this point we have been mainly interested in the activation of the muscles of the limbs and body trunk. The pyramidal system also has a large component concerned with muscles of the head and neck. Axons traveling in the pyramidal system turn off from it in the lower brain stem and synapse upon various nuclei located in this region, then leave the brain stem and travel via the cranial nerves to the appropriate muscles in the head and neck areas. The system is extremely complex, with a single cranial nerve carrying axons from several or many of these nuclei.

The Extrapyramidal System
While it would be incorrect to imply that the motor functions of the *extrapyramidal system* are well known, we do have some grounds for making general statements about them. Basically, the extrapyramidal system is in-

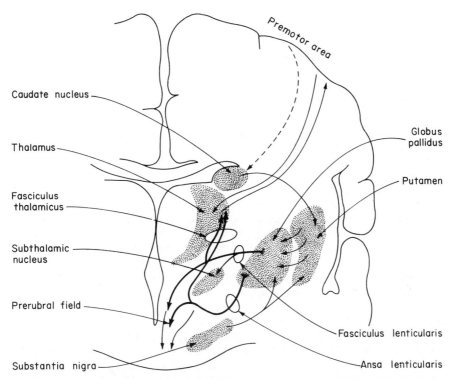

Caudate nucleus

Thalamus

Fasciculus thalamicus

Subthalamic nucleus

Prerubral field

Substantia nigra

Premotor area

Globus pallidus

Putamen

Fasciculus lenticularis

Ansa lenticularis

FIGURE 6-10–Diagramatic view of a coronal section through the brain showing the various structures comprising the extrapyramidal system. (From J. T. Manter and A. J. Gatz. *Essentials of Clinical Neuroanatomy and Neurophysiology.* Philadelphia: Davis, 1961.)

volved with facilitating or "smoothing out" muscle movements initiated by the pyramidal system. Destruction of the various components of the system results in jerky, uncoordinated movements which generally accomplish their purpose in a very uneconomical way.

The pyramidal system is so named because in the lower brain stem areas it has a pyramidal shape (Figure 6-9). The extrapyramidal system refers to those fibers reaching the spinal cord through routes other than the pyramidal and corticospinal tracts. There are several extrapyramidal routes from the brain to the spinal cord, and we will discuss the majority of them individually in later sections.

Figure 6-10 shows a diagrammatic view of the structures involved in the extrapyramidal system. The primary cell bodies of origin of this system exist in the central core of the cerebral hemispheres, at such sites as the *caudate nucleus, putamen, globus pallidus, red nucleus,* and *substantia nigra.* Many of these structures send axons directly to the *descending reticular formation,* which, as described in Chapter 3, exists in the core of the brain stem. From here axons travel to the appropriate neurons in the spinal cord. In the spinal cord itself, these axons tend to travel around the central gray matter.

Perhaps our best insights into the functions of the extrapyramidal system have come from selectively stimulating and/or destroying various parts of the system. Electrical stimulation of the globus pallidus, for example, has been found to enhance reflex movements as well as those movements initiated by electrical stimulation of the prefrontal gyrus (area 4). By the same token, destruction of the globus pallidus tends to result in a lack of spontaneous movements in animals and a generally passive animal which will remain in unusual postures when placed in such positions. The caudate nucleus seems to be primarily a structure that inhibits movements initiated by the pyramidal system. Stimulation of the caudate nucleus in the awake animal, for example, often suppresses the ongoing motor behavior. Bilateral destruction of this area in cats has been found to produce a motor pattern which is called *obstinate progression.* An animal subjected to such a lesion will continue to walk forward even though further locomotion is impossible because a barrier has been placed in its path. The animal will literally place its head against a wall and push, all the while showing appropriate loco-motive behavior in its four paws. Such animals are also hyperactive in that they constantly pace back and forth in their cages, etc.

Parkinson's disease is due mainly to damage to the extrapyramidal system. The affected patient shows rigid muscles which strongly resist passive movements, and there is a tremor in these same muscles when they are at rest. Some evidence indicates that the disease is a result of damage to the substantia nigra. This nucleus is thought to inhibit the globus pallidus to some extent, and when its inhibitory powers over the latter are destroyed or lessened, the tremor and rigidity follow. Support for this position comes from the fact that the symptoms of Parkinson's disease can be partially or totally eliminated by surgically destroying portions of the globus pallidus.

Reticular Influences upon Motor Activity

As mentioned above, a prime recipient of extrapyramidal inputs is the descending component of the reticular formation. From here, axons travel directly to the appropriate areas in the spinal cord. Electrical stimulation of the reticular formation can cause either facilitation or inhibition of ongoing motor activity. The reticular formation is thought to exert its extrapyramidal motor influences through the gamma motor neurons. Recall that gamma efferents control the sensitivity of muscle spindle afferents and that activa-tion of gamma efferents facilitates reflex contractions and voluntary move-ments. Stimulation of those points in the reticular formation which facilitate movements increases the rate of discharge of the gamma efferents while stimulation of those points which inhibit movements decreases activity in the gamma system.

A second pathway by which the extrapyramidal system can influence or modulate pyramidal function involves a collection of nuclei in the thalamus. These nuclei receive direct inputs from the various cortical components of the extrapyramidal system and, in turn, pass this influence on to the cortical areas from which the pyramidal system originates.

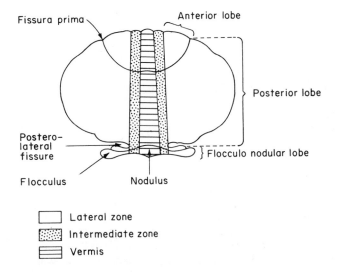

Lateral zone

Intermediate zone

Vermis

FIGURE 6-11–Diagram of the cerebellum laid out flat, in dorsal view. The anterior and posterior lobes comprise the cerebellar cortices. (From D. Bowsher. *Introduction to Neuroanatomy.* Oxford: Blackwell Scientific Publications, 1961.)

The Cerebellum

The *cerebellum* sits atop the lower part of the lower brain stem just above the fourth ventricle (Figure 6-11) and is connected to the rest of the brain by six large fiber bundles called the *cerebellar peduncles.* It has two basic components or subdivisions: the *flocculonodular lobe* and the *cerebellar cortices.* The flocculonodular lobe is situated at the base of the cerebellum and is its most primitive part. The cerebellar cortices in man have paralleled cerebral cortical development. The cerebellar cortex is highly convoluted and like its cerebral counterpart consists of an outer mantle of gray matter (cell bodies) which covers the cerebellar tracts or white matter.

Inputs to the cerebellum come from a variety of sources: the spinal cord, the cerebral cortices, the reticular formation, the vestibular system, and some extrapyramidal nuclei. In turn, the cerebellum projects to these same structures. Assigning a general function to the cerebellum is easier than pointing out specific functions in a given motor behavior. The cerebellum ultimately receives sensory input from all five senses and can influence both reflex and voluntary movements. Thus it is a primary center for sensorimotor coordination.

Electrical stimulation of the anterior portions of the cerebellum can cause decreased muscle tonus if it is of high frequency and increased tonus when the stimulus is of low frequency. There is evidence that these effects are due both to influence on the gamma motor system and to a direct influence on the alpha motor neurons themselves.

Stimulation of the posterior cerebellum can result in eye movements but, more important, both facilitates and inhibits voluntary movements. These effects are thought to be mediated through the cerebellum's influences on the pyramidal and extrapyramidal systems.

The behavioral impairments caused by destruction of the cerebellum in man and lower animals are certainly compatible with the notion that this structure is a primary sensorimotor coordination center. Cerebellar lesions lead to flaccid muscles, postural disturbances, and "intention tremors." A patient with an intention tremor has great difficulty performing precise voluntary movements. Reaching for a piece of chalk, for example, becomes a decided chore, the patient's movements being jerky and missing the mark many times.

Motor Lesions—General Considerations

Alpha motor neurons (the final common pathway) ultimately mediate all movements—both reflex and voluntary—in the body trunk and limbs. A lesion *completely* destroying this pathway to one limb results in a complete loss of movement in that limb. If all of the dorsal or afferent fibers which supply a given limb are destroyed, and the final common pathway is left intact, the patient will lose reflex movements to pain stimuli, for example, but will be able to move the limb voluntarily. Destruction of the corticospinal tracts (the pyramidal system) impairs voluntary movements in a given limb while reflex movements are still intact. Voluntary movements are seldom, if ever, lost completely since the extrapyramidal system can mediate some of them. Total destruction of both the pyramidal and extrapyramidal systems would conceivably cause the loss of all voluntary movements, but such destruction is extremely unlikely even in the event of a massive lesion.

The Vestibular System

Technically, the *vestibular system* is a sensory one and should have been considered in the previous chapter. While it does provide information about the position of the head and neck in space, it is also intimately involved in postural adjustments and various reflex responses.

Existing within the inner ear, the vestibular apparatus consists of three *semicircular canals* which connect to a saclike structure called the *utricle* (Figure 6-12). The utricle in turn connects with another larger sac structure called the *saccule.* The semicircular canals are situated in three different planes at right angles to each other. Each canal is filled with fluid and enlarges at its base where it attaches to the utricle. This enlarged portion is called the *ampulla* and contains hair cells called *cristae.* The cristae project from the inner wall of the ampulla into the fluid medium. Rotary movement of the head causes the fluid of the semicircular canals to distort the cristae, which distortion activates the fibers of the vestibular nerve surrounding each crista.

The fluid of the semicircular canals is continuous with that in the utricle and saccule. Since almost nothing is known about the functions of the saccule, we will not discuss it any further.

The utricle also contains receptor hair cells which project into the fluid medium. They are covered by a gelatinous substance containing calcium carbonate particles. The receptor cells plus their gelatinous covering are

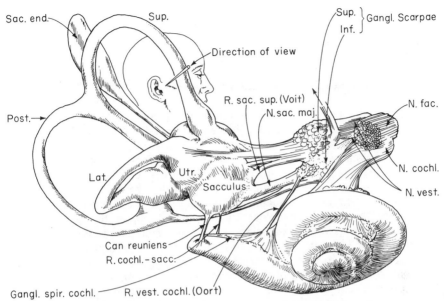

Sac. end. Sup. Direction of view Sup. } Gangl. Scarpae Inf.

R. sac. sup.(Voit) N.sac. maj. N. fac.

Post.

Lat. Utr. Sacculus N. cochl.

N. vest.

Can reuniens R. cochl.-sacc.

Gangl. spir. cochl. R. vest. cochl.(Oort)

FIGURE 6-12–Nerve supply of the vestibular apparatus and cochlea. (From M. Hardy, *Anatomical Record*, 1934, *59*, 412.)

referred to as the *macula.* The semicircular canals, as mentioned above, respond to rotary motion of the head around any axis. The receptor cells of the utricle are activated by linear acceleration such as takes place when an automobile begins to move forward from a standing position.

Efferent fibers leave the vestibular apparatus traveling in the vestibular component of the eighth cranial nerve. Their immediate destination is the vestibular nuclei in the brain stem. Fibers leave these nuclei and travel to a variety of places in the brain. One set goes to oculomotor centers in the brain stem to mediate reflexes such as movement of the eyes to the left when the head rotates to the right. Other fibers go to the cerebellum and the reticular formation. A third group travels to nuclei in the thalamus which project directly to the cortex. Finally, a group of axons travels from the vestibular nuclei to the spinal cord (the vestibulospinal tract) where they synapse on internuncial neurons influencing both alpha and gamma motor neuron activity.

A person suffering from unilateral damage to the vestibular apparatus exhibits a variety of symptoms. Head movement causes nausea, disorientation, distress, and frequent vomiting. Interestingly enough, the fact that these symptoms disappear in a relatively short time (a few days or weeks) indicates some ability of the central nervous system to adapt to the new situation of vestibular input coming from only one side. Bilateral destruction of the vestibular apparatus causes none of these symptoms; however, the patient does show some loss in ability to stand upright when his eyes are closed. There is also evidence linking the vestibular system with motion sickness.

Electrical stimulation of the vestibular apparatus can produce the nausea and vomiting characteristic of this ailment. Bilaterally destroying the connections between the vestibular apparatus and the cerebellum has been found to render the organism immune to motion sickness.

Levels of Motor Control (Decerebrate Rigidity)

One of the early attempts to understand the role of higher neural centers in motor behaviors consisted in isolating them surgically or cutting them off from the spinal cord. The experimental work has been done primarily in higher mammals such as cats.

A complete section of the spinal cord, of course, renders the areas below the cut insusceptible to any higher neural influences. In higher mammals the initial reaction to such a cut is a condition known as *spinal shock.* All spinal reflexes either are reduced substantially or disappear altogether. The duration of the period of spinal shock depends upon the phylogenetic position of the organism in question. In cats, for example, it may last only a few minutes while in man it may continue as long as several weeks. Spinal shock does not seem to be the result of the actual physical trauma involved, but rather of the cutting off of the normal descending influences from higher neural centers. Evidence for this view comes from the finding that transection below the point of original section does not once again produce the symptoms of spinal shock.

The first reflexes to return after the period of spinal shock are protective flexion reflexes to painful or harmful stimuli. In time these reflexes become exaggerated and may involve components normally not included, such as urinating and sweating. The extensor reflexes, on the other hand, seldom if ever redevelop their presection state. The extensor muscles remain flaccid, with decreased tonus. Chronically affected animals are able to stand upright if properly positioned; however, they cannot right themselves if placed on their backs, nor can they walk.

If one transects the brain stem above the vestibular nuclei but below the red nucleus in the upper part of the brain stem, a condition known as *decerebrate rigidity* results, characterized by marked rigidity of the extensor muscles (Figure 6-13). This state is thought to occur because the excitatory influences of the reticular formation upon these muscles are no longer checked by inhibitory influences from centers above the point of transection. An animal so prepared cannot walk or right itself. If the cerebellum too is isolated from the decerebrate preparation, the extensor rigidity becomes even greater.

Section of the brain stem just above the red nucleus (such a preparation is called *high decerebrate*) does not cause marked decerebrate rigidity. After an initial recovery period, the animal can right itself and is able to walk and even run and climb in some cases. The onset of these complex motor behaviors is, however, delayed for several weeks after the transection. There is a mild decerebrate rigidity in the animals when they are at rest but it disappears when the animal is moving.

Surprisingly, *decorticate* animals or animals which have the neocortex separated from the rest of the brain are somewhat similar in terms of motor

FIGURE 6-13–Typical posture of the cat in decerebrate rigidity. Note the marked and rigid extension of the forelimbs, the forward extension of the neck, and the extension of the tail. (From L. J. Pollock and L. Davis, *Journal of Comparative Neurology,* 1930, *50,* 384.)

behavior to those having a transection just above the red nucleus. In the decorticate preparation, of course, the extrapyramidal structures are intact and able to exert their influences upon motor behaviors. Any differences between high decerebrate and decorticate preparations could be at least partially attributed to the influences of the extrapyramidal system. Comparing the motor behaviors of the two preparations could give further insights into the functions of the extrapyramidal system. The decorticate animal, in contrast to the high decerebrate, does show walking and climbing behavior immediately after the operation. Decerebrate rigidity does exist in the decorticate animal when at rest but is certainly less prominent than in the high decerebrate. About the only long-term difference between the two preparations according to present knowledge is that the high-decerebrate animal is apparently more impaired in locomotive behavior than is the decorticate animal.

All in all, the decerebrate and decorticate preparations have given us little specific knowledge about the functions of the extrapyramidal system. Perhaps with more sophisticated behavioral testing techniques greater differences would be found. There is also the possibility that the rather gross technique of transecting or isolating large areas of the brain is inappropriate for a detailed analysis of motor function.

Role of Learning in Motor Behaviors

Complex motor behaviors such as driving a car, typing, or playing a piano are certainly not innate, and the human organism must spend long hours acquiring and practicing these skills. They are probably performed best when they are performed automatically, without the organism's having to plan or think about the next movement in a sequence. Needless to say, the neural mechanisms involved in the learning and performance of such complicated skills are not yet understood even on a general level.

Several points, however, can be brought up for consideration. Very young children first learning to reach for objects go through a fairly typical sequence which seems to be dependent not upon maturation but rather upon simple practice of motor skills. The earliest motions involve not just the hand but the entire body. Only after considerable practice do precise movements utilizing the arm and fingers alone occur. The infant seems to experience a long period in which the movements get closer and closer to the most efficient motion.

Adults acquiring new and complex motor behaviors go through much the same sequence. The initial attempts are rather gross and rely heavily on visual verification of success or lack of it. If the movement does accomplish its goal, it is usually in a very uneconomical way. After some practice, however, the motor sequence becomes smooth, precise, and in some sense automatic in that the organism no longer finds it necessary to actively consider or correct the various components of the total movement.

There is speculation that well-practiced motor skills in their final form are almost reflex acts. The proprioceptive feedback from a previous component of the motor sequence is thought to act as a stimulus for the next movement of the chain. This formulation is interesting in that it leads to the possibility that different anatomical structures or areas are involved in the acquisition of a motor skill and its final performance. A given area might be necessary for the trial-and-error process of mastering a given motor skill but no longer be involved once the skill has become automatic or reflex-like. If this were the case, it would account for the finding that very complex motor behaviors often remain intact after extensive damage to prime motor areas in the cortex.

MEMORY AND LEARNING

CHAPTER 7

Almost all general definitions of learning emphasize the fact that it is a process which involves a change in behavior. Most of them state that the change is brought about by repetition or practice of a certain response. Furthermore, according to many theories this change in behavior can come about only if there is reinforcement. Benton Underwood, a psychologist interested in verbal learning, has pointed out that a number of considerations have to be examined in trying to define learning operationally. For example, the change in performance from which learning is inferred must result from practice, and the response measured must show an increment or improvement as a result of practice. Also, learning is a process of acquiring new responses or improving the way old responses are performed.

Most psychologists distinguish between learning and performance. They view learning as a process of acquiring a new response (whether reinforcement is involved is a separate issue; and performance as a steady state process, i.e., the execution of the response once the acquisition phase is completed. For example, attaining the responses necessary for driving a car is clearly a learning process; because it involves acquiring a large number of new responses which have to be executed in a definite order and with great skill. Once we receive our license and supposedly drive well, driving is a performance process. At this point we do not need to think about how to execute each response but perform it "automatically." As time goes on, driving becomes more refined; and we may develop shortcuts such as slowing down at a stop sign instead of stopping. If we are punished for making such incorrect responses, they will be unlearned or extinguished (along with the driver, in some cases) and, we hope, replaced by the proper habits.

One reason it is important to distinguish between learning and performance, especially with regard to physiological mechanisms, is that brain systems involved in the acquisition of a response may be different from those involved in its continued performance. Hence, some brain lesions disrupt the acquisition of a response but do not affect the execution of a response once it has been learned. Information gained from studies of such lesions clearly demonstrates that learning and performance are different processes.

A concept central to the psychology of learning is reinforcement and (in this regard) the question of whether reinforcement is essential for learning. Is it true that learning occurs only if correct responses are rewarded (positive reinforcement) or incorrect responses punished (negative reinforcement)? Are all rewards overt, that is, do all rewards satisfy specific motivational needs, such as hunger, thirst, sexual needs, or are some of the rewards which might be utilized in the learning process "internal"? In man, internal rewards include the satisfaction gained when a task is done properly or social approval for an action taken. Do animals also work for some kind of internal reward not essential for survival but necessary for psychological well-being?

Some psychologists have argued that reinforcement is not necessary for learning to occur. If an animal is placed in a maze and allowed to run through it without reinforcement, the experience of free exploration will result in enhanced learning at a later time if reward is introduced for correct responding. This phenomenon, called *latent learning,* was of particular interest to Tolman as he formulated his learning theory. In part, the theory viewed the learning process as cognitive and not necessarily dependent upon external reinforcement. Other theories of learning have maintained that without reinforcement of a primary motivational need, such as hunger or thirst, learning cannot exist at all.

At this point it should be stressed that learning cannot be characterized by any single process. Learning to drive a car largely involves complex motor coordination and the development of rapid automatic responses to specified stimulus signals—a stop sign, police whistle, etc. In contrast, learning to derive proofs or solve problems in modern algebra is a highly abstract task which excludes the motor system. Still another type of learning, such as learning the names of the Presidents of the United States or elements in the periodic table, is referred to by psychologists as a rote memory task. In each of these three cases new skill or information has been acquired, and new responses or behaviors are added to the individual's behavioral repertoire. Nevertheless, the role of reinforcement may be quite different for each of these types of learning and so may be the neural events underlying it. Even today the issue of whether the reinforcement of responses is basic to all types of learning is not resolved. In fact, to try to specify every possible source of reward and punishment in a learning situation, particularly in the case of complex human tasks, becomes meaningless and subjective.

Physiologists are interested in what is occurring in the nervous system during those behavioral changes called learning and memory. Is an "engram" or physical record stamped into the brain, either electrically or chemically, while learning is taking place? What is the role of memory in learning? How is information stored in the brain and how is it drawn upon by the organism? What are the processes involved in selecting and dredging out a memory of the far distant past, in forgetting something, in learning new information or revising old ideas? Clearly it is artificial to consider memory and learning separate processes since learning cannot exist if there is no mechanism available for the storage and recall of information.

As we have seen, either electrical or chemical stimulation of the nervous system can elicit emotions or enhance motivational states. Is it then unreasonable to assume that alterations in electrical activity of the brain might reflect changes in the learning process and that alterations in the chemistry of the nervous system might affect the degree to which learning can take place or memories be established? From modern research which asks the question comes the hope for the future that perhaps deficient memory and learning can be enhanced by alterations in brain chemistry if learning rate and memory capacity can be shown to be dependent upon changes in levels of brain chemicals. As we shall see later on, some significant progress has already been made in this direction.

TYPES OF LEARNING

Let us now consider types of learning commonly studied by physiological psychologists: classical conditioning, operant conditioning, discrimination learning, and complex learning. These four types of learning are employed in physiological research because they not only are useful for determining the effect of brain damage or central stimulation on the learning capacities of the organism as a whole but can also be applied to discrete portions of the nervous system. At one time, for instance, there was considerable interest in whether the spinal cord was capable of being conditioned. Or we may ask how a cortical neuron in the visual system discriminates between two wavelengths (colors). As we shall see, classical and operant conditioning procedures have the advantage that stimuli and responses can be specified. Furthermore, these procedures can be automated so that specific stimuli are presented to the subject and responses recorded automatically whether they occur in the intact organism or in a portion of its nervous system. Automation of stimulus presentation and data collection makes it possible for learning procedures to be carried out in a controlled environment.

Classical Conditioning

Classical conditioning as a research technique developed primarily from the work of Ivan Pavlov done in the early part of the twentieth century and is often referred to as Pavlovian conditioning. It is the major type of learning procedure studied experimentally today in the Soviet Union, where it is the basis for a large body of theoretical work leading to ideas concerning the modification of human behavior. Because of its apparent simplicity Pavlovian conditioning provides a good model for neurophysiologists to study electrical changes occurring in the nervous system during the learning process. Further, the experimenter has strict control of stimulus presentations, which is essential to the study of neural coding.

Classical conditioning involves the presentation of a conditioned stimulus (CS) followed by the presentation of an unconditioned stimulus (UCS). For example, to condition a dog to move a paw in response to the sound of a bell, we can present the dog with the bell sound, then quickly apply an electric shock to the paw we would like the dog to move. If the interval between the CS and the UCS is short enough, conditioning will progress rapidly. At first the dog will respond only slightly to the bell and then withdraw the paw sharply when shock is presented. After a number of trials the animal will anticipate the shock and begin to withdraw its leg between the time it hears the bell and the time it receives the shock. This type of conditioning is known as *nondiscriminative* classical conditioning. A single CS, here the bell, is paired with a single UCS, the shock, until the conditioned response (CR) of paw withdrawal occurs. In the final stages of conditioning the animal will withdraw its leg to the sound of the bell before the shock occurs. At this point the shock can be eliminated, and leg withdrawal will continue to occur for some time on presentation of the conditioned stimulus. In a second form of conditioning, called *discriminative,* the animal is required to distinguish between two conditioned stimuli. For example, the bell could be paired with shock (CS+), a buzzer, with no reinforcement (CS−).

Many investigators refer to classical conditioning as stimulus substitution. That is, the animal responds to the bell by withdrawing the leg as if the bell were a shock. The notion of stimulus substitution is only partially correct since the response to the CS is slightly different in intensity and duration from that following the UCS. It is probably more correct to say that the bell becomes a warning signal and the dog's response of leg withdrawal is an attempt to minimize the pain of shock. The example just presented illustrates conditioning of an escape response, because by withdrawing the leg in response to the CS the animal removes it from the shocked surface. As training proceeds, the response appears earlier in the CS-UCS interval in anticipation of the shock.

It is also possible to condition an appetitive response—a response dependent upon the presentation of food and water. Pavlov worked with the very famous salivation response when he trained a dog to salivate to the sound of a bell in anticipation of food. In that case the food was the unconditioned stimulus and the bell the conditioned stimulus. Discriminative conditioning is more often used with appetitive responses than avoidance responses, so that a bell (CS+) could signal food and a buzzer (CS−), no food.

In classical conditioning the order of stimulus presentation is critical for successful learning to take place. If the unconditioned stimulus, for example, is presented before the conditioned stimulus, no conditioning develops; backward conditioning is not possible. Also, in employing classical conditioning one has to be aware of a phenomenon known as *sensitization,* which involves a response without the presentation of the CS. If an unconditioned stimulus is presented many times, a response may be elicited by a number of extraneous stimuli, none of which have been paired previously with the UCS. An animal may be given an electric shock as a UCS to produce leg withdrawal and then at some point a bell is presented which has never been paired with the shock, yet a response occurs. By analogy, a person can be made so anxious or frightened that he will "jump at anything." Sensitization also occurs where there is a response to the CS after a number of CS-UCS presentations but where these presentations are not systematically related or paired during training. This type of sensitization effect has been termed "pseudoconditioning."

It has been shown that the most effective interval between the CS and the UCS is one-half second and that generally the fewer the trials during each training session and the greater the time between trials, the more rapid the learning. Furthermore, the stronger the UCS and CS are, up to a point, the more rapidly the conditioning takes place. If the conditioned stimulus is repeated many times after conditioning has been established but is not followed by a UCS, the conditioned response will begin to disappear or be *extinguished.* Extinction is an active process, not simply a matter of forgetting, as is shown by the fact that if the CS and UCS are again paired after extinction is complete the reacquisition of the response is much more rapid than the initial learning. Following extinction, moreover, the conditioned response will spontaneously reoccur after a lapse of time, even without further training.

Operant Conditioning

A second type of learning procedure, which has been very popular in the United States and Great Britain, is called operant conditioning. Any animal has a large repertoire of responses, some involved in seeking food, others in mating, and still others in escaping a predator. An experimenter can choose any one response and so manipulate stimuli as to increase the probability that the animal will repeat that response. Simply stated, the experimenter can "lead the animal on" to make a given response, which is within the animal's capabilities, more frequently.

B. F. Skinner is primarily responsible for the development of the operant technique, which, in fact, he discovered quite accidentally. One day Skinner came into his laboratory to observe some pigeons that were housed together there, as he had on many previous days. He found the pigeons engaged in a strange series of behaviors. Some of the animals were standing on one foot, hopping around. Others were lying on their backs with their feet in the air. Still others were walking with their heads dragging on the ground. At first he thought all the animals had become infected with some strange disease, but upon closer examination he noticed that periodically a small amount of pigeon food would drop onto the floor of the cage because of a leak in the food dispenser supplying the cage. Each time this happened, the animals would run over and eat the food, then go back to their previous odd behavior. Skinner reconstructed events as follows: First, some food would occasionally fall upon the cage floor. Second, whatever a particular pigeon was doing at the time the food fell was reinforced by the appearance of the food. If an animal happened to be standing on one leg at the instant the food appeared, it "hypothesized" that standing on one leg made the food fall; this response, therefore, would be repeated. Skinner was careful not to describe these events in such cognitive terms but he did write a paper dealing with superstitious behavior in pigeons. A similar thing happens in humans and is the basis of our own superstitions. At one point in somebody's life, he must have gotten hurt while walking under a ladder. Consequently, walking under a ladder is considered by the superstitious a bad practice. Perhaps someone was punished at the same time a black cat happened to wander across his path, and over a period of time the superstition developed that black cats bring bad luck. Skinner's pigeon "thought" that standing on one leg or rolling over on its back would bring food, and its responses became reinforced and strengthened when food did, in fact, appear.

Operant conditioning simply involves choosing a response and then presenting reinforcement when the response is made. A response may be a somatomotor one, such as pecking at a key or pressing a lever, or an autonomic one, such as contraction of the bladder or change in heart rate. It could even be a response within the nervous system—a change in the frequency or amplitude of neural activity such as a spike or an EEG response, for example. All that is necessary to strengthen the response is to "reinforce" it appropriately. To increase the probability that an animal will press a lever, we reinforce each lever press by presenting a small quantity of food and in a short time the animal will acquire the lever-pressing response for food. The response can be made even stronger by rewarding the animal periodically (partial reinforcement) rather than continuously, i.e., by rewarding the animal after every five presses of the lever instead of for every single lever press, thus making the animal work harder for each reinforcement. This is known as a "ratio schedule" of reinforcement; in this case, one reinforcement is given for each set of five responses.

Another schedule of reinforcement is known as an "interval schedule." The animals are rewarded after a certain period of time has elapsed no matter how many responses were made during the period. On such schedules animals might be reinforced once every minute, regardless of when the animal is responding during the minute interval. There are a number of other schedules of reinforcement, most of them combinations of ratio and interval schedules.

Discrimination Learning

There is a large class of learning tasks which fall in the category of discrimination learning. In these tasks the subject is trained to acquire a response which indicates that it can differentiate between two or more stimuli. Can a monkey tell the difference between two tones? Can it distinguish between two colors? Can it tell which one of three objects is different if two are the same? Can it distinguish a smooth object from a rough object?

Discrimination tasks can be set up in a number of ways. To establish a discrimination between two objects, a runway can be used which is formed in the shape of a T or a Y. As one might expect, these devices are known as T mazes and Y mazes. The animal is reinforced for responding to the correct and not reinforced for responding to the incorrect object. In the Y maze, if the animal is to distinguish between a square and a circle, we can always offer reinforcement when the animal runs down the arm of the maze that has the circle at the end. The position of the square and the circle must be randomly varied from trial to trial so that the animal does not learn to respond simply on the basis of position, left or right. In an alternative method the stimuli are placed in front of the animal and the animal simply chooses the desired stimulus and moves it, uncovering a food cup containing the reward. More sophisticated types of apparatus, used primarily for monkeys, involve opening a door or a series of latches on doors to get to the reward.

The operant paradigm also lends itself to discrimination tasks. For example, the animal learns that when a bright light is on, lever pressing will lead to food delivery but when a dim light is presented, no food is available, i.e., a condition of extinction has been imposed.

A variation of discrimination learning depends upon the development of a "go, no-go" response. The animal is *rewarded* for making the correct response (go) or *punished* for making the incorrect response (no-go). If an animal is to be trained to discriminate between a triangle and a circle, with responses to the triangle being reinforced, such a differential response may be established simply by punishing responses to the circle. The go, no-go task is particularly useful if one is trying to separate sensory deficits from certain types of motor response deficits. For example, Rosvold and his colleagues showed in 1961 that following ablation of portions of the prefrontal lobes monkeys could not distinguish between two different visual stimuli in a go, no-go task. They responded to both correct and incorrect stimulus in the same way. However, when the severity of the punishment was increased for the no-go response, the animals stopped making irrelevant responses. These results indicated that following prefrontal damage there was no deficit in the animals' visual capacities, but there may have been a deficit either in attention or in the capacity for the subject to withhold incorrect responses. The use of a go, no-go task in this experiment made it possible to distinguish between a sensory (visual) and a nonsensory deficit following brain damage.

Complex Learning

A last category of learning tasks may be called complex learning tasks. These procedures are used to assess complicated behaviors, such as maze learning. The so-called problem box has been used with monkeys to examine the effect of cortical damage upon "reasoning." The task entails manipulating a number of latches in order to open a cage containing food. The assessment of human abilities, neurological damage, and intelligence is largely through complex tasks rather than through classical or instrumental procedures.

All of the types of learning discussed here are useful in appraising the effects of brain lesions, drugs, and brain stimulation upon behavior. However, it must be kept in mind that the same lesion which renders an animal incapable of learning an operant response might actually improve certain aspects of classical conditioning and that a lesion which destroys auditory discrimination might have no effect at all on visual discrimination. From the point of view of proper methodology, then, one must assess the effect of any type of brain manipulation, whether it be electrical stimulation, ablation, or chemical stimulation, by a variety of behavioral tasks. All too often conclusions regarding the function of the various brain regions are based upon a single testing procedure or very limited types of procedures. Such experimentation is of dubious value; in some cases initial conclusions based on one task or procedure had to be abandoned or even reversed when performance was evaluated in other situations.

MEMORY

Underlying all learning processes is the phenomenon of memory. Since memory is believed to be a brain function and since many brain manipulations which enhance or inhibit learning may do so through actions on memory mechanisms, the concept of memory should be discussed. First, memory is an inferred process. That is, it is useful to postulate a process which we call memory as an explanation for the continuation of behaviors that we have learned. Second, there are probably many types of memory. Some people can recall in great detail things they have seen; others can repeat verbatim conversations heard. Perhaps specific types of memory are organized along the lines of the different sensory modalities: visual, auditory, tactile, etc. There also seems to be a motor memory. For example, a good pianist can usually learn to play many selections without the music. To this end the sequence of motor responses which represent the playing of the sequence of notes in the selection must have been stored and a recall mechanism set up for its retrieval. To be able to understand memory, investigators must be able to determine what types of memory exist. Since memory appears to be at least sensory or motor specific, it is not unreasonable to suggest that the sensory and motor areas of the cortex are directly involved in the processing of these kinds of memory.

A more general consideration is that the electrical activity of the brain is ultimately dependent upon chemical processes; therefore, disruption of the brain's electrical or chemical functions is likely to lead to an interference with memory and hence with learning. One of the classic experiments designed to test this assumption was carried out by Duncan in 1948. Using electroconvulsive shock (ECS) as a means of "deranging" the brain's electrical activity, Duncan showed that memory and learning could be disrupted. He taught rats to leap from one compartment to another in a two-compartment box in response to a conditioned stimulus paired with shock. This is an example of *avoidance conditioning.* After different groups of rats had learned the problem to a given criterion, each group was given an ECS via electrodes connected to the ears and delivering a strong electrical current. Some rats received ECS 40 seconds after they had finished the learning task; others 1 minute after; others after 15 minutes; and still others as long as 14 hours later. If the ECS was given one hour or more after the problem had been learned, Duncan found, there was virtually no effect on retention of the task. If the ECS was given within 15 minutes of completion of the problem, retention was severely disrupted.

Duncan proposed that the effect of the ECS was to disrupt the memory process which was going on immediately after the task was learned. Memory involves the *consolidation* of information by the brain; and immediately after a task, such as memorizing a list of familiar words, is accomplished the memory of the list is unstable until consolidation takes place. During the "consolidation phase," memory can easily be destroyed. ECS is a convenient way of destroying the consolidation process, but once the consolidation is complete (presumably after 15 minutes or so in the case of Duncan's animals), it is virtually impossible to destroy the memory. A number of investigators have considered memory a two-part process, the first part being a consolidation of short-term memory and the second a storage and utilization of long-term memory. There are several ways to disrupt the first process. As we shall see later, certain types of brain lesions seem to interfere with recently learned material but not with later material. The same is true of some drugs and, we have just seen, ECS.

It is another story with old memories. In people with considerable brain damage, as in the case of the senile brain in which the blood supply has been severely diminished and a large portion of the cortex may be dying, childhood memories often seem to persevere after almost all new learning has ceased and recent memory is lost. Such data clearly indicate that very old memories are strongly fixed as compared with recent memories and well protected from the ravages of time and most types of brain damage. The behavioral effects, as noted by Duncan, indicate that memory is not dependent upon *current* activity within the nervous system but somehow reflect neural activity which has been *translated* and *stored*. How does neural activity become stored? Probably via some type of chemical process since electrical events in the brain are dependent upon such chemical processes as the formation of neurohumors, the separation of ions, and the change in the permeability of membranes.

With the recent discoveries in the field of biology that genetic coding might be accomplished by means of chemical messages stored in the DNA molecule, theorists began to hypothesize that if genetic information can be stored chemically, and even passed from one generation to another, perhaps learned information can too. Indeed, it is possible that the memory storage mechanism is similar to that used genetically and involves DNA or some similar substance. The first theory proposing this possibility was that of Katz and Halstead in 1950. They suggested that memory is stored in the brain in the form of RNA molecules and protein. Specifically, they suggested that neurons contain protein molecules randomly scattered which become ordered by incoming neural impulses and that as these proteins are arranged into different patterns they encode a specific output to be passed from one neuron to the next. This point of view remained virtually forgotten until almost 10 years later when a large number of investigations and theoretical papers began to emerge again examining the relation between memory and biochemical events.

Molecular Basis of Memory

In 1954 F. H. C. Crick proposed that DNA was the major substance universally involved in encoding genetic information for transmission from one generation to another. DNA also became a candidate for the coding of individually acquired information. A number of investigators have examined the effect neural stimulation has on the rate of DNA synthesis and have measured changes in the rate at which related substances such as RNA are formed. It is now clear that, whereas no changes take place in the synthesis of DNA, there is a change in RNA metabolism which seems to mirror the intensity of stimulation. Thus, intense stimulation of the vestibular system increases the rate of RNA formation in the vestibular nuclei of the brain stem but not in other areas. Intense visual stimulation increases the RNA in retinal ganglion cells. On the other hand, prolonged visual deprivation, experienced by monkeys living in complete darkness for months, has been shown by A. H. Riesen to decrease the quantity of RNA found in retinal cells.

Because of the extreme stability of DNA necessary for its being involved in the passage of genetic information from one generation to another, attention has shifted to RNA, which is more labile than DNA, as a potential memory molecule. Some recent evidence indicates that RNA levels change as a function of learning. A study done by Holger Hydén in Norway showed that in animals trained to walk up a tightwire placed at an angle of 45 degrees to the floor in order to obtain food there was an increase in the amount of RNA found in cells of the brain stem vestibular nuclei. This would be expected since a great deal of "vestibular learning" is involved in overcoming balance problems associated with climbing such a steep incline. Some people reviewing this experiment felt that it was not a good demonstration of learning because the task involved was primarily a motor task and simply required the refinement of already present responses. It would have been more convincing to show that there is a change in RNA content, let us say in association cortex, when an animal learns to run a maze.

Although the preceding examples illustrate a positive approach to the problem, a negative approach is also of value. Can it be shown that if RNA synthesis is vastly diminished or even shut off learning will not take place? There are a number of ways to find out. RNA synthesis can be either enhanced or interrupted by means of a series of drugs. One experimentally used substance which interferes with RNA synthesis is known as 8-azaguanine. Administration of this chemical, a metabolic inhibitor of RNA, can disrupt certain types of maze learning. On the other hand, after a maze has been learned, administration of 8-azaguanine does not produce a deficit. This finding leads to two possible conclusions: one, that once memory is encoded in RNA, the RNA becomes metabolically inert and therefore disruption can occur only during the consolidation of memory; the other, that RNA subserves the encoding of memory but the storage and recall of memory involves some other chemical substance. There is some evidence that proteins rather than RNA may be more aptly considered memory molecules.

A second approach using drugs is to show that increasing the rate of RNA metabolism enhances learning. At the present time there is no *clear-cut* evidence pointing in this direction although some very weak evidence indicates that a substance known as magnesium pemoline, which may enhance RNA synthesis under certain specialized conditions, possibly leads to an improvement in *performance.* However, magnesium pemoline probably acts as a stimulant, and while it may produce faster acquisition of skill in maze running this is primarily a stimulant effect; any residual effects on "learning" are hard to defend.

The most dramatic single finding with respect to RNA as a memory molecule is credited to Cameron, who in 1958 claimed to have found a marked improvement in memory of aged, senile humans following continuous administration of yeast RNA. In later studies Cameron maintained that there were increases in intelligence levels and notable improvement in retention tasks as well as in the speed of acquisition of new material following RNA therapy. The main argument leveled against this research is that RNA may have a stimulating function, or impurities present in the RNA extracts may have had stimulating effects that enhanced responses much as a "pep pill" such as amphetamine enhances it. Also Cameron's subjects had not been paired with appropriate control groups, i.e., people who had been given either amphetamine, caffeine, or some other stimulant substance. A further possibility is that in aged, sick, or undernourished patients impaired in bodily function any stimulant might improve performance on memory tests simply by increasing alertness. At present this issue has not been resolved, and it is not clear whether Cameron's work shows a true effect of RNA administration on memory or one which is mainly an artifact of stimulant effects.

The last set of substances which have been considered as memory molecules are specific proteins produced as a result of RNA-directed metabolism. A substance which has been shown to increase RNA-directed protein metabolism is known as tricyanoaminopropene (TCAP). In 1966 Solyom and Gallay reported that TCAP significantly increased the output of responses in a Skinner box. Other investigators have found improvement in other types of learning tasks. In contrast, Churchill showed in 1967 that pregnant rats, if deprived of protein during the second half of their gestation period, produced offspring severely deficient in learning of mazes.

Transfer of Learning by Chemicals

The most dramatic research on the molecular basis of memory concerns the transfer of "learning" from one animal to another by means of chemical extracts. Earlier work in this area was done with a flatworm (planaria). Present work frequently involves training of a mouse or rat in a task, removal of its brain, extraction of RNA from its brain, and injection of the extracted material into a naive animal which is then trained in the same problem. The idea is that if memory is a biochemical phenomenon such a procedure will enhance the learning of the specific task by the naive animal. This is getting very close to the science fiction notion of learning a foreign language by taking a pill, or, better yet, by extracting RNA from the brain of a linguist and injecting it into our own nervous system.

Let us consider first the planaria research. Figure 7-1 shows a diagram of the planarian nervous system. The planaria has the interesting property, shared by many lower invertebrates, of being able to regenerate completely if it is cut in half, producing two normal animals. This property makes it ideal for studying molecular basis of memory. The planaria is also one of the simplest animals to have a bilaterally symmetrical nervous system consisting of a cerebral ganglion and parallel strands of nerve fibers running the length of its body. The cerebral ganglion is the largest single collection of neurons in the animal's nervous system and is considered by some people to be a primitive brain.

A study carried out by McConnell and his colleagues in 1959 at the University of Michigan showed that planaria could be classically conditioned. They could learn to contract lengthwise or turn to the presentation of a light paired with shock. Now, if such animals are conditioned and then cut

a.

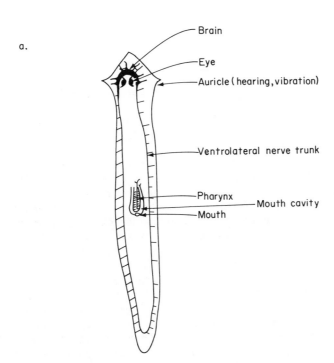

b.

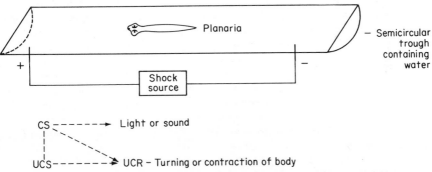

FIGURE 7-1–(a) Dorsal view of the planaria Dugesia showing the nervous system and other main structures. The mouth opens ventrally. **(b)** General setup used for classical conditioning of planaria and conditioning procedure.

in two and allowed to regenerate, it is found that both the head, which had to regenerate a new tail, and the tail portion, which had to regenerate a new head, are able to retain the learning. That the head part of the worm, which regenerates a new tail, retains the task is not surprising since the cerebral ganglion is left intact. But the fact that the tail portion, which has to regenerate a new head, and hence a new cerebral ganglion, also retains the learning indicates that some encoding of what has been learned takes place in the tail region and is transmitted to the embryonic tissue forming the new head, where it is organized by the new brain as the latter is formed. Indeed, the tail portion tends to remember the problem better than does the head portion.

Another ingenious way of looking at memory coding in the planaria was presented by Corning and John, who felt that RNA played a central role in this respect. They classically conditioned planaria and cut them in two but placed the regenerating tails in a ribonuclease medium. Ribonuclease is an enzyme having the property of disrupting the formation of new RNA. The regenerated animals, therefore, had heads which were deficient in new RNA, and such animals were deficient in retention of the task. This and similar experiments by these investigators clearly pointed to the serious consideration of memory as a molecular phenomenon since its very existence can be disrupted by an enzyme which destroys the proposed memory molecule.

More recent and even more spectacular work by Jacobson and his colleagues involved training rats on an operant learning task or maze problem, removing their brains, extracting the RNA, and injecting this RNA into naive animals which were then trained on the same problem. Jacobson and his co-workers claim that this radical procedure produced enhancement of learning. Control groups were tested in which animals received the brain extracts of naive donors and no enhancement of the learning task was found. The effect, therefore, was presumed by the investigators to be specific to the task studied.

Jacobson's results, although seemingly of tremendous significance for the future of psychology and medicine, are not as clear-cut as had first been expected. Immediately upon publication of these experiments, an army of researchers throughout the world tried to replicate them. Only a small percentage of the attempts succeeded. This is an unresolved issue at present, and it is not possible to state whether interanimal transfer of learning exists or is simply an artifact due to some methodological flaw. Nevertheless, a growing body of data indicates that memory, which provides a basis for learning, is a biochemical phenomenon. It is the hope of psychologists and physicians alike that we shall soon be able to unlock the secret of the biochemical memory code so that deficient memory may be restored and normal memory enhanced.

Location of Memory Storage in the Brain

Is memory stored throughout the brain or are there special regions set aside for memory storage? This is different from asking whether memories are stored biochemically, for even if they are, the processes might take place only in certain regions of the brain. The problem of localizing memory has been approached in two ways. One is to try to find specific types of brain damage that will disrupt memory; the other is to determine whether electrical stimulation of the brain somehow alters memory functions or perhaps elicits memories from their storage sites.

The *hippocampus* has been more clearly implicated in memory functions than any other specific brain region, largely through work carried out in the mid-1950s with humans by the neurosurgeons Penfield and Scoville and a clinical psychologist, Brenda Milner. These investigators found that after bilateral removal of most of the human temporal lobe, including portions of the hippocampus, as a treatment for severe motor epilepsy, there were persistent memory losses. In fact, in some subjects memory for events occurring as much as three years before surgery and memory for new information acquired after surgery was virtually destroyed. Old memories, such as those from childhood, were left intact. The results support the earlier notion that memory involves two processes, a recent transient storage process and a permanent storage process. They also implicated a specific brain region, the temporal lobe and hippocampal formation, with the latter as a possible site for the storage of recent information.

These findings in human patients instigated a large number of animal studies in which the hippocampus was removed in order to determine whether or not recent memory storage occurs there. Unfortunately, as is also the case for molecular memory research, results in animals are not clear. In fact, deficits which arise from hippocampectomy can in general be more readily interpreted as deficits in learning *how* or *when* to respond to stimuli rather than in remembering what response to make (retention) or learning to acquire new information.

Recently it has been suggested by two of the present authors (Schmaltz and Isaacson) that different results are obtained from animals suffering lesions of the hippocampus and from human patients because the human patients all had been suffering from temporal lobe epilepsy before surgery. Electrical dysfunctions of the temporal lobe in man are now commonly believed to reflect abnormalities of function which tend to produce a confusion of recall for recent events. This confusion may not be dramatic but it can almost always be demonstrated with strenuous testing of the patients. Perhaps the surgical removal of the temporal lobe areas merely enhances a preexisting deficit in memory caused by the same abnormal processes that produced the abnormal electrical activities. To test this possibility, Schmaltz and Isaacson injected substances into the hippocampus in animals which caused electrical abnormalities and produced damage somewhat similar to that found in naturally occurring epileptic conditions. Then they removed the hippocampal formation contralateral to the hippocampus receiving the injection, which was normal. These animals, with one hippocampal area removed and the other exhibiting peculiar electrical activities, evidenced behaviors similar in many ways to the symptoms found by Penfield, Scoville, and Milner in human patients. They seemed unable to acquire new habits, yet older memories remained intact. The implication is that in the normal animal memories, whether recent or old, do not depend upon the integrity of the hippocampus but that abnormal discharges or activities of the hippocampus tend to produce disturbances of memory. An animal with only an abnormal hippocampus cannot demonstrate learning of recently acquired responses.

The portion of the hypothalamus known as the mammillary nuclei, which receives information directly from the hippocampus via Papez's circuit (see Chapter 3), has also been implicated in memory functions. Interestingly, acute alcoholism, which in its final stages often produces severe derangement of memory, confounding of speech, and a deficit in a variety of cognitive tasks, damages the mammillary nuclei through the vitamin deficiencies and general malnutrition associated with the disease. Destruction of the mammillary nuclei in man by tumors and brain abscesses has also been shown in a number of clinical investigations to correlate with deranged memory function. Since the mammillary nuclei receive their major input from the hippocampus, it might not be unreasonable, at least in humans, to view dysfunctions of either or both of these structures as a cause of disturbances of the memory processes.

Some work done with animals has been useful in localizing memory functions. Kaada and his colleagues in Norway found that hippocampal lesions produce deficits in the acquisition of a maze running habit in a complex multiple T maze. Furthermore, the degree of impairment seems to be related to the size of the lesion. Such a result could clearly be interpreted as a memory loss. That is, the animal cannot remember from one trial to the next or from one choice point to the next which way in the maze to turn. However, the result is also interpretable on the basis that the animal is unable to hesitate appropriately at each choice point and make a decision but instead perseveres in one direction so that it is always bearing to the left or always bearing to the right at each intersection. Especially with animals, deficits due to difficulties in responding appropriately are hard to separate from deficits which may actually be due to memory loss. For this reason it is not a simple matter to determine whether the hippocampus is a primary organ for the storage of recent events.

A second approach to the problem of localizing memory is to search the brain with stimulating electrical probes to determine points at which memory disturbance can be found. The general procedure used in human neurosurgery in probing for damaged brain regions involves the stimulation of different regions and the elicitation of responses. Unlike most surgical procedures, an operation on the human brain can be carried out while the subject is awake and conscious. Local anesthetics are sufficient because stimulation of the brain itself does not produce the sensation of pain. In a patient in whom it is suspected that a region of the brain is not functioning properly, one way to track down the damage is to touch various portions of the cortex with a small stimulating probe and observe the responses elicited. If an exaggerated motor movement or a deficient sensory response is elicited from a region, the site of the damage has been located.

A noted investigator who has used this method for over a quarter of a century is Wilder Penfield of McGill University. Penfield has uncovered some fascinating facts about memory storage. Specifically, he has shown that stimulation in the temporal regions of the brain often elicits a complete memory sequence. A subject may begin telling in great detail a story of something that happened to him many years ago which he thought he had completely forgotten. The memories are so clear and perfect that they often amaze the patient. Unfortunately these episodes have seldom been checked for accuracy. If the findings could be authenticated, they would strongly support the idea that most of what we learn or experience is retained, and the reason we cannot remember everything is that we lack adequate means for recalling stored information. However, the application of direct stimulation to the brain can apparently unlock long-hidden information from its cerebral vault. There are some individuals who have "photographic memories" and seem to be able to retain and use almost everything. This ability is usually more prevalent in children and disappears with age. No neurosurgical patients with this ability have been examined. Finding such patients might be of great value in helping us understand memory storage and recall processes. It must be pointed out again that these results of human brain stimulation have been obtained from abnormal brains to begin with.

Since memories can be elicited by electrical stimulation, the laying down of information in the brain must involve (in addition to a chemical process) certain electrical processes such as the transmission of information from one neuron to another and changes in membrane potentials. An increasingly popular way to study the physiological basis of learning is to look for electrical changes in the central nervous system which correlate with the learning of specific problems. Let us now turn to a discussion of electrical changes possibly associated with memory formation or storage and learning. Here we are considering only gross activity capable of being reflected in electrical recording, not activity directly associated with the crossing of ions from one side of a membrane to another.

ELECTRICAL CORRELATES OF LEARNING

Two types of electrical processes occur in the nervous system: slow processes and rapid changes. Slow processes are most easily measured by means of the electroencephalograph (EEG). Brain rhythms such as the alpha rhythm or the delta rhythm or any other generally slow activity can be easily recorded with the EEG and analyzed by means of modern equipment, which can average responses and describe dominant frequencies occurring in a segment of recorded activity.

Rapid activity such as postsynaptic potential changes and action potentials from single neurons (units) is beyond the grasp of the EEG and is best measured by an oscilloscope. Modern techniques have made it possible not only to measure "on line" activity—that is, activity as it occurs—but to store a complete record of the electrical brain activity on frequency-modulated tape. The tape can be played back later through an oscilloscope and the wave forms observed and analyzed. There are also electrical devices for averaging responses and comparing one set of electrical activities with another set. These "computers of average transients" have revealed much about the electrical activity of single neurons, groups of neurons, fiber tracts, etc. Virtually nothing, however, is known about electrical activity of cellular components such as cell nuclei and cytoplasmic components or about the electrical contributions of the supportive glial cells. Therefore, all of our information dealing with electrical correlates of learning is thought to reflect the function of large groups of neurons.

Because there is so much rhythmic activity in the nervous system at all times, it is possible that many correlations exist between a given ongoing electrical activity and a given learning process. But correlation does not necessarily imply causation. It has to be shown that the same electrophysiological change is consistently related to the same learning phenomenon, and this is a far more difficult problem.

Electrical Changes in Classical Conditioning

Let us consider first the types of electrical changes that occur during classical conditioning. As mentioned earlier, classical conditioning involves presentation of a neutral stimulus, or conditioned stimulus, and its eventual pairing with an unconditioned stimulus. With successive pairings the conditioned stimulus will elicit the unconditioned response. If we present a novel stimulus to an animal for the first time, a stimulus we wish eventually to use as a conditioned stimulus, we elicit a reaction. This reaction has been referred to by investigators throughout the world as an *arousal reaction* or *orientation reflex* to a novel stimulus. Behaviorally, the animal might tilt its head, move its ears, or, if the stimulus is very intense, actually turn toward the stimulus. At the level of autonomic responses the animal might show pupillary dilation and a variety of sympathetic responses which will be more or less apparent depending upon the intensity of the stimulus and whether it has any particular significance for the animal. Within the animal's nervous system there is a change in the overall EEG pattern, from spontaneous background activity to clear arousal which consists of low voltage and high frequency. However, since the arousal stimulus is usually modality specific— that is, auditory, visual, or whatever—it is reasonable to assume that changes in the electrical activity of the nervous system depend to some extent upon which sensory areas are receiving the stimulus. If an auditory stimulus is used, there will in fact be a greater amount of arousal reaction, or desynchronization, apparent in the region of the auditory projection cortex which receives the stimulus from the auditory system than in other portions of the brain. In addition, if the stimulus is repeated several times, there seems to be a "tuning in" of the nervous system so that the area receiving the input stimulus becomes sensitized to it. Its threshold for the receiving of additional information decreases whereas the threshold of nearby surrounding tissue increases.

If the stimulus is repeated many times, a new process is initiated. The orienting response begins to disappear as a result of nonreinforced stimulus presentations, and the electrical activity tends to recede to the base line of background activity. The arousal reaction disappears, and eventually the stimulus has no effect whatsoever. This process, referred to as *habituation,* is illustrated in Figure 7-2. Habituation is not only an overt behavioral phenomenon but an electrophysiological one as well. In this case, then, a behavioral and an electrophysiological phenomenon show a clear correlation. It is not unreasonable to assume, in fact, a close relationship between the return of the physiological arousal response to a spontaneous activity and the decreased behavioral response to the stimulus. Habituation is known to be specific to the stimulus used and is considered a very simple form of learning.

A more detailed analysis of these processes shows that there are

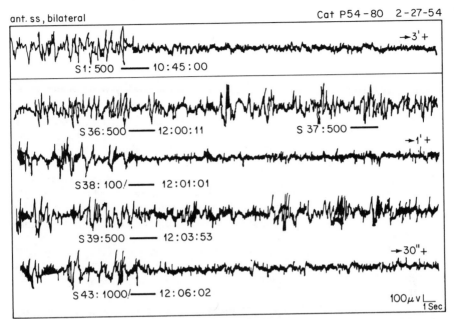

ant. ss, bilateral   Cat P54-80   2-27-54

FIGURE 7-2—Cortical electrograms from the suprasylvian gyrus of a normal cat showing typical habituation of the arousal reaction to a 500-cycle tone after about 30 trials.
In the first tracing the response to the first presentation of the 500-cycle tone is
shown (S1:500). The solid bar shows the duration of the stimulus followed by the time
in hours, minutes, and seconds (10:5:00). The second tracing shows the 36th and
37th trials (S36 and S37). Then a novel tone of 100 cycles is presented in the 38th
trial (S38:100) followed by a repetition of the habituated tone (S39:500) and then another novel tone (S43:1000!). The figures at the right above the EEG traces indicate
the duration of the activation in each trial. (From Sharpless and Jasper. *Brain,* 1956, *79,*
655–680.)

differences within the cortex in the rate at which habituation occurs. The
neocortex in mammals is a six-layered structure. Some layers are used
primarily for the reception of sensory imput; others, mostly for the production of responses; and still others, for gathering information from the sensory
side and passing it to the response side. Layer 4 from the top of the cortex is
known as the *internal granular layer.* This is the sensory input layer, and in
areas of the brain which are specifically designed to receive sensory information—auditory cortex, for example—it is much enlarged and contains
numerous granular cells, which are small multipolar neurons. In cortex which
is known to be associational in function, layer 4 is similar to the other layers
in size. In cortex which is involved in motor output, such as motor cortex,
layer 4 tends to be very small. In sensory receiving cortex, where this fourth
layer is large, it is found that habituation, although it occurs in all cortical
layers, takes longest to occur in the fourth. This kind of detailed information
is a result of recent advances in the techniques of microelectrode implanta-
tion into individual neurons within a cortical layer.

Another interesting finding is that the orientation response, or orientation reflex, disappears before the habituation (as measured electrically) occurs. That is, the animal stops showing an overt behavioral response to the stimulus, i.e., appears habituated, before its EEG or electrical activity has habituated. E. Roy John, who has done research on the electrophysiological basis of learning, interprets these phenomena underlying habituation by saying that novel stimuli exert an influence over a large region of the brain and that information about unexpected changes in the environment is distributed over many systems, both cortical and subcortical. However, as the information is repeated but not paired with the conditioned stimulus, the animal learns that the information is irrelevant—it signifies nothing—and therefore habituation occurs. The influence of the stimulus is gradually excluded from one system after another in the brain and eventually disappears from all systems but lastly from the sensory pathways which originally brought this information in. As Dr. John goes on to say in essence, the fact that information can be selectively habituated is clear evidence that habituation is a learning phenomenon.

Once a response has been habituated to a novel stimulus, we can pair it with an unconditioned stimulus and try to produce classically conditioned responses. Unconditioned stimuli, such as shock, differ from conditioned stimuli in that they do not habituate nearly as well and in some cases not at all. The unconditioned stimulus produces a more pronounced arousal response than the conditioned stimulus although electrically the same pattern of changes occurs with both. The earliest attempt to explain how classical conditioning takes place was that of Pavlov himself. Pavlov believed that when a conditioned stimulus and an unconditioned stimulus are paired, changes are produced in the nervous system in the specific areas which mediate these two stimuli, and the changes eventually link CS and UCS. He wrote about the formation of temporary connections between the conditioned stimulus receiving area and the unconditioned stimulus receiving area, a connection that ultimately allows a response to be elicited by the conditioned stimulus.

Although Pavlov devised this theory almost half a century ago, only now is it becoming clear that some kind of connection must be formed between the CS and the UCS within the nervous system. Specifically in support of this notion, Kogan in the Soviet Union has shown that desychonization in the sensory receiving area for the CS becomes limited more and more to a small region with a decreased threshold for response as the CS is presented and paired with the UCS. This finding is in line with Pavlov's idea that the responses to the CS also become consolidated. One way to set up a specific linkage between a conditioned and an unconditioned response is to pair presentation of light to the eyes of the anesthetized animal and shock to the animal's motor cortex. The shock will produce a limb movement. By pairing the light and the shock, one can eventually elicit the limb movement with the light alone. Since the light is registered in the visual cortex and the shock is registered in the motor cortex and after a while the visual stimulus will elicit a limb movement, it is assumed that some sort of temporary connection has been set up between the two regions. There is consolidation at both the CS receiving area and the motor cortex.

How are temporary connections formed? Three possible means have been proposed. The first is by spreading across the cortex from one region to another. Such spread would be primarily through the dendritic plexus or connections found in the uppermost or molecular layer of the cortex, and it is known as *ephaptic* transmission. A second means might be through axons which normally run from the visual cortex to the motor cortex. These axons pass from the output layers of the sensory cortex through the white matter of the brain and into the input layers of the motor cortex. From the output layers of the motor cortex information is then passed down to the muscles. When we say "temporary connection formation," we do not imply that new connections are grown but only that existing connections are utilized by changing their electrical responsiveness. This is a reasonable point of view; there is such an enormous number of possible fiber tracts in the brain that the learning of new information probably involves a switching onto circuits which are not at the moment in operation but are there and ready to be used at any time. The third method by which a temporary connection might be formed is from the output of the sensory receiving area through subcortical regions and then over to the motor area. There may be connections that are set up from the visual cortex down to limbic and hypothalamic regions and back up to the motor cortex. Another possibility obviously not to be discounted is that all these means of linkage are employed simultaneously.

It has been shown in a few experiments that conditioned responses set up in the way described can be abolished by *undercutting* the motor cortex. Undercutting is simply a way of cutting the fiber tracts to the motor cortex from either subcortical regions or other cortical regions (see Figure 7-3). It does not eliminate the possibility of ephaptic transmission across the cortex; but since the conditioned response is abolished following the undercutting of the cortex, clearly the cutting of subcortical connections (or cortical connections via white matter tracts) is sufficient to abolish the phenomenon. Ephaptic transmission does not have to be invoked as a possible means of connection formation.

Finally, some remarkable work by Olds and Olds (1961) presented evidence showing that operant conditioning might take place at the cellular or unit level. Earlier research by Olds (1954) had shown that rats will self-stimulate (press a lever) to deliver reinforcing electrical stimuli to their own brains through implanted electrodes. The septal area and medial forebrain bundle are two anatomical regions within the limbic system in which lever-pressing rates for self-stimulation are very great. To determine whether single units (neurons) can be instrumentally conditioned, Olds and Olds applied stimulation to the medial forebrain bundle as a reward. The response to be rewarded was spontaneous activity recorded via a microelectrode from a single unit in some other brain region such as the hippocampus, hypothalamus, or neocortex. The results of this procedure were striking. Some subcortical units showed an increase in discharge rate after only 15 reinforcements. It seems plain that the basic processes underlying learning can be reflected within single neurons, particularly in view of recent findings that memory and learning may be represented by biochemical events which are also believed to occur within single neurons.

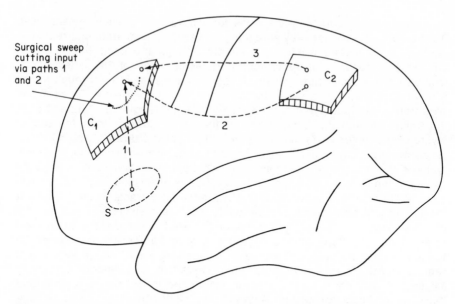

FIGURE 7-3–The lateral surface of a primate brain showing two cortical regions C_1 and C_2 and a subcortical region S. C_1 receives subcortical input from S and association fibers from C_2. In addition, transcortical or ephaptic spread is shown following path 3 from C_2 to C_1. Surgical undercutting of C_1 would eliminate input via paths 1 and 2 but still leave the possibility that influences could be exerted on C_1 via path 3.

In summary, the evidence is good that there are electrical changes mirroring the conditioning process which seem to indicate some type of neural linkage between the area receiving the conditioned stimulus, the area receiving the unconditioned stimulus, and the area initiating the response. Clearly, if this is the case in classical conditioning, it is not unreasonable to assume that stimuli might be linked together with responses in other types of conditioning—operant conditioning, discrimination learning, maze learning, etc. We have already seen tentative evidence for the operant conditioning of single units. There appears to be a fundamental property of the nervous system, a built-in plasticity so that it can associate stimuli and responses. This is a basic property which one would expect in order for learning to exist.

Reponse to Repetitive Stimuli

Another property of the nervous system is important: its ability to respond to repetitive stimuli. If a flickering light at 8 flicks per second or a clicking at 10 clicks per second is presented, it is possible to drive units (neurons) in either the visual or auditory cortex to follow these specific inputs. A 10-cycle-per-second flickering light will produce a 10-cycle-per-second response in many units in the visual system. This ability to follow repetitive input is limited by the response abilities of the neurons, but for low frequencies it is the most direct way to code information.

In 1960 John and Killam showed that during operant conditioning one can record specific electrical changes from various regions, both subcortical and cortical. The interesting thing is that as bar pressing is reinforced by presentation of milk to a hungry cat, for instance, there is a sharp rise in activity recorded from the hippocampus, the reticular formation, and the visual cortex. This increase was most prominent in the visual cortex as learning progressed and indicated that specific changes occur in the nervous system not only as a function of the problem learned but also as a function of time. The basic principle illustrated here is that not only do electrical changes occur in the nervous system as a function type of learning—a shuttle box response, let's say, as different from an operant conditioning response—but *different* electrical changes occur as learning progresses.

In a 1959 study of avoidance learning in the cat John and Killam showed that frequency-specific responses can be recorded in visual cortex and visual pathways as well as in portions of the limbic system during the initial presentation of the conditioned stimulus. Their stimulus consisted of a 10-cycle-per-second flickering light. After continuous presentation of this stimulus without reinforcement habituation occurred and the frequency-specific "labeled responses" disappeared. When shock was paired with the conditioned stimulus, the labeled responses reappeared in primary visual pathways but not in the limbic system structures. As the conditioned stimulus and the unconditioned stimulus were paired on succeeding trials, changes were noted in the form, particularly in the amplitude, of the electrical responses in different regions of the brain. There was a shift in the appearance of responses from the visual pathways to less specific regions such as the reticular formation. At various points in the conditioning procedure a dominant response would again appear from time to time in the major visual paths. The most striking finding was that when the animal had learned to respond 100 percent of the time to the conditioned stimulus, a 40-cycle-per-second burst of activity appeared in the amygdaloid complex. This was the clearest electrical change found in the study. Whether a causal relationship should be implied here is questionable. Perhaps when an animal has mastered the problem, a response appears in the amygdala signifying that all linkages or temporary connections have now been completed between the sensory receiving area and the motor output regions. Since many studies show that certain types of amygdaloid lesions produce severe deficits in both acquisition and retention of a conditioned avoidance response in a shuttle box, damage in the amygdaloid complex, which would of course abolish such an electrical response, might be assumed to be disruptive of this type of avoidance learning.

Prediction of Behavior
One of the great hopes of electrophysiologists studying electrical phenomena underlying learning is that these phenomena may have a predictive value. Some day it may be possible to look at a portion of a record from an animal's nervous system and say, "The animal has not yet mastered the problem" or "The animal will master the problem in a few trials" or "This animal will never learn the problem." Ability to predict behavior would have

great implications for human learning, in particular, if the information could be obtained by scalp electrodes in man rather than through intervening in the nervous system. Modern technology has already enabled us to record evoked potentials and to average them from simple scalp electrodes in man; the day may come when learning processes can be monitored electrophysiologically. Even more exciting is the possibility that one can tell a human subject before he makes a response in a discrimination task that, even though he is not yet consciously aware of the fact, he is going to make the wrong choice in the next trial. There is some evidence obtained by Ross Adey, a neurophysiologist at the University of California, that the choice behavior of a cat in a visual discrimination task on a specific trial before a response is overtly performed can be predicted on the basis of the electrical activity recorded from the animal's brain.

We have seen, then, that in the learning of even such simple tasks as habituation of responses to novel stimuli a large number of cerebral structures are involved—sensory receiving areas, motor response areas, and the vast association regions in between consisting of limbic nuclei, hypothalamic nuclei, and cortical regions of various types. A second method utilized in trying to understand the role of the nervous system in learning is the *ablation technique.* What happens if brain damage is produced experimentally in regions which are known to participate in the learning process? Is learning disrupted in a specific predictable way that might indicate the function of these regions, or is there just a generalized nonspecific decrease in learning ability? Fortunately, it has been found that learning deficits are quite specific to some of the damage produced. Let us now turn to a discussion of the effects of central nervous system damage on learning.

ROLE OF CENTRAL NERVOUS SYSTEM STRUCTURES IN THE LEARNING PROCESS

During the past half-century much research has shown that a number of subcortical structures and large portions of the neocortex are involved in various types of learning. It has already been pointed out in Chapter 3 that limbic system as well as cortical structures are intimately involved in the mediation of emotion as well as the emotional states. Learning depends heavily upon the motivational condition of the animal particularly since most learning procedures involve reinforcement. Emotion too plays a central role in determining the course of a learning experience. Strong emotions in man and animal alike can inhibit certain kinds of learning, especially in humans being tested by complex cognitive tasks. On the other hand, strong emotion may facilitate avoidance as in learning to avoid an electric shock in a conditioning task. An animal that either does not feel an electric shock or is indifferent to it would have great difficulty in learning such a task. The fact that the limbic system mediates emotion and motivation, which are, in turn, processes essential to the learning phenomenon, implicates it in learning.

An important methodological problem being attacked by modern psychologists and physiologists derives from the fact that it is experimentally difficult to distinguish between deficits in the performance exhibited during learning tasks due to alterations in motivation or emotion and those due to alterations in "learning" per se. For example, if an animal has a hard time mastering an avoidance task in a shuttle box, a variety of factors may be involved: (1) The shock is not felt; therefore the animal does not respond. (2) The shock is felt, but the animal does not respond appropriately because of a defect in emotionality and therefore learns very slowly if at all. (3) The shock is felt, and the animal is sufficiently motivated, but some kind of motor deficit prevents the animal from initiating the response. These performance deficits are confounded by alterations in the animal's motivational or emotional state or its ability to produce appropriate movements. Most difficult to handle is the possibility (4) that the animal's sensory reactions to the shock and its perception of the situation are normal, its motivational state is unaltered, but it does not "understand the problem." This can be called a *cognitive impairment.* Perhaps the animal cannot link the stimuli together with the response because of some deficit in higher functions. Since such deficits are hard to describe, it is a real challenge to pin them down structurally. In instances of human cortical damage this type of deficit is often found. There may be no change in sensory thresholds or in the general ability to perceive, no change in emotional or motivational state, yet the subject is unable to learn a maze problem or a word association task.

One way to approach the problem of separating emotional, motivational, and cognitive deficits is to set up behavioral tasks pitting these three possibilities against one another, as follows: If a deficit is a result of a motivational change, effect A should be produced; if it is a result of response alterations, effect B should be produced; if it is a result of an emotionality change, effect C should be produced. A number of studies have been designed with such a model in mind since this is a reasonable procedure for specifying brain damage.

A particularly useful approach to interpreting behavioral deficits observed following damage to the limbic system is to employ active- and passive-avoidance tasks. In the active-avoidance task an animal is required to actively avoid punishment by making a specified response—for example, to leap over a hurdle in a shuttle box in response to a conditioned stimulus such as a light or a buzzer in order to avoid impending shock. In the passive-avoidance situation the animal is punished for making a specified response and can avoid the punishment by withholding this response. If it drinks from a water dish which is electrified so that a shock is delivered directly through the mouth with each contact, it can avoid shock by simply not drinking. The term "passive avoidance" is misleading but has remained in the literature by default. The problem is that, although an animal can avoid punishment by not responding, it is still inhibiting a response to food or water, usually in the face of deprivation. The inhibition of a response is an active process, not a passive one. The advantage of the active-avoidance task is that it is good for testing motor deficits. If an animal's brain has been damaged so that use of a limb has been lost, not only should the animal be unable to acquire an active-avoidance response, but it should show obvious signs of motor difficulty. On the other hand, the passive-avoidance paradigm might be good for assessing a loss of inhibitory control in the nervous system. It is well known that certain types of motor damage will make animals unable to control their movements appropriately. Lesions of the caudate nucleus will cause animals to start walking in a certain direction and continue doing so even when an obstacle has been encountered. Like a wind-up toy, they will try to walk in a forward direction against a wall. This is known as "obstinate progression." A task that punished such an animal for walking into a compartment where a shock was delivered would reveal a deficit in response inhibition because the animal would be unable to stop its forward movement. These are the more obvious cases (i.e., motor deficits) which can be examined with active- and passive-avoidance tasks.

More difficult is the question of how to distinguish a deficit due to an emotional change from one due to a motivational change or a change in response capabilities. A brain-damaged animal might be deficient in a passive-avoidance task requiring it to inhibit approach responses to a dish containing food and water because it is thirstier and/or hungrier than a normal animal. It might be "overresponding" because it is unable to inhibit its response even though no overt sign of motor damage is present. It might be responding in the face of punishment because it is no longer afraid of the shock or it may not even feel the shock. How does one separate one deficit from the other? In the active-avoidance task an animal might not learn to avoid a buzzer paired with shock because of some kind of motor difficulty, even though it is not grossly apparent; or because it does not feel the shock and therefore cannot respond; or because, although it feels the shock, its emotional reactions have been affected and it is now not afraid of the shock. The animal may be, on the other hand, so frightened by the shock on account of alteration of its emotional state that its only response is to "freeze." Freezing in response to shock is more easily learned than the more appropriate and adaptive escape or avoidance response. Needless to say, the confounding of these variables—emotion, motivation, learning, memory, etc.—is no less apparent in active- and passive-avoidance tasks than it would be in deficits found in discrimination tasks, operant conditioning tasks, maze learning tasks, and so on. Let us now turn to some specific experimental findings relevant to understanding the role of brain regions in learning.

Role of Brain Regions in Learning

The interest in passive-avoidance problems in the assessment of brain damage may be traced to an often cited experiment reported by R. A. McCleary (1961), a physiological psychologist at the University of Chicago. It had been shown earlier at the University of Oslo by B. R. Kaada and his colleagues that stimulation of the septal area and surrounding cortex in both anesthetized and awake cats produced a loss of motor tone, inhibition of blood pressure, decrease in heart rate, and slowing of respiration. Kaada proposed that this region of the brain, known as the subcallosal area since it lies right under the head of the corpus callosum and just in front of the septum, be labeled an inhibitory region for the control of autonomic and

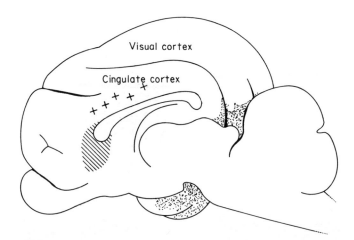

FIGURE 7-4–Medial view of the cat's brain showing two areas which act to modify motor responses in opposite ways. The hatched area represents the subcallosal area, which is an inhibitory zone, whereas the region designated by plus signs, the cingulate cortex, is a motor facilitatory area. Lesions in the subcallosal region produce deficits in passive-avoidance behavior; lesions in the cingulate cortex in rats produce active-avoidance deficits. In the cat, however, active-avoidance deficits are probably due to damage to fiber tracts on route to the overlying visual cortex. (Modified from R. A. McCleary. *Journal of Comparative & Physiological Psychology,* 1961, *54,* 606.)

motor functions. In contrast, stimulation of the middle of the cingulate gyrus increased autonomic activity. Kaada proposed that the middle portion of the cingulate region might act as a facilitatory area for the autonomic nervous system and perhaps also for portions of the motor system (see Figure 7-4). In these two areas of the limbic system, then, stimulation produces opposite results. McCleary, who had worked in Kaada's laboratory, designed a simple experiment to show that behavioral predictions might be borne out regarding the effects of lesions on certain types of learning tasks. He reasoned that if stimulation of the septal area or subcallosal cortex produces inhibition, removal of this region should cause a net facilitation; i.e., the animal might not be able to control or inhibit its motor responses. McCleary tested this hypothesis by using a passive-avoidance task in which normal cats and cats with subcallosal damage were allowed to eat from a food dish that delivered shock to the mouth after several days of unhindered eating from the dish. He clearly showed that animals with subcallosal or septal damage were deficient in withholding responses to the dish; they would, that is, take more mouth shocks than normal animals.

McCleary reasoned further that removal of the cingulate cortex, a facilitatory area, might produce a net inhibition, and an animal so inhibited might have difficulty initiating an escape or learning an avoidance response calling for rapid movement. He tested such operated cats in a two-way version of the active-avoidance task. Here an animal is required to jump from the left to the right compartment of a two-compartment apparatus on one trial and

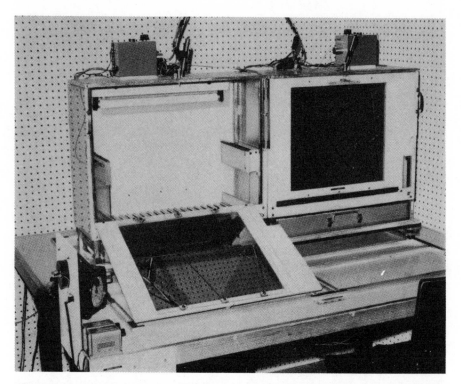

FIGURE 7-5–Active-avoidance apparatus used for cats. The boxes can be moved independently on the track system, which is mounted on the table. In the two-way or shuttle response the animal is required to avoid by jumping from the left box to the right box on one trial and from the right box to the left box on the next trial. This alternation continues with each succeeding trial. In the one-way test, the animal jumps from the left box to the right box on all trials. The position of the boxes is interchanged by moving them on the tracks after each trial is completed. (From J. F. Lubar, C. J. Schostal, and A. A. Perachio, *Physiology and Behavior*, Vol. 2. Elmsford, New York: Pergamon Press, 1967. Facing p. 180.)

from the right to the left compartment on the next trial (see Figure 7-5). Severe deficits in the acquisition of the two-way avoidance response occurred. Many animals were not able to learn at all; others took many more trials than control animals to learn. In contrast to these findings, McCleary reported that septal operated cats, which are deficient in passive avoidance, are normal in active avoidance and perhaps master this task even faster than normal subjects. On the other hand, cingulectomized animals deficient in active avoidance showed no deficit in passive avoidance. McCleary based his interpretation of the effects of cingulate and septal lesions upon Kaada's earlier work and viewed deficits obtained as deficits in the initiation of responses.

The role of the cingulate and the septal area in avoidance conditioning looked clear until a few years later when J. Harvey and his colleagues at the

University of Chicago showed that animals with septal lesions consumed more water than normal controls and could learn to lever press for water more rapidly than normal animals on several different schedules of reinforcement. This finding suggested an alternative interpretation to McCleary's experiment. Septal operated animals may be deficient in passive-avoidance behavior not because they cannot inhibit their responses but because they are thirstier and thus more motivated for the water than normal animals. The important problem which now faced investigators was a matter not merely of devising more behavioral tasks and getting more phenomena to look at in septal ablated animals but of determining which of these two hypotheses was more cogent in explaining the effects of septal lesions in passive avoidance.

A third factor had entered into the argument by this time: the possibility that animals with septal lesions are not as frightened by the shock as normal animals. It is observed in the passive-avoidance situation that when a normal animal is shocked for making the consummatory response it not only leaps out of the compartment where the electrified water is located but will often run to the opposite corner of the box and sit there freezing (terrified), a normal reaction if an animal has been severely punished. The septal operate, however, will jump back in response to the pain produced by the shock but then wander around the box and come back and take additional shocks as if it were relatively unafraid of the consequences. It had been shown earlier by Brady and Hunt that septal operates were deficient in the formation of a conditioned emotional response to shock (a conditioned emotional response, it will be recalled, is a constellation of responses produced when an animal is frightened, consisting of freezing and sympathetic signs). So the third interpretation relevant to the passive-avoidance situation is that the septal operated animal, since it does not readily freeze, is less frightened of the shock and, being as thirsty as a normal animal (if not more so), will respond in the face of punishment. Now we have covered the three interpretations that were discussed earlier: change in response capabilities, change in emotionality, and change in motivational state.

It could also be argued that the septal operate does not remember from one trial to the next what has occurred previously, but various learning tasks have shown that such an animal is capable of performance indicative of normal memory function. In a recent series of experiments by one of the present authors (Lubar) and his colleagues, an attempt was made to differentiate between the increased water intake and the loss of response inhibition seen in septal operated animals. Septal lesions have been shown to produce largely similar deficits in rats and cats in passive-avoidance behavior. For the particular experiment to be described rats were used. It was suspected that the reason septal rats increase their water intake is that the lesion produces a deficit in the utilization of antidiuretic hormone. There are, we know, direct projections from the septal area to the supraoptic nucleus of the hypothalamus. It was hypothesized that if the septal area is damaged the projections to the supraoptic nucleus might also be damaged, so that no message could be sent to the supraoptic nucleus telling it to release antidiuretic hormone. The effect of a septal lesion would be expected to be similar to the effect of a supraoptic lesion. In the latter case no antidiuretic hormone is available because the system for it is destroyed. The animal loses water through urination and in compensation drinks large quantities of water. This is the syndrome of diabetes insipidus, to be discussed in the next chapter.

In our experiment a number of animals with septal lesions were monitored for daily water intake, and a sustained increase was found, as expected. Antidiuretic hormone was then administered to these animals to try to compensate for the hormone which had not been released, and the water intake was normalized; i.e., with hormone replacement therapy the septal operated rats drank the same amount of water as normal animals. Next, both septal operated and normal animals with and without antidiuretic hormone replacement therapy were tested in the passive-avoidance task, and it was found that the hormone made no difference. Septal rats that had been on the hormone as well as septal rats that had been given a placebo injection showed equally large deficits in passive avoidance. Moreover, the increase in water intake only occurred when the lesion extended into the posterior septum whereas the deficit in passive avoidance seemed to be independent of lesion placement. The experiment shows clearly that the deficit in passive avoidance cannot be explained by the change in water intake. One cannot hypothesize that septal damaged animals are deficient in water-motivated passive avoidance because of a changed motivational state or a greater need for water. This is an example of how one of the alternative interpretations for behavioral deficits seen in a specific behavioral task can be eliminated.

The septal operated animal shows, then, a number of behavioral changes following the ablation including a hyperreactivity to stimuli, an increase in water intake, and a deficit in passive-avoidance behavior. In addition, the fact that it exhibits no increase in general activity in an open field indicates that any loss of response inhibition is not so gross as to cause the animal to move continuously. Septal operates can and do inhibit some of their responses. Perhaps, indeed, they have no difficulty in controlling their responses, and all of the effects seen in behavioral tasks which look like response deficits can be attributed to a deficit in emotionality.

Septal damaged animals show two other clear-cut behavioral changes, one of which, at least in rats, is an enhancement of performance in two-way active-avoidance problems. In two-way avoidance, it will be recalled, the animal has to go from the left compartment to the right on one trial and from the right compartment to the left on the next. Again, in this type of task septals are *superior* to normals. However, in a one-way active-avoidance task septal operated rats are *deficient* in comparison to normal animals (see Figure 7-5). This is one of the most perplexing findings reported in the recent literature. Normal animals compared in one- and two-way tasks have been shown by many investigators to learn the one-way task in half the number of trials required to learn the two-way task (Lubar and Perachio, 1965). Normal rats may learn the one-way task even more rapidly than that.

The fact that a septal operated animal is enhanced in its acquisition of a two-way task is not unreasonable since a two-way task involves both an active- and a passive-avoidance response. The active-avoidance response is getting out of the box where shock is going to be delivered before it comes.

The passive-avoidance response occurs as follows: On a given trial the animal has to leave the compartment it is in, in order to avoid shock, and enter the opposite compartment (which in a two-way task is the compartment where it was shocked on the previous trial). A conflict is thus set up for the animal—leaving the compartment where it is to avoid shock or jumping into the one where it has just been punished. In fact, when the conditioned stimulus comes on, the animal often runs up to the hurdle separating the compartments and then backs away from it, approaches and backs away again. This is a case of an approach-avoidance conflict between competing responses—the active-avoidance response and the passive-avoidance response. In the septal operated animal deficient in passive avoidance, however, the passive-avoidance response component is altered and the conflict is absent. The animal is willing to leap into the compartment where it was previously shocked. Since it has no active-avoidance deficit either, the net result is an enhancement in learning the task as measured by fewer trials to a criterion and faster responding on each trial. On the other hand, septal operated animals are deficient in learning a simple one-way avoidance response: always to jump from the same compartment (i.e., always from the left to the right compartment). This one-way deficit is not found in cats but only, thus far, in rats. At present we have no suitable explanation of this bizarre behavioral phenomenon.

The hippocampus is another limbic system structure that is similar to the septum with regard to active- and passive-avoidance behavior. Both hippocampal and septal lesions produce deficits in the acquisition of the one-way response, enhancement in the acquisition of the two-way response, and deficits in passive-avoidance behavior. On all three measures hippocampal damaged and septal damaged animals seem indistinguishable from one another. On the other hand, hippocampal damage in humans has produced deficits in memory, and some experiments show that animals with hippocampal lesions are deficient in learning complex maze tasks whereas those with septal lesions are not (Kimble, 1963; Ain et al., 1969). More to the point, it has recently been shown that septal operated rats are not deficient in the learning of the complex Hebb–Williams maze, in which an animal is given a number of problems of varying difficulty. Septal rats respond as rapidly as normal animals and make no more errors than normal controls in learning the series of complex maze problems. However, the hippocampal damaged animals do show a deficit in learning Hebb–Williams maze problems. This is important information if one is trying to make distinctions between the hippocampus and the septal area.

Still another structure implicated in both emotion and learning is the cingulate cortex. As has already been mentioned, lesions of the middle portion of the cingulate gyrus produce a deficit in two-way active-avoidance learning in cats (McCleary, 1961). This finding has been replicated in rats by a number of investigators. Thomas and Slotnick, Peretz, and others have clearly shown that anterior and middle cingulate lesions produce deficits in the acquisition of both the one-way and the two-way response. In the case of the cat, however, a second factor has to be considered. Recent work by Lubar and his colleagues reveals that deficits in avoidance conditioning ascribed to the cingulate gyrus are due to damage to the overlying visual cortex (see Figure 7-4). The striate or visual cortex, which is the primary receiving area in the visual system, lies directly above the cingulate cortex in the cat. In making a cingulate lesion it is easy to inadvertently cut the visual radiations which pass from the lateral geniculate body in the thalamus to the visual cortex lying above the cingulate. It was found that removal of the visual cortex, independent of any damage to the cingulate gyrus, is sufficient to produce a severe deficit in two-way avoidance response once it has been learned. Even more interesting, removal of only 25 percent of the total visual cortex is sufficient to cause these avoidance deficits in acquisition and retention.

A question raised by these findings was that perhaps the animal cannot learn because of some kind of visual difficulty. But a recent experiment by Lubar, Schostal, and Perachio (1967) showed that cats with lesions in the visual cortex are not deficient in learning a visual pattern discrimination and display no gross abnormalities in locomotion, visual placing, or coordination. Nevertheless, a severe deficit in acquisition of the two-way avoidance response was again found. If primary visual processes are not affected, what is the cause of the deficit? It was proposed that the visual cortex might mediate nonvisual functions as well as the usual visual functions ascribed to it.

Earlier work by Lashley and his colleagues in the 1930s had shown that, if the visual cortex of a rat is removed, a deficit in maze learning can be demonstrated. This is not an unreasonable finding. Yet if the animal is peripherally blinded, there will also be a deficit in maze learning, and this too would be expected. The more interesting finding was that removal of the visual cortex *plus* peripheral blinding of the animal produced a deficit which was greater than that produced by either peripheral blinding or cortical damage alone. Since addition of cortical damage in the peripherally blind animal caused a further deficit in learning, some other type of function must have been affected, perhaps a nonvisual function relevant to the learning process.

This suspicion has recently been confirmed in Lubar's laboratory, using cats. Lesions placed in the striate cortex of animals that were functionally peripherally blinded with opaque contact lenses produced a greater deficit in the acquisition, retention, and relearning of the two-way avoidance response than in animals that either sustained only damage to the striate cortex or were intact but being tested with opaque contact lenses. Furthermore, animals with striate damage showed no difficulty whatsoever in crossing the hurdle in the avoidance apparatus, in general locomotion, or in any other type of observed visually guided behavior. The deficit itself consisted not of an inability to respond but of an inability to reach a criterion of 9 out of 10 avoidance responses in a single daily session. The animal acted as if it did not "understand the problem," in that on many trials it would respond to the CS by running back and forth rather than by leaping to the other box.

Not understanding the problem is similar to the deficit seen in humans who have sustained damage in the association cortex of the visual system: visual agnosia. This is not a disruption in the ability to see but a defect in the ability to interpret what is seen. A human with cortical damage might be able to describe an apple by saying, "It is round," "It is red," etc., but not be able to tell what it is. Such a loss in recognition and interpretation is clearly not a primary visual defect so much as a cognitive or intellectual one. It is very difficult to say whether a true visual agnosia has been found in the cat that cannot learn an avoidance task with visual cortex damage but can learn a visual discrimination. At present it can only be said that something of a nonvisual type of deficit seems to exist.

The cingulate gyrus does not appear to be directly involved in mediating avoidance conditioning in the cat. In the rat the visual cortex lies more posterior than in the cat, and it is therefore more likely that cingulate cortex lesions in the rat do produce some type of avoidance deficit, although a thorough investigation of the possibility that the visual cortex is also involved has yet to be carried out.

Continuing Problems

We have seen that many regions of the brain are involved in memory and learning processes. In the case of memory it may be true that virtually the entire cortex and many subcortical regions are involved. Perhaps different aspects of memory are stored in different places; visual aspects may be processed by the visual cortex, auditory aspects by the auditory cortex, etc. Perhaps recent memories are processed by the hippocampus, and the final storage of memory is carried out by association cortex. This is the best evidence we have, grounded in brain stimulation performed by Penfield and others in humans, findings dealing with hippocampal damage in man and work on the molecular basis of memory. Learning also involves a large number of structures. Motor learning is carried out by motor cortex, motor nuclei, and peripheral motor nerves. The learning of a visual discrimination is mediated by the visual cortex; auditory discrimination by the auditory cortex. The motivational aspects of learning (that is, the linkage of stimuli and responses based upon reinforcement or punishment) seem to be strongly mediated by those limbic regions which are involved in the mediation of emotion and motivation.

Modern experimentation has been aimed at devising experiments to separate the various effects of brain damage or stimulation from one another and to assess relative strengths of each of the possible contributing factors. Only limited progress has been made, as we have seen in the detailed account of the septal area. More complex types of learning deficits are found in the case of the cortex, and we have noted one example in which visual cortex, traditionally thought of as only processing visual information, also is implicated in nonvisual learning. Perhaps sensory cortex does more than simply process sensory information. It may contain mechanisms for the interpretation and evaluation of incoming stimuli rather than simply recording the stimuli according to the modality through which they enter. Another factor must be considered in the learning process: the state of attention mechanisms. Therefore, the reticular formation and portions of the forebrain which control sleep-wakefulness cycles are critical in determining how much learning takes place.

Finally: If the entire brain is involved in learning, what accounts for differences in intelligence in man? Thus far it is clear that we cannot differentiate between levels of human intelligence on the basis of anatomical appearance, vascular structure, biochemistry, etc. Somewhere there must be a difference. To say that individuals differ in intelligence because of a genetic difference is simply sweeping the matter under the rug. Obviously genetics play an important role in determining intelligence. In some families special abilities such as musical talent seem to appear generation after generation—notably the Bach family. In these cases one cannot discount the role of heredity. Certainly genetic predispositions tend to make it possible for some individuals to have unusual mathematical ability, others to have amazing memories. Environment, of course, has some modulating effect on these abilities, but we cannot see the effects of environment directly in the brain any more than we can see the effects of genetics. At present we have little more than an underlying faith that, since there is a genetic predisposition in the determination of intellectual function, the genetic predisposition must express itself in some structural or chemical manner.

SUGGESTED READINGS

Gurowitz, E. M. *The molecular basis of memory.* Englewood Cliffs, N.J.: Prentice-Hall, 1969.

John, E. Roy. *Mechanisms of memory.* New York: Academic Press, 1967.

Lubar, J. F., Schostal, C. J., & Perachio, A. A. Non-visual functions of visual cortex in the rat. *Physiology & Behavior,* 1967, *2,* 179–184.

McCleary, R. A., & Moore, R. Y. *Subcortical mechanisms of behavior.* Basic Topics in Psychology, Ed. G. Boring (Ed.). New York: Basic Books, 1965.

Olds, J., & Olds, Marianne E. Interference and learning in paleocortical systems. In J. F. Delafresnaye, A. Fessard, R. W. Gerard, & J. Konorski (Eds.), *Brain mechanisms and learning.* Oxford, England: Blackwell Scientific Publications, 1961.

Penfield, W. Studies of the cerebral cortex of man. A review and interpretation. In E. D. Adrian, F. Bremer, H. H. Jasper, and J. F. Delafresnaye (Eds.), *Brain mechanisms and consciousness.* Springfield, Ill.: Charles C Thomas, 1954.

Scoville, W. B., & Miller, B. Loss of recent memory after bilateral hippocampal lesions. *Journal of Neurology, Neurosurgery and Psychiatry,* 1957, *20,* 11–21.

EMOTION AND MOTIVATION

CHAPTER 8

EMOTION

Emotion has in recent years come under extensive investigation, particularly from the point of view of determining the physiological mechanisms underlying emotional behavior. One of the outstanding problems involved in the study of emotion is that we do not really have a clear picture of what to look for. The term "emotion" is one of the most difficult of all psychological concepts to define. We speak of gross classes of behavior—love, hate, anger, defensiveness, anxiety, pleasure, and so on, and some of these are strong emotions. There are also more subtle forms of behavior which may be more properly defined as moods—the feeling of well-being, the feeling of tenseness, and so on. Furthermore, different people stress differing aspects of emotion. Some stress internal changes. Others look at overt behavior or effects on learning or performance. But since emotion encompasses overt behaviors, expressed feelings, and changes in internal body states, all must be taken into account in a complete description of emotion. Present-day investigators tend to emphasize one aspect or the other, and each believes that he is studying emotion.

The problem of defining emotion becomes even more complex when we try to determine the causes of different emotional experiences. Are emotions classes of behavior arising out of past experiences, or do they perhaps even have an instinctual basis? That is to say, does the complement of emotions one is capable of feeling result from the kind of experiences one has had, or are there also certain types of behavior which we could call emotional that are programmed from the very beginning of life? A related problem is the difficulty of studying emotion in animals as compared with that in studying human emotion, in spite of the lack of a clear definition of the term "emotion." At least when we talk about love, fear, anger, or any of the other classes of behavior which we consider emotional in man we have a fairly good idea of what we mean. But when we observe an animal engaged in a certain type of behavior—a cat with its teeth bared, hissing, spitting, its hair standing on end (piloerection), vocalizing—how do we classify the behavior? Is it what we would call in humans anger, or is the animal frightened? Maybe the animal is experiencing some kind of sadistic pleasure! This is a critical definitional problem because a large proportion of the research being done today in the mechanisms of both normal and pathological human emotion is based upon animals and not humans.

Furthermore, saying an animal is angry because it "looks angry" is anthropomorphizing. Even in the case of man it is possible for one person to make incorrect judgments concerning the emotional state of another based upon observed facial expressions and his own feelings. The latter aspect exemplifies what psychologists call *projection,* in which anxiety in oneself is reduced by attributing one's own feeling, usually in exaggerated form, to others. Certainly the lack of complete objectivity inherent in human interpersonal judgments makes generalizations to animals even less meaningful.

Several approaches can be taken in trying to describe the emotions of both man and animals. One is to characterize the behavior objectively, as in the preceding example of the cat, and then to look for underlying changes in the subject's somatic and neural systems which might correlate with the overt behavior. It might be discovered that when the cat, for instance, has its claws and teeth bared, its hair standing on end, etc., it is at the same time undergoing an increase in heart rate, an increase in respiration, and an inhibition of peristalsis. From its central nervous system signs of increased activity in the cortex can concomitantly be recorded with an electroencephalograph, and perhaps it could also be shown that certain subcortical structures are undergoing pronounced changes in activity, as reflected by electrical recording while the animal is exhibiting the observed behavior. This is a fruitful way to begin to explore the problem. If the peripheral and central changes described *always* occur when the cat is exhibiting these responses, a series of physiological correlates of the behavior has, in fact, been defined. The semantic problem arises in naming the behavior. An easy solution is to take an anthropomorphic point of view and say that the animal is "angry" because in man anger is associated with a similar behavioral or physiological pattern. Thus, anger is defined by a series of discrete physiological changes which occur both peripherally and in the central nervous system. Perhaps the same can be done for other emotions. Critically speaking, however, it has not been *proved* that the animal is really angry or frightened, and we still rely on a judgment partially based on human behavior. So the problem of defining emotions across species is not satisfactorily resolved.

Another approach to the definitional problem is to take the pragmatic view that most higher animals, including man, show similar classes of behavioral responses as categorized by many psychologists. Higher animals are capable of showing anger, fear, fight, and flight behavior when attacked. These are rather gross emotional responses. Subtle emotions and moods cannot be handled so easily. It is not possible to say that an animal shows love to a familiar human as opposed to tolerance, although anyone who has owned a pet dog or cat will claim that the emotion we call love is definitely a part of the animal's capabilities. Again, this is a judgment.

The following discussion explores the problem of physiological correlates of emotion from the point of view of both peripheral and central mechanisms and closely examines the hypothesis that specific peripheral and central changes underlie different emotional states.

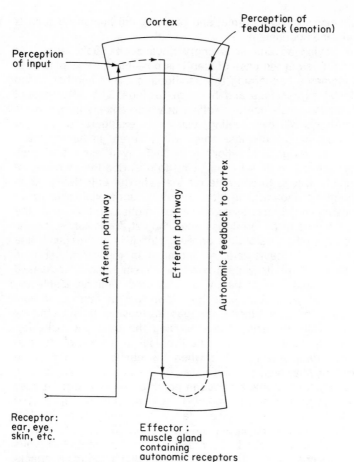

FIGURE 8-1–Schematic representation of events which according to the James–Lange theory of 1884 underlie emotion.

Peripheral Theories of Emotion

One of the earliest modern theories of emotionality was proposed by William James in 1890 in his *Principles of Psychology*. James expressed the belief that "bodily changes follow directly the perception of exciting facts (stimuli) and that our feeling of these same changes as they occur is the emotion." He is saying that emotion is determined or encoded peripherally. Figure 8-1 presents a diagrammatic representation of James's theory.

First to occur in the chain of events leading to emotion is the transmission of sensory information from peripheral receptors to the cortex by means of the classical afferent pathways. When the information has reached the cortex, it is perceived and evaluated in some still unknown fashion, then transmitted presumably to motor areas which can send it on to skeletal muscles to elicit a response. Let us imagine that we are sitting in a quiet room and suddenly the door opens and a grizzly bear 9 feet tall enters with its teeth bared. First comes the reception of the visual image of the bear by our eyes and the transmission of this information to the visual cortex. From the visual cortex the information is spread to association areas, and somewhere in this chain of neural events the stimulus is evaluated. If the evaluation is the following: *Object viewed is dangerous—escape!* then impulses will be transmitted to the motor cortex and from there sent down to the skeletal muscles. The expected reaction of jumping up as rapidly as possible and running out of the room can then occur.

Up to this point, James would say that no emotion has been experienced. The perception of emotion comes in as follows: While the skeletal nerves are producing the escape response, proprioceptors in the skeletal muscles are being activated. Feedback from the proprioceptors is sent to the cortex, and the *perception* of this feedback is the felt emotion, which presumably would be intense fear. An alternative way an emotion might be produced is by feedback not only from skeletal muscles but also from visceral organs. Once the visual image of the bear has been evaluated, not only is information sent to the skeletal muscles to produce the escape response, but impulses are sent simultaneously to visceral organs innervated by the autonomic nervous system. These organs will produce a variety of effects, such as an increased heart rate in order to provide more blood for the brain and muscles, a stopping of the digestive process, a redistribution of the blood in the body, and the secretion of chemical substances—adrenalin (epinephrine), for one. These autonomic changes supposedly act to maintain the escape response and to increase its strength. The visceral responses also activate proprioceptors located in the walls of internal organs. Perception of the feedback from visceral proprioceptors is received centrally as well, and that feedback, combined with the feedback of skeletal muscles, is the emotion. James's theory is often described by saying that we are scared because we run; we react to the stimulus first and then feel the fear. A second investigator, Carl Lange, restated James's theory and added that feedback from the circulatory system might also be an adequate stimulus. Both viewpoints together are known as the James–Lange theory of emotion.

Many examples of behavior can be cited in support of the James–Lange theory (cf. Magda Arnold, 1960). A driver whose automobile is about to collide with another car usually reacts immediately to the danger by trying to control the car so as to avoid the collision. Once avoidance is accomplished, the experience of fear, anxiety, panic, and sometimes shock will then occur. It should be pointed out, however, that the James–Lange theory of emotion, although regarded as a peripheral theory, is not entirely peripheral; because the first step in establishing an emotional reaction is the evaluation of the stimulus at the cortex. If the stimulus is not perceived and evaluated at the cortex, there is no way to "tell" the viscera or the skeletal muscles which response to execute. This means that at the cortical level there is some kind of previous processing of information which signals how the stimulus is to be regarded. Exactly what the mechanism may be is still unknown. Nor do we understand what is involved in the processes of perceiving and evaluating the incoming information, but surely memory is one factor. If we do not already know that the bear is an object to be avoided, there is no way for a coordinated response and emotional experience to occur.

In this regard one should not discount the fact that many animals exhibit emotional behaviors elicited by certain classes of stimuli without any evidence that learning is involved. The behavior may be accountable for in terms of structural connections between brain regions which mediate specific stimuli and responses and the physiological processes occurring in these structures. Such connections may form the basis for a variety of instinctive behaviors. Recently, for example, it was discovered that the visual system of some animals contains specialized receptors which produce a strong response linked with food getting if the appropriate stimulus is presented. In the frog retina, receptors have been found which discharge if an insect is presented to the visual field. Presentation of the insect will produce lashing out of the animal's tongue, and if the coordination is proper, the frog will succeed in catching it. This is an example of a neural circuit linking a specific receptor to a specific response. The frog "sees" the insect and automatically responds. The discovery of such specialized receptors may, in fact, mean that certain responses are actually "preprogrammed" for each species and on a genetic basis. Some of these responses could form a part of an emotional expression and as such are characteristic of the species. However, the overall experience of an emotion, including internal changes and the perception of the emotional experience, is built upon past learning and emotional experiences. This is not to deny that some reflexive responses such as quick withdrawal of the hand from a hot stove cannot give rise to powerful emotions—fear in this case.

Walter B. Cannon's Thalamic Theory of Emotion

A large body of important research bearing upon the physiological basis of emotion was done by Walter B. Cannon during the early part of this century. Cannon's experimentation revealed a variety of problems arguing against the James–Lange point of view. In 1927 he wrote a critique of the James–Lange theory in which he pointed out the following objections: First of all, removal of viscera in man and animals does not produce a general loss of emotion; moreover, removal of specific visceral organs does not cause a loss of specific emotions. Cannon cited work by Sherrington in 1900 which showed that if the spinal cord of a dog is transected at the cervical level, thus completely eliminating all of the sympathetic output to the viscera (and presumably destroying all possibility of proprioceptive feedback), the dog is still capable of normal rage reactions. He also noted Dana's citation, as early as 1921, of the case of a 40-year-old woman who suffered a transection of the spinal cord at the upper cervical spinal level and became a quadriplegic. In addition to sustaining this motor damage, she was unable to experience cutaneous sensation. Not only was proprioceptive feedback destroyed but so was the primary transmission of sensory information from the body surface and viscera. Nevertheless, the woman reported a full range of emotions. Cannon concluded that the visceral changes so critical to the James–Lange theory were essential neither to the experience nor to the expression of emotion. He also presented results to show that the same visceral changes can occur in all emotional states. The same changes, in fact, may take place in the peripheral autonomic nervous system during such diverse states as hypoglycemia, chills accompanying fever, being under the influence of certain drugs, as well as during the emotional states of fear and anger; yet peripheral autonomic reactions under the conditions of ill health do not automatically elicit fear or anger, or any other specific emotion. This means that emotion is not coded solely by a specific pattern of visceral feedback, and that there is no such thing as an "autonomic profile of specific responses" correlated with specific emotional states.

Another important objection to the James–Lange theory is that the reactivity of visceral organs is usually too slow to be a direct cause of the conscious awareness of emotion because smooth muscles have a long response latency. Nevertheless, psychologists have known for some time that if certain words, phrases, or pictures are presented for a very brief time an immediate emotional response can be elicited. The latency of such responses may be shorter than the estimated length of time necessary to traverse the entire circuit (see Figure 8-1) indicated by the James–Lange theory. Evidently, as soon as sensory information is received by the cortex, emotional reactions can rapidly follow, and autonomic changes then occur; they are more reasonably a by-product of emotion and not a cause.

In 1927 Cannon proposed an alternative theory of emotion which has become known as the "thalamic theory." It is diagrammed in Figure 8-2. Sensory impulses, Cannon stated, receive an emotional "quale" in transit through the thalamus to the cortex. The normal function of the cortex is assumed to inhibit the expression of emotion; however, in situations in which the cortical suppression or control of the incoming thalamic bombardment is not powerful enough to contain emotion, it is "released." Once the emotion is released, two things can happen: first, discharge over peripheral efferent pathways to produce the somatic expression or reaction; second, discharge over autonomic pathways to produce those internal changes which can be observed and measured during the experience of emotion. The role of the thalamus, Cannon said, is not only to transmit sensory information to the cortex through the specific sensory thalamic relay nuclei but to add "emotional toning" to this sensory input. The same problem exists with Cannon's theory as with the James–Lange theory: How does the thalamus know which emotional response to produce? Nevertheless, Cannon's theory did avoid some of the other objections to the James–Lange theory.

What was the evidence for Cannon's proposal that emotion has a release phenomenon? First, early experiments by Bard, Mountcastle, and others showed that if an animal was decorticated a pattern of behavior known as "sham rage" appeared. "Sham" refers to the observation that the rage was general, poorly directed, and elicited by a variety of stimuli. For example, animals would exhibit intense rage and attack behavior upon being handled or even upon the presentation of a bright light or a loud sound.

During light ether anesthesia there is also an inhibition of cortical activity, associated with a period when animals are very excitable and agitated. Some animals may make violent movements. These reactions are often seen when ether is used as an anesthetic. Humans undergoing ether

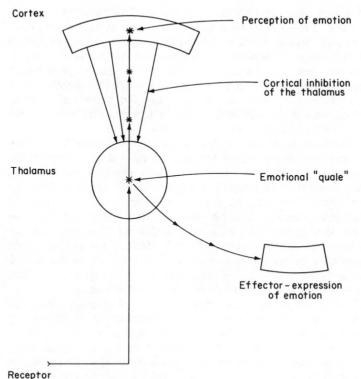

Cortex

Perception of emotion

Cortical inhibition
of the thalamus

Thalamus

Emotional "quale"

Effector - expression
of emotion

Receptor

FIGURE 8-2–Walter B. Cannon's thalamic theory of emotion. The diagram attempts to show that emotion is considered a release phenomenon.

anesthetization have been reported to engage in prolonged weeping or laughter.

Unfortunately, the Cannon thalamic theory itself was prone to a number of problems. In 1928 Bard showed that in diencephalectomized cats (cats with both cortex and thalamus removed) sham rage still occurred. Moreover, sham rage in decorticate animals was a temporary phenomenon and usually disappeared after a brief postoperative period. This *may* mean that sham rage is nothing more than a manifestation of some kind of temporary postoperative irritation. But the most relevant evidence to argue against the Cannon thalamic theory comes from the work of a European investigator, W. R. Hess. Hess has shown in a series of ingenious experiments that various emotional behaviors can be elicited by electrical stimulation of the brain of intact, awake animals. The primary areas of interest were located in the diencephalon and more specifically in the hypothalamus. Some of the responses elicited by stimulation are shown in Figure 8-3. Relatively few emotional responses were elicited by thalamic stimulation. From Hess's work it has become increasingly apparent that perhaps the hypothalamus and not the thalamus is one of the critical regions in the nervous system for the generation of emotion.

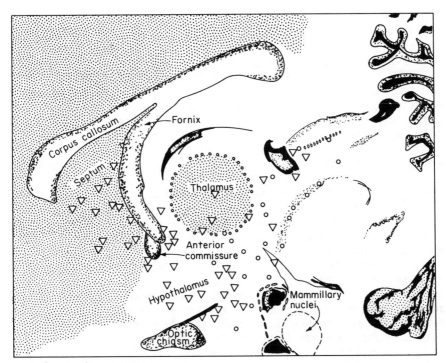

○ Ergotropic responses

▽ Trophotropic responses

FIGURE 8-3–Map of the thalamus and hypothalamus showing points from which W. R. Hess elicited ergotropic (sympathetic) and trophotropic (parasympathetic) responses using brain stimulation.

Schachter's Research

Still the attempt to link specific emotional behaviors to specific central or peripheral physiological states is beset with problems. Stanley Schachter has pointed out that similar alterations of bodily state can produce different emotional experiences depending upon the context in which they occur. Thus, he discusses an observation reported in 1924 by Maranon, who found that administration of adrenalin to several hundred subjects was followed by a variety of behavioral and physical changes. Some reported no altered emotion; others felt afraid, happy, anxious, or angry. In this specific case adrenalin, which has very similar physiological effects on subjects, produced *different* affective or emotional states. Schachter has shown in his own research that such a lack of identity between bodily state and emotion is the rule and is therefore in opposition to the earlier viewpoints of James and Lange.

The solution of the problem of understanding the relationship between bodily state and emotion, Schachter believes, lies in examining a person's perception of his bodily state and how he interprets this perception in terms of the present context and his past experience. Simply stated, a substantial body of Schachter's research says that we can similarly alter the bodily state of people (e.g., by administering a drug) and then elicit very different emotions and feelings by placing the subjects in different social situations. To some extent Schachter's point of view can be considered an arousal theory. As he himself puts it, "It is my assumption that the label one attaches to a bodily state, how one describes his feelings, [is] a joint function of such cognitive factors and of a state of physiological arousal." He goes on to illustrate: "Imagine a subject whom one somehow managed to inject covertly with adrenalin, or to feed a sympathomimetic agent, such as ephedrine. Such a subject would become aware of palpitations, tremor, etc., and at the same time be utterly unaware of why he felt this way" (Schachter, 1967). The subject would label his bodily feelings according to context. "Should he be watching a horror film, he would probably decide that he was badly frightened. Should he be with a beautiful woman, he might decide that he was wildly in love or sexually excited. Should he be in an argument, he might explode in fury or hatred."

In summary, the research of Schachter and his colleagues has substantially extended the main ideas embodied in the James–Lange theory, showing that, although peripheral autonomic responses or states are not linked to specific emotions, peripheral autonomic states can determine the degree of arousal. Arousal in conjunction with social context (environment) results in specific emotions, feelings, or moods. These considerations, however, do not completely explain the mechanism of emotion. Somehow peripheral states and environmental factors must be centrally processed. We have already seen that the central nervous system plays a role in mediating emotion. Let us now explore the roles of various central nervous system structures in emotion: the hypothalamus, the limbic system, and the cortex. Then we will return to a discussion of the role of the peripheral autonomic system in emotion and look at the interaction of peripheral and central systems.

Central Nervous System Structures in Emotion

Hypothalamus   It has been pointed out that one of the major pioneering efforts in mapping the responses of the hypothalamus to electrical stimulation was the work of W. R. Hess. Specifically, Hess found that stimulation of the anterior and lateral portions of the hypothalamus gave rise to rage responses, and he suggested that perhaps these responses are part of the mechanisms normally involved in the mediation of attack, defensive, and flight behaviors. Concurrent with central stimulation, a number of autonomic responses were observed peripherally. The autonomic responses that were correlated with the defensive, flight, and attack behaviors were primarily those produced by activation of the sympathetic branch of the autonomic nervous system, i.e., increased respiration, pupillary dilation, and increased heart rate.

Other investigators have studied hypothalamic functions by making lesions in various portions of this structure. One of the earliest hypotheses derived from this approach was advanced by Ranson, who reasoned that, if stimulation of the hypothalamus elicits intense emotion, then destruction of such tissue should result in a diminution of emotionality. Many more experiments have been carried out with this idea in mind. Ranson and his colleagues in fact found that most large hypothalamic lesions were accompanied by a decrease in emotionality, a marked increase in sleeping, and a general lack of responsiveness. A highly dramatic lesion study of the hypothalamus was undertaken by Wheatley in 1944 with cats. He found that small lesions made in the region of the ventromedial nucleus of the hypothalamus resulted in intense savage attack behavior coupled with a voracious appetite. Over a postoperative period of several months the animals showed an enormous gain in weight because of their increased food intake. The importance of Wheatley's finding is that the rage behavior elicited from the animal with the ventromedial lesion is very different from the rage behavior obtained from the decorticated animal. In the latter, only sham rage reactions are observed; in the former, the attack response is clearly directed toward the investigator and has been described as extremely savage. It is the intensity, directedness, and long duration of the attack that differentiates this type of rage from sham rage. Generally speaking, then, a large variety of emotional responses may be elicited from the hypothalamus.

Behaviors which are elicited from the hypothalamus by stimulation seem to form a pattern. Stimulation of the more anterior portions of the hypothalamus usually evokes less intense emotional responses than stimulation of the lateral or posterior portions. Stimulation in the extreme anterior hypothalamus and preoptic area can cause diminution of activity and sleep whereas stimulation in the extreme posterior hypothalamus may elicit attack and rage behavior. Concurrently, stimulation of the anterior hypothalamus tends to evoke, peripherally, parasympathetic responses in the internal organs whereas stimulation of the posterior hypothalamus usually brings sympathetic responses. Lesion effects are generally opposite to stimulation effects; a lesion of the posterior hypothalamus will characteristically cause lethargy. Lesions in the anterior hypothalamus and preoptic area often lead to enhanced activity.

Hess recognized this functional dichotomy almost 20 years ago and has designated two functional zones in the hypothalamus. He named the anterior zone the *trophotropic* region and the posterior zone the *ergotropic* zone. The trophotropic zone controls parasympathetic activity, both peripherally and centrally; stimulation there results in an enhancement of parasympathetic activity. The ergotropic zone activates sympathetic centers and gives rise to intensified behaviors and strong emotion. That the hypothalamus may have dual centers for the control of emotion as well as autonomic function is a unifying principle which not only has become stronger during recent years but has been the basis for recent theories of emotion and diencephalic functions (cf. Gellhorn, 1961, and Bovard, 1961).

Limbic System The limbic system, first described by Broca in the 1890s, consists of a ring of structures, both cortical and subcortical in origin, surrounding the thalamus and hypothalamus (Figure 8-4). Anteriorly is found the septal region. Ventrally and laterally lies the amygdaloid complex. Ventrally and posteriorly is located the region of the entorhinal cortex and hippocampus, and dorsally is found the cingulate cortex. The structures of

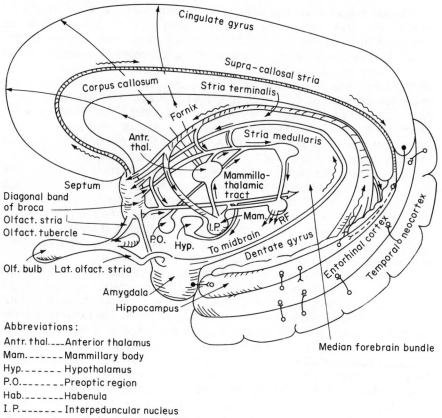

FIGURE 8-4—The limbic system and related structures. Arrows represent the direction in which information is believed to pass from one structure to another.

the limbic system are very old phylogenetically; in fact, most of them exist in the brains of reptiles although they have usually undergone marked evolutionary changes since their first appearance.

Anatomists of the beginning of the present century hypothesized that the primary function of the limbic system was olfaction. C. Judson Herrick, a well-known early twentieth-century anatomist, was of this opinion because of the correspondence in the size of limbic structures in animals known to have large olfactory bulbs. Furthermore, physiologists were successful in recording olfactory evoked responses in some limbic structures. Broca himself believed that the limbic system had olfactory functions but changed his mind after studying the brain of the porpoise. The porpoise is a member of the order Cetacea, which includes whales and other sea mammals. Porpoises are unique in having no olfactory bulbs and therefore no sense of smell; nevertheless, they have highly developed limbic structures. Clearly, then, the limbic system in these and other animals must mediate functions other than olfaction.

A second important fact concerning the limbic system is that most of its structures not only are connected to one another but channel information downstream to the hypothalamus and beyond to lower centers in the brain stem, which relay it to autonomic effectors and neuromuscular junctions. This would indicate that whatever the limbic system does, it does by acting through the hypothalamus, and its effects are ultimately reflected in peripheral autonomic functions.

To go one step farther: The limbic system participates in the control of the hypothalamus. Since the hypothalamus is concerned with controlling a variety of responses in both the autonomic and the emotional realm, as well as playing an important role in motivational states, limbic control of the hypothalamus might imply programming of emotional and motivational behaviors. The limbic system also controls hypothalamic "output channels" to effectors for expressing these behaviors at the level of both autonomic and somatomotor function. Considerable evidence supports this point of view.

Many studies carried out in the last 30 years have indicated that destruction (ablation) or stimulation of limbic structures can profoundly alter emotional behavior. James W. Papez recognized this fact in the late 1930s and in 1937 wrote a significant paper entitled "A Proposed Mechanism of Emotion." He described in detail a limbic-hypothalamic circuit which might mediate emotional behavior. Papez's theory of emotion is diagrammed in Figure 8-5. Simply stated, it is that rage behavior is produced by the hypothalamus. He also differentiated between the expression of emotion and the experience or feeling of emotion and believed that the experience of emotion was correlated with specific activities of the neocortex. The expression of emotion was mediated by hypothalamus and effectors. The cortical center which Papez believed played the key role in receiving information necessary for the experience of emotion was the cingulate cortex. This area, he felt, added emotional "coloring" or, to use Cannon's phrase, emotional "quale."

The chain of events that takes place in the generation of emotion, according to Papez, can be described as follows: First, sensory information received by the primary afferent pathways is relayed to the thalamus. Thus, visual information is passed to the lateral geniculate; auditory, to the medial geniculate; and somesthetic, to the ventrobasal complex. In the thalamus some of this sensory information is transmitted to primary sensory areas for sensory processing, but some is relayed by short fiber tracts to portions of the hypothalamus which regulate visceral activities and emotional expression. Within the hypothalamus, then, there is some coding of the sensory information as it may affect emotional responses. From the hypothalamic centers the information is finally projected to the mammillary nuclei and the posterior hypothalamus, which simultaneously receives information from the neocortex, and this combined information is then processed and passed from the mammillary bodies to the anterior nuclear group of the thalamus. From there the impulses are relayed to the cingulate cortex, where the emotional experience is added, and then transmitted by means of the cingulum bundle to the hippocampus. The hippocampus organizes the information, and finally it is relayed from the hippocampus back to the mammillary bodies via the fornix. This closed circuit has been referred to as *Papez's circuit* and repre-

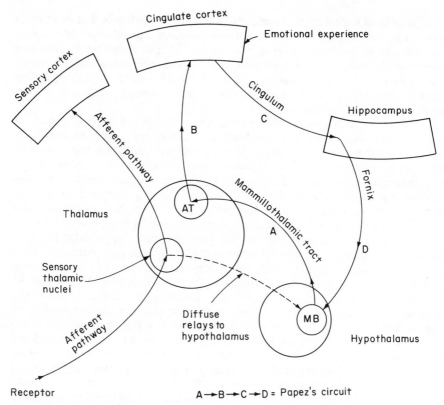

FIGURE 8-5–James W. Papez's (1937) proposed mechanism for emotion.

sents what Papez has called "the stream of feeling." Since the time of Papez's proposal, it has become plain that other limbic system structures play a role in emotionality—for example, the septal nuclei and the amygdaloid complex. Any modern theory of emotion based on anatomical structures must take into account recently implicated brain regions as well as their interconnections.

In 1949 another experimenter, MacLean, extended Papez's theory by clarifying the role of the limbic system in controlling visceral (autonomic) responses. MacLean pointed out that in lower animals olfaction is important because it is critical for primary drive states. For example, smell is essential for food getting, the detection of enemies, and mating behavior. It has been suggested that the hippocampus plays a part in these behaviors because it does receive olfactory input and that it influences brain regions which in turn influence visceral functions via the autonomic nervous system. MacLean deemphasizes the role of the cingulate and instead states that the hippocampus and the amygdaloid complex are the two structures most closely related to the experience of emotion. Furthermore, MacLean organizes the responses of the limbic structures into two categories: those concerned with the preservation of the self, such as fighting and fleeing behavior, and those concerned with preservation of the species, such as choice of a sexual partner, mating, and maternal behavior.

A recent theory that has grown out of the earlier notions of Hess's ergotropic and trophotropic behaviors is Gellhorn's, concerned with the "tuning" of the somatic and autonomic systems. Gellhorn believes that proprioceptive feedback from sensory endings in muscles, tendons, and joints modulates the hypothalamus and in turn the state of arousal within the organism. Specifically, when we express an emotion by means of a muscular action (e.g., run from a predator), such action excites proprioceptors in the skeletal muscles. This feedback passes to the ergotropic portion of the hypothalamus, and there the emotional state is intensified. Gellhorn calls this process "ergotropic tuning" and states that it can also be brought about by lowering blood pressure and by procedures (drugs or stimulation) that increase the excitability of the posterior or decrease the excitability of the anterior hypothalamus. The state of balance between the ergotropic and trophotropic systems determines the direction of emotion or moods. The limbic system plays an important role in the process through its anatomical projections to the hypothalamus.

Investigations over the past 10 years have dealt more with the functions of individual limbic system structures than with trying to integrate all that is known about them into complete theories of emotion. Let us now turn to a brief discussion of the role of some of these limbic components in emotional behavior.

AMYGDALA. The amygdala has been considered by most investigators a central structure in the control of emotional behavior. Papez, however, in laying out his circuitry for emotion in 1937, failed to recognize its role. One of the earliest and most important investigations of amygdaloid functions was carried out by Klüver and Bucy in 1937. They showed that the removal of the temporal lobe and amydaloid complex in primates produces a striking array of behavioral changes, part of which could be interpreted as profound alteration in emotion and part as motivational change. Postoperatively, the monkeys became tame and friendly. They seemed to feel neither fear nor anger. A marked increase in oral behavior was noted. The animals would pick up objects from the environment and put them in their mouths. Whether they were inedible (screws, bolts, nails, dirt) or edible, all were mouthed continuously. This change in behavior was described as a visual agnosia—inability to interpret the meaning of visual stimuli. Other behavioral changes included an increase in sexuality, and in sexual responses which were directed not only toward appropriate females but also toward other males and even other species. There were also changes in dietary habits. Normally vegetarian, the monkeys became meat eaters. In total, this behavior pattern is known as the Klüver–Bucy syndrome.

The Klüver–Bucy syndrome has been interpreted several ways. A recent theorist, Magda Arnold, has proposed (1960) that the role of the amygdala is to determine imagination and that amygdalectomy changes the ability to imagine and to evaluate stimuli. Thus, the visual agnosia, the alteration in sexual behavior, and the alteration in diet all come about as an inability to determine the proper response to stimuli. Another interpretation is that ablation of the amygdala results in a loss of normal inhibitory control over responses and that the animal tends to overrespond to stimuli—hence the placing of objects in the mouth, the eating of both proper and improper food, and the overresponse in the sexual realm. This theory tends to place too much emphasis on the amygdala. It has been known for some time that the visual agnosia was probably due to damage to the overlying infero-temporal cortex. Such an interpretation certainly weakens the position that the amygdala alone mediates evaluation and "imagination."

One of the most comprehensive studies of the amygdala and its functions was done by a Norwegian investigator, Holger Ursin. It is Ursin's opinion that because the amygdaloid complex, which is really composed of a variety of subportions (nuclei), is so heavily interconnected with other limbic structures (as well as with portions of the hypothalamus), its functions are most appropriately analyzed by stimulation of discrete points within that structure. A large portion of Ursin's research has been devoted to functional localization within the amygdaloid complex. His results are striking and clearly point out that placing lesions in the amygdala is too gross a technique to employ in trying to demarcate between closely adjacent points that have different functions.

Prior to Ursin's work it was known, at a more general level, that the amygdaloid complex could be functionally divided into two main zones. The older zone phylogenetically is called the *corticomedial division* and receives primary olfactory input. It is the subcortical region for olfaction analogous to the visual and auditory cortex. In the newer division, the *basolateral area,* a large variety of behaviors can be obtained following stimulation. Using small electrodes and low levels of stimulation, Ursin found that the responses observed fell into rather discrete categories. One type is comprised of attention responses. The animal will show alerting head movements and orientation reflexes and at higher intensities of stimulation may actually raise its head, stand, and look around as if it sees something. Attention responses are accompanied by cortical EEG arousal. A second type of behavior falls in the category of emotional responses—fear and anger responses, which are clearly differentiated anatomically from each other. In fact, there seems to be better functional localization for fear and anger responses than for any of the others found by amygdaloid stimulation (see Figure 8-6). But it is also evident from the figure that the zones from which various responses were obtained do not correspond to specific nuclear groupings within the amygdaloid complex. That is, anatomical boundaries within the amygdala do not delimit specific functions. A third class of responses is composed of autonomic responses: salivation, urination, and defecation. A fourth type of response pattern could be called visceral; it includes sniffing, chewing, and licking— responses that are associated with eating. In short, it seems that the amygdala can mediate alerting and attention; it can also mediate responses associated with eating, responses associated with the peripheral autonomic nervous system, and responses that are clearly emotional. It serves as a response programming center for the sorting and transmission of different classes of responses to points downstream where they can finally influence

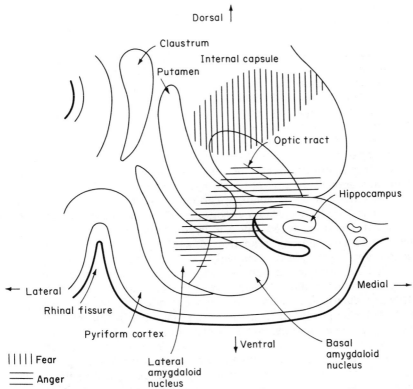

FIGURE 8-6–The amygdala of the cat represented in cross section showing the regions from which fear and anger responses were elicited by electrical stimulation of the unrestrained animal. (From Ursin and Kaada, 1960.)

motor and autonomic effectors. Anatomically, the amygdala is strongly interconnected with the hypothalamus and hence may act as a link to the hypothalamus for responses generated by the limbic system.

Whereas stimulation of the amygdala elicits a variety of emotional behaviors, amygdalectomy can counteract the vicious attack behavior that occurs after lesions are placed in the ventromedial nucleus of the hypothalamus. It would appear, then, that the amygdala acts upon the ventromedial nucleus directly and that both structures work together to determine the balance or direction of emotionality.

HIPPOCAMPUS. The hippocampus is less directly involved in emotionality than are other limbic system structures. According to MacLean, stimulation of the hippocampus with implanted chemicals results in enhancement of attack behavior to specific environmental stimuli. Vocalization and defensive behavior have also been reported. In conjunction with these responses are the expected autonomic reactions such as pupillary dilation and salivation, primarily sympathetic responses. Another important link between the hippocampus and emotional behavior may be through the endocrine system. In 1961 Fendler and his colleagues found a marked increase in ACTH secretion following ablation of the hippocampus. Others have shown that stimulation of the hippocampus produces a reduction in ACTH level (e.g., Endroczi *et al.*, 1959). ACTH is known to play an important role in stress reactions. Nevertheless, the role of the hippocampus in emotional behavior is far less clear than is the case for the amygdala. Stimulation and ablation do not produce distinct and consistent patterns of emotional change, and certainly there is no indication of discrete functional localization as has been found for the amygdala.

SEPTAL REGION. The septal area has been strongly implicated in emotional behavior. From Figure 8-4 it can be seen that the septum receives major input from both amygdala and hippocampus. It supplies output to the hypothalamus as well as several limbic system structures. One of the most pronounced results of septal ablation, particularly in the rat, is an intensified rage response. Brady and Nauta reported (1953, 1955) that lesions in the ventral septal region produced rage and hyperemotionality. The animals also show an enhanced alerting response to auditory or visual stimuli. This effect, however, usually disappears within a short time postoperatively. Now it is felt that the stronger responses obtained after septal ablation are not due to any change in the animal's emotional state but represent a hyper-reactivity particularly to sensory stimulation. Amygdalectomy, moreover, abolishes septal-lesion-produced rage, indicating that there is a specific interplay between these two structures. Some observers have found that in cats septal ablation often results in a marked increase in pleasure reactions and affectionate behavior, as exemplified in the "compulsive following" behavior of cats with septal lesions (Bond *et al.*, 1954; Lubar, 1963). This reaction consists in a marked tendency of the animal to follow humans or other animals coupled with a strong propensity to seek cutaneous stimulation. The cat will rub against the legs of other animals or humans and follow them tirelessly around the room in search of bodily contact. When held, it will often engage in licking and other forms of affectionate behavior similar to that seen in a young puppy. Typical feline independence appears to have been destroyed. Sometimes the animals will respond vigorously to rubbing or petting, arching the back (lordosis) or rolling over to have the stomach rubbed. Usually such stimulation elicits purring, but occasionally the vocalization will suddenly turn into growling, hissing, and spitting, and without warning attack may occur. Septal lesions generally cause an animal to appear to be deficient in expressing normal fear, and it has been shown experimentally that the animal is impaired in acquiring conditioned emotional responses.

CINGULATE GYRUS. In 1944 W. K. Smith described the effect of cingulectomy in monkeys as leading to a loss of aggressiveness. Ward extended Smith's findings and described cingulectomized monkeys as having lost their "social consciousness." Such animals, he said, do not show affection for their companions but treat them as inanimate objects. The monkey will walk over its companions, take food from their hands, and appear to be unaware of the consequences. When it is attacked, it simply acts as though nothing has happened by ignoring the attacker. It does not show any hostility or try to escape.

The cat and the rat react quite differently. There is enhancement of fear and an increase in the strength of conditioned emotional responses. In fact, these responses may be so strong that they lead to freezing behavior in conditioning situations and hence impair the learning of avoidance responses (Lubar, 1965). It must be pointed out, however, that there are anatomical differences between the cingulate of carnivores and rodents and that of primates and man. Stimulation of the cingulate region, depending on the site of stimulation, produces a variety of autonomic effects. Generally, stimulation of the anterior cingulate results in the inhibition of heart rate and respiration and a decrease in blood pressure, whereas stimulation of the middle cingulate strengthens these responses (Kaada, 1961). In 1964 Brutkowski reported that cingulectomized animals tend to be aggressive and vicious and that these emotional changes are due to removal of the inhibitory influence of the anterior portion of that structure. The finding that removal of the middle cingulate region enhances fear, freezing behavior, and associated autonomic reactivity is in accord with the results obtained from stimulation—that is, facilitation of autonomic responses. However, these results obtained from ablation studies emphasize again the dual and opposed nature of the anterior and middle cingulate.

Neocortex The cerebral cortex has grown in size with the evolution of the mammals and reaches its greatest development in man. Superimposed upon the development of the cortex (corticalization) has been the elaboration of the frontal and prefrontal areas of the brain as well as an enlargement of the posterior parietal association areas. In the rat and cat, for example, less than 10 percent of the neocortex is relegated to the prefrontal association areas whereas in man more than 35 percent is designated for prefrontal association functions. Furthermore, it has been shown anatomically that there are strong interconnections between portions of the prefrontal association areas and limbic system structures. Even more important, a series of fiber tracts passes from the orbital part of the prefrontal region to the hypothalamus. The prefrontal lobe receives its major input from the dorsomedial nucleus of the thalamus, which in turn receives its major input from the anterior nuclei. The latter, it may be recalled, are found in Papez's circuit. This anatomical arrangement indicates that the prefrontal lobe is ideally suited to act as either a control or perhaps a programming center for the limbic system.

In 1935 Fulton and Jacobson reported that, following frontal damage, frustration responses observed in normal chimpanzees under conditions of nonreward disappeared. Tantrums and anxiety vanished, and the animals acted as if there were no reason to be angry or disappointed. Fulton found that even the most vicious animals seemed to become docile. It was largely through these and similar findings that psychosurgery in man became an accepted practice in the 1930–1955 period for the alleviation of intense anxiety, obsessional behavior, and, in the most extreme cases, rage behavior.

Karl Pribram has suggested that the prefrontal association areas may be considered "association cortex" for the limbic system. That is, the prefrontal lobes may direct the activities of the various structures in the limbic system, and the prefrontal lobe plus the limbic system may direct the activities of the hypothalamus. Human clinical evidence indicates that in man the prefrontal lobes play a role in the evaluation of the consequences of behavior. One of the effects of prefrontal lobectomy in humans is loss of social awareness. Subjects sustaining such damage are often reported to be tactless and to behave inappropriately in social situations (i.e., to use vulgar language and display inappropriate mannerisms). At times they are described as incapable of expressing feeling for other people's problems and not having an understanding of their own. They are unable to make decisions for the future, live virtually in the immediate present, and seem to have a general dulling of the emotions. There are many similarities between these behavior patterns and inappropriate social behavior sometimes found in intact humans. A detailed discussion of the state of frontal lobe research can be found in a publication by Warren and Akert (1964).

In summary, it is clear that the cortex, the limbic system, and the hypothalamus act in concert to produce emotional responses. Modern research indicates that the cortex and to some extent the limbic system are probably responsible for the evaluation of stimuli and that through the limbic system and the hypothalamus, in conjunction with the motor cortex, the appropriate response is initiated. Changes in the peripheral autonomic nervous system that accompany emotion, therefore, are probably the result of one's experiencing emotion rather than the cause of the emotionality.

Before leaving the subject of emotion, let us turn to the autonomic nervous system and ask two final questions: Is there any evidence that changes in the peripheral autonomic system do correlate with emotional states? and Is there feedback from these peripheral changes in the sense proposed by James or Lange that might alter or enhance ongoing emotion?

Autonomic Correlates of Emotion

Functionally, the autonomic nervous system is composed of two main divisions—the parasympathetic and the sympathetic. The *parasympathetic* division is primarily concerned with maintenance functions (homeostasis); the *sympathetic* system, with emergency functions. It is believed that during strong emotional states there is dominance of activity in both the peripheral and the central portions of the sympathetic nervous system whereas during quiet or restful states the parasympathetic system predominates. However, at all times both divisions of the autonomic system are functioning.

The extent to which emotion is correlated with either sympathetic or parasympathetic activity can be illustrated by several examples. Stimulation of the body by warmth is generally thought to be pleasant. Taking a warm bath is relaxing. Warm stimulation produces vasodilation, i.e., an increase in the diameter of blood vessels. On the other hand, stimulation of the parasympathetic system will also produce peripheral vasodilation. According to the James–Lange point of view, vasodilation resulting from parasympathetic stimulation sends feedback to the central nervous system, which in turn induces the feeling of pleasantness. The contemporary position would support the hypothesis that warm stimulation both produces peripheral vasodilation and at the same time is a pleasant experience.

Eating, tasting, the feeling of food in the mouth or in the internal organs, and the consumption of alcohol are generally considered pleasant experiences. Eating and digesting food are activities which discharge peripheral parasympathetic receptors. Salivation that accompanies anticipation of eating is also a parasympathetic activity. On the other hand, one must not make the mistake of assuming that whenever the parasympathetic system is active one is experiencing pleasant emotion or that pleasant emotions are always accompanied by parasympathetic activity. Gellhorn pointed out that crying, smelling bad odors, and the gastric contractions which lead to vomiting all occur when the parasympathetic system is discharging, yet they are unpleasant experiences. Further, the motor activity of the bladder and rectum which leads to urination and defecation during intense fear, as in the conditioned emotional response (CER), is a parasympathetic activity and is certainly associated with unpleasant emotions.

Although there is obviously not a perfect correlation between pleasant emotion and specific autonomic activity, a relationship does exist. During intense emotion such as fear, anger, or stress, the sympathetic system *is* dominant. Salivation, peristalsis, and secretion of digestive enzymes are all inhibited. There is usually retention of feces and urine, increase in heart rate, vasoconstriction in the intestines, accumulation of blood in the brain and muscles—all in preparation for emergency action. Finally, sweating, erection of the hair, and dilation of the pupil take place. Now the question can be asked: Since there is some relationship between sympathetic and parasympathetic activity and emotional state, may there not be different patterns of activity for specific emotions? Thus far only one type of autonomic profile change has been shown to differentiate between two emotional states. Albert Ax in 1953 and Funkenstein in 1955 found that under conditions of anger the circulating levels of norepinephrine increase whereas under conditions of fear the epinephrine levels increase. Furthermore, injection of epinephrine can temporarily produce fear or enhance ongoing fear; injection of norepinephrine can enhance ongoing anger. In terms of the James–Lange theory we might say that fear and anger can be differentiated on the basis of this one biochemical change. Perhaps altering the epinephrine-norepinephrine balance through some type of feedback mechanism would make it possible to enhance ongoing emotions. This is the strongest piece of evidence in support of the original James–Lange point of view. Again, we must realistically state that most autonomic changes follow rather than precede the experience of emotion.

In overview, emotion may be considered the total of both certain internal changes and observable behaviors in the context of a given environment. We have seen that while an emotion is being expressed changes are taking place in the peripheral autonomic nervous system. For the most part, they are the result or correlate and not the source of emotion. Centrally the activity of hypothalamic, limbic, and certain cortical centers is altered. The fact that central stimulation can elicit specific emotional states indicates that neural structures, particularly in the limbic system, control the expression of the emotion via the somatic musculature. The perception or interpretation of the emotional state is in large part a cortical function. Cortical damage, especially in the prefrontal lobe, leads to misperception and the display of inappropriate emotional responses. Finally, according to Schachter how one subjectively "feels" depends upon his state of arousal and upon the environment in which he is placed.

MOTIVATION

Traditionally, when psychologists speak of motivation, they refer to primary drives—states of behavior that are essential to the maintenance of the organism. These typically include hunger, thirst, and reproduction or sexual behavior, but animals show other types of motivational behavior which are not nearly so well understood but may also be necessary for well-being: curiosity, manipulation of objects, and exploratory behavior. There is a strong relationship between motivation and emotion. Thus, many animals when frightened will not eat. Wild animals sometimes die of starvation in captivity. Some people react to anxiety by overeating and others by not eating enough. Sexual behavior varies as a function of ongoing emotion; anxiety can lead to sexual unresponsiveness in both human males and females. Compulsive drinking has been noted in both man and animals (psychogenic polydipsia) and is believed to be a condition brought about by emotional upset.

There are a number of ways of looking at motivational variables. In the case of thirst, one can look at the base rates of water intake for an animal that is allowed freely to explore its environment and drink whenever it so desires (ad libitum). One can look at water intake under conditions of deprivation or drive in which the animal is allowed to drink for only a short time each day after a period of water starvation has been introduced. Or one can look at water intake in animals learning to run a maze for water reward or to press a lever for water reward. These different situations are important, because in some cases animals drink a large quantity of water when left alone (ad libitum) but refuse to drink when required to work for the water by performing a behavioral task even though physiological needs for water become very strong.

Some psychologists are interested in the interplay of motivational or drive states with the ongoing behavior of the animal. Others are interested in the underlying physiological mechanisms of the motivations. An early point of view regarding hunger, thirst, and sex drives was that bodily needs enhanced perception of certain sensory stimuli. Theories based on this view were referred to as *local state* theories. Stomach contractions or "hunger pangs" were perceived as hunger, local dryness of the mouth signaled thirst, and accumulation of seminal fluid in the male led to sexual arousal. The local state theories are also called peripheral theories of motivation because they assume that motivational states arise from changes in peripheral receptors. Questions must still be asked: Are there only peripheral factors that lead an animal to drink, or is drinking governed by central factors? Where do the neural impulses originate that initiate drinking and how do they control behavior? What makes an animal stop drinking after a certain amount of water has been taken into the body? Because of the complexity of the subject, no single approach to the research has developed in the area of motivation. The following discussion will be limited to primary drives—states vital to either survival of the self or survival of the species, specifically hunger, thirst, and sexual behavior—and we will consider peripheral and central factors which are involved in the maintenance of each drive state.

Hunger

Hunger and, as we shall later see, thirst are extremely complex processes. Hunger is difficult to define precisely because it can be defined in so many ways. For example, psychologists usually talk about central versus peripheral factors. Peripheral factors subsume such things as state of the body including the composition of the blood, state of the digestive processes, and amount of food already in the system. In addition to these variables, one has to consider the subject's level of deprivation, or how long it has been since food was ingested. How much did the subject eat previously? How old is the subject; what kind of diet has it been fed; what is its body weight? All these factors interact in determining a number of operational variables (i.e., measurable factors such as the survival state of the animal and the strength of its drive to seek food), and these in turn interact with past learning and nutritional needs. Another peripheral factor in hunger motivation is the state of receptors in the mouth, including taste and cutaneous receptors. Then there are the central factors: the states of hypothalamic and limbic regions that are sensitive to food intake and may be responsible for initiating the food-seeking process. Both central and peripheral factors must be considered in trying to determine the physiological basis for hunger.

Peripheral Factors   Peripheral theories of hunger were proposed as far back as the 1700s when Haller set forth the hypothesis that hunger arises from stimulation of the sensory nerves of the stomach during contractions or peristalsis. The sensory nerves in turn are responsive to the intensity of the contractions, which increases when the stomach is empty. Johannes Müller restated Haller's position a century later. During the early part of the present century Walter B. Cannon asserted that the adequate stimulus for hunger arises from contractions of the stomach and that the adequate stimulus for drinking or thirst arises from dryness of the mouth and throat.

These investigators had not considered that perhaps hunger came first and the stomach contractions occurred afterward. An important similarity can be seen between this reasoning and that which we employed in the discussion of emotion. The central problem is confusion between cause and correlation. Hunger may be initiated entirely by central processes, but contractions of the stomach may occur at the same time. Perhaps eating satisfies centrally initiated needs, and the feedback from the decrease in peristalsis which occurs when food is placed in the stomach simply acts as a regulatory mechanism to stop further food intake. We will explore this possibility later in more detail.

Even at the time of Cannon's proposal experiments had shown that removal of the nerve supply to the stomach by cutting the vagus nerve does not cause any appreciable change in hunger; as a matter of a fact, combined cutting of the vagus and the splanchnic nerves which eliminates afferent impulses from the intestinal system does not appreciably affect food intake. Clinical case histories dating back to the last century indicate that in people who have had portions of the stomach, esophagus, or intestine removed no contractions can occur, nor are there secretions which could act as stimuli for feedback to the brain concerning the state of the stomach, yet a normal desire for food and a reasonable regulation of diet still exist. Furthermore, in the case of human starvation, contractions and "hunger pangs" are reported to cease after 3 to 5 days while hunger persists. Rats that have had their stomachs removed can still learn to run a maze or runway for food reinforcement. One must conclude that stomach and intestinal peristaltic contractions are not adequate stimuli for hunger but may simply contribute to it. Stated another way, feedback from such contractions may act as a regulatory mechanism for controlling the amount of food ingested but cannot be the only source of peripheral control.

Schachter has provided a novel explanation for human obesity. His view is that the normal individual responds to his bodily state, in this case stomach contractions, to determine when he is hungry. His eating is based upon his *local state.* The obese individual is largely incapable of perceiving hunger based on local state but uses environmental cues to guide his food intake. The obese person may eat because it is time to eat, because he is with others who wish to eat, because he sees food, or always eats when reading, etc. In other words, the overweight condition results from ingesting food sometimes when the local state signals hunger and sometimes when the body is actually satiated. Because he is not responding appropriately to local state, the overweight person will actually eat more of a palatable food and less of a tasteless food than will a normal person.

Schachter has gone even further in suggesting that obesity is determined largely in infancy. In babies who are fed to stop their crying the pattern for obesity is set up since the child cannot later discriminate true hunger from misperceived hunger based upon environmental cues. So, for example, the child may eat when he is unhappy. The wise mother, realizing that a baby cannot always be hungry, times the feedings to parallel digestion so that the child is fed when hunger is felt. Later this type of feeding will be conditioned to local state. As a result, the individual of normal weight has less difficulty than the overweight person in turning down the offer of a banana split at 2 P.M. because he ate at noon and is not hungry. The overweight person is not "hungry" either but might accept the dessert because it looks too good to refuse. Schachter has made a valuable contribution to the study of obesity and also has shown that peripheral or local state can play an important role in the regulation of food intake.

PERIPHERAL HORMONAL FACTOR. A second proposal which arose in the early part of the present century was that, if peristaltic contractions did not act to initiate eating, perhaps the peripheral control of hunger was exerted through a biochemical factor. The reasoning is simply that when food is digested chemical changes do occur in the blood composition; glucose level increases, digestive enzymes are released, and so forth. These biochemical changes may be adequate stimuli for the initiation of feeding or may even help regulate food intake.

An experimental approach to the problem was developed by Robins and Boyd in 1923. From excised denervated gastrointestinal tissue in which the blood supply was left intact they constructed a small, artificial stomach bag called a "Heidenhain pouch." Implanting this pouch in the body cavity, they found that it exhibited peristaltic rhythms which were relatively synchronous with those occurring in the stomach. Furthermore, like the stomach, the pouch varied its rhythms in accordance with how long it had been since food was digested (deprivation state). If food was placed in the small intestine, the contractions in the pouch decreased. On the other hand, if nutrients were put directly into the pouch, there was no change in intestinal contractions. Thus it would seem that when food passes through the gastrointestinal system some type of chemical change is produced which reaches the pouch via the circulatory system and inhibits the contractions there. However, since the pouch itself is attached in such a way that it depends upon information from the stomach or intestines to respond, the placing of nutrients in the pouch affects only its *own* contractions and not those occurring elsewhere in the digestive system.

An earlier experiment, often cited in the literature, was performed in 1915 by Luckhardt and Carlson, who reported that transfusion of the blood from a starving dog would stimulate peristaltic contractions in animals that had eaten a full meal. They further suggested that a decrease in blood sugar might be the adequate stimulus for initiating hunger. Other early investigators showed that intravenous injections of glucose decreased gastric motility in hungry animals and might, therefore, act as an adequate stimulus for regulating food intake. One of the strongest statements to this effect has been attributed to Jean Mayer, who proposed a glucose regulation of food intake and hunger. Mayer's *glucostatic theory* assumed that within the central nervous system were located specialized receptors (*glucoreceptors*) that were sensitive to the level of blood sugar and could initiate food-getting behavior whenever the level of blood sugar fell below a certain critical value. The theory has undergone several modifications as a result of more recent evidence, and in 1955 Mayer suggested that the glucoreceptors, supposedly located in the hypothalamus, may be sensitive to the rate of *utilization* of glucose sufficient to affect its availability in the brain. In other words, Mayer is saying that a decrease of blood sugar in the circulatory system produces a decrease in central (brain) sugar utilization and that this in turn stimulates the central mechanism for the regulation of food intake.

Unfortunately, evidence in support of Mayer's theory is weak. For example, according to the theory, injection of glucose into a food-deprived animal should be sufficient to make the animal satiated, yet it remains ravenously hungry. The strongest support comes from a series of experiments showing that if gold-thioglucose is injected directly into the brain of an animal the result is a marked overeating (hyperphagia) and a prominent weight gain. Gold is a toxic substance, and the effect of the gold-thioglucose injection is presumably to destroy the glucoreceptors in the hypothalamus. With the control mechanism for feeding destroyed, the subject overeats since there is no signal to stop ingestion except a physical limitation imposed by size of the digestive organs. These results bring us directly to the problem of central regulation.

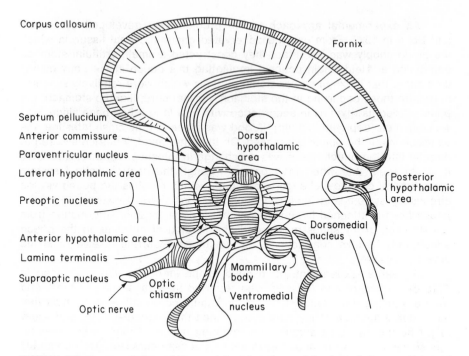

Corpus callosum

Fornix

Septum pellucidum

Anterior commissure

Paraventricular nucleus

Dorsal
hypothalamic
area

Lateral hypothalmic area

Preoptic nucleus

Posterior
hypothalamic
area

Anterior hypothalamic area

Dorsomedial
nucleus

Lamina terminalis

Mammillary
body

Supraoptic nucleus

Optic
chiasm

Optic nerve

Ventromedial
nucleus

FIGURE 8-7–Representation of the nuclei and regions of the hypothalamus. (Adapted from House and Pansky, 1960.)

Central Mechanisms for the Regulation of Food Intake   Research over the past two decades indicates that two centers, located in the hypothalamus, are primarily responsible for the regulation of food intake (see Figure 8-7). These are the lateral hypothalamic feeding center and the ventromedial hypothalamic satiation center. Earlier work by Brugger in 1943 and Wheatley in 1949 demonstrated that lesions placed in the ventromedial nucleus of the hypothalamus caused a tremendous increase in food intake followed by a very large weight gain. In our previous discussion of emotion, it was pointed out that lesions in this same region produced savage behavior. Whether these are related or independent effects is not yet certain. The overeating or hyperphagia has been found in rats, cats, and monkeys with the ventromedial lesions. Anand and Brobeck suggested that the ventromedial nucleus is a "timing" center. That is, its normal function is to stop feeding when enough food has been taken in. Presumably the signals which tell the brain that enough food has been ingested come from the peripheral nervous system (receptors) or possibly from hormonal changes in the blood. Nevertheless, it has been shown that stimulation of the ventromedial region will cause a feeding animal to cease feeding whereas, as we have seen, ablation of this region causes the hyperphagia. In contrast, Anand and Brobeck found that lesions placed in the lateral hypothalamus produce a dramatic aphagia which can lead to starvation. Conversely, stimulation of this lateral region will initiate feeding even in animals that have already been fed.

Although the lateral and the ventromedial hypothalamus appear to exert opposite effects upon food intake, it is unlikely that they are the only portions of the brain involved in this function. Teitelbaum and Stellar in 1954 showed that, although lateral hypothalamic lesions produced a dramatic cessation of feeding which often led to starvation, it was possible to get the animals to eat again provided they were kept alive by artificial feeding and given very palatable food. The fact that lateral hypothalamic operated animals *can* recover the function of feeding indicates that other areas of the brain are capable of taking over the lost function. Direct evidence of the participation of other neural centers comes from an experiment by Morgan and Coisman in 1959 showing that lesions in the amygdala can lead to hyperphagia. Clearly, therefore, there is limbic control as well as hypothalamic control of food intake. In fact, modern evidence indicates that the amygdala contains a satiation center which perhaps helps regulate the satiation center in the ventromedial nucleus of the hypothalamus. Further, the ventromedial nucleus exerts control over the lateral hypothalamus so that under normal circumstances when an animal receives peripheral information indicating that it is time to initiate feeding, the lateral hypothalamus becomes active and the animal searches for food. Once the stomach has been maximally distended by ingestion, the proper amount of calories has been ingested, or the oral receptors have been sated (it is not yet clear which of these, or maybe even other factors, is most critical), signals are sent to the amygdala, then to the ventromedial nucleus, and feeding ceases. Whether the adequate stimuli for the amygdala and hypothalamic regions are hormonal or neural or both is not known. It is unlikely that something as simple as circulating levels of glucose is sufficient to account for the degree of control of food intake that we have seen occurs.

One of the more interesting recent findings was contributed by S. P. Grossman, who carried out numerous experiments from 1960 to 1964 using cannulas implanted in the lateral hypothalamus of rats. He injected several different chemicals directly into the lateral hypothalamic region. Injections of adrenergic transmitter substances such as norepinephrine and epinephrine elicited voracious and prolonged eating in animals that were fully satiated. Injections of cholinergic transmitter agents such as carbachol into the *identical* site elicited pronounced and vigorous drinking behavior (see Figure 8-8). This important discovery might mean that the same lateral hypothalamic center controls the initiation of both feeding and drinking behavior, and that in the case of feeding, the brain operates on the action of adrenergic synapses, whereas in the case of drinking, cholinergic synapses are active. If a link between these two types of neural transmitters and events occurring in the peripheral nervous system (receptors) could be established, perhaps an understanding of the peripheral events and their central coding would be possible.

Thirst

The same basic scheme obtains in the case of thirst as in feeding behavior. Peripheral, perhaps orai, and central factors are involved, and there is hypothalamic and limbic system control of water intake. Peripherally, changes occur once water has been assimilated into the system. One of the

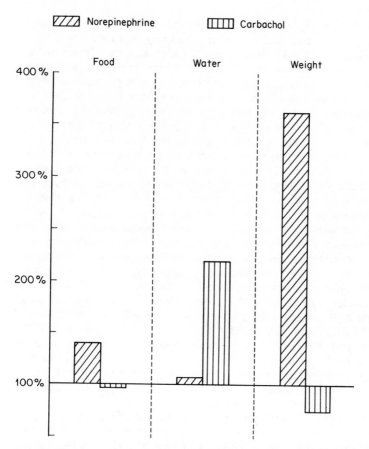

FIGURE 8-8–Effects of adrenergic and cholinergic stimulation of the hypothalamus on food intake, water intake, and weight for the 24-hour period following stimulation. The ordinate expresses the percentage increase or decrease in the measures as compared with their control levels. (From S. P. Grossman, *International Journal of Neuropharmacology,* 1964, *3,* 48.)

primary effects of water intake is a change in the concentration of solids in the blood; the plasma fraction of blood is diluted. Another way of expressing this dilution is to say that the osmotic pressure (a measure of the relative concentration of solids in a liquid medium) of the blood has decreased or that the blood becomes hypotonic with respect to its normal state, which is defined as the isotonic state. In contrast, when an animal is deprived of water for long periods of time, the plasma fraction of the blood becomes more concentrated or hypertonic. Plenty of evidence suggests that the brain has *osmoreceptors,* which probably detect the sodium content or osmotic pressure of circulating proteins. The reaction of the osmoreceptors to the peripheral state of hydration may initiate water intake.

Another factor which is effective peripherally is the volume of circulat-

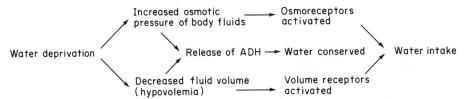

FIGURE 8-9–Relationships between two peripheral determinants of water intake (osmotic pressure and fluid volume) and a cerebral factor (antidiuretic hormone level).

ing intravascular fluids, such as blood plasma. When a great deal of water is taken in, the volume of intravascular fluids increases. This condition is known as *hypervolemia.* On the other hand, water deprivation leads to decrease in intravascular fluids or *hypovolemia* (see Figure 8-9). In 1966 Striker and Wolfe postulated that there may be volume or volemic receptors which are sensitive to this type of physical change. No information is yet available as to whether the proposed volume receptors are peripheral or are centrally located.

Thus two factors seem to tell the brain to initiate or to stop drinking: the concentration of solids (tonicity) of the blood and the volume of intravascular fluid. Besides any direct effect that volumetric or tonicity changes may exert upon central mechanisms for the control of water intake, a third factor has to be considered: the role of antidiuretic hormone (ADH).

ADH is a substance that is stored in the supraoptic and paraventricular nuclei of the hypothalamus. Information received from osmoreceptors causes

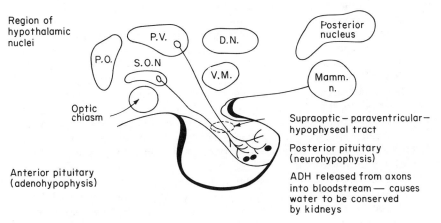

Legend:
P.O. = Preoptic region
P.V. = Paraventricular nucleus
D.N. = Dorsal nucleus
V.M. = Ventromedial nucleus
Mamm. N. = Mammillary nucleus
S.O.N. = Supraoptic nucleus

FIGURE 8-10–Hypothalamic control of water balance via ADH.

ADH to be released and to flow along axons from the hypothalamus to the posterior pituitary and then into the general blood circulation (see Figure 8-10). ADH acts peripherally upon the posterior renal tubules of the kidney, allowing them to reabsorb water from the urine. The result is a conservation of water. Thus the role of ADH is to control the amount of water lost through urination. In man, hypothalamic damage brought about by a brain tumor, etc., occasions a clinical syndrome known as *diabetes insipidus,* characterized by an enormous increase in the amount of water drunk. Diabetes insipidus has been studied clinically in humans and produced experimentally in animals. It is directly due to a loss of ADH function.

Disruption of the ADH system causes dehydration; presumably, the dehydration in turn peripherally results in the excitation of both volume receptors and osmoreceptors. These receptors act to initiate drinking through some incompletely understood hypothalamic mechanism. Drinking replaces the water which has been lost, but the water taken in is conserved for only a short time before it too is lost through further urination. In diabetes insipidus we say that the polyuria (increased urination) is a primary effect and that the polydipsia (increased water intake) is a secondary effect. The latter is a compensatory mechanism necessary to maintain water balance as much as possible. In a normal individual with undisturbed hypothalamic functioning the drinking of large quantities of water will produce general *hydration.* As this hydration is reflected centrally by an inhibition of ADH release, urination will increase and the hydration will fall toward normal levels. In the process of such recovery, drinking may occur. On the other hand, depriving an animal of water will create the opposite set of conditions. *Dehydration* will occur, resulting in centrally directed feedback and an increase in the amount of ADH released. Urination will then be decreased in an attempt to conserve water. It can be seen that there is direct interaction among the state of volume receptors and osmoreceptors, peripheral conditions such as blood and plasma tonicity, and the central mechanisms which regulate ADH release. Thus, perhaps unlike hunger, thirst is more directly controlled by hormones.

Central Mechanisms   We have seen that the kind of information which is transmitted to the central nervous system deals with the tonicity and perhaps volume of body fluids. Tonicity information is processed by osmoreceptors located in the hypothalamus. They exert an influence through the pituitary gland via the antidiuretic hormone. ADH in turn acts to produce a state of water conservation. These are the peripheral aspects of water balance, but there is still the question of thirst motivation.

What makes an animal seek water? In 1954 Teitelbaum and Stellar showed that small lesions placed in the lateral hypothalamic region at the level of the ventromedial hypothalamus produced not only a complete loss of eating behavior, as was mentioned earlier, but also adipsia or avoidance of drinking. The adipsia was so complete that it actually could lead to the death of the animal. In contrast, Andersson, in a series of studies using goats, discovered that stimulation in a portion of the lateral hypothalamus, specifically in regions which may contain the osmoreceptors, would elicit drinking in animals that were already satiated. Many studies performed over the last 20 years have clearly shown that certain regions in the lateral hypothalamus will, upon stimulation, initiate behavioral drinking whereas lesions in these same areas produce a loss of drinking.

From the point of view of brain biochemistry, drinking is probably a cholinergically mediated phenomenon (see Figure 8-8), as demonstrated by Grossman in 1962. By implanting small crystals of cholinergic substances in the lateral hypothalamus by means of small tubes or cannulas, Grossman found that drinking could be elicited. We have already seen that in the *same brain areas* implantations of an adrenergic substance will produce eating behavior. Further support for this hypothesis comes from the finding that the effects of central stimulation leading to drinking behavior can be eliminated by previous administration of a cholinergic blocking agent such as atropine. In similar fashion, previous injection with an adrenergic blocking agent such as dibenzyline will lead to a cessation of eating elicited by central stimulation.

Thus a new way of looking at brain functions has been revealed. Rather than viewing the brain as a set of neuronal aggregates (nuclei) and fiber tracts and attempting to identify correspondences between structure and function, one can consider the brain a series of chemical systems. Functions may be more meaningfully tied to chemical differences (i.e., different concentrations of types by neurohumors and varying reactivity of different tissues to implanted substances) than to anatomical differences. Instead of searching for an "eating" or "drinking" nucleus in the hypothalamus or limbic system, one may find that the same region can subserve both functions, depending upon how it is chemically stimulated.

Other portions of the brain, notably in the limbic system, are also involved in the central regulation of thirst. A recent study by Lubar, Schaefer, and Wells (1968) shows that lesions in the septal area result in a marked and sustained increase in water intake. Perhaps the septal area exerts control over the hypothalamus and specifically on the supraoptic region, which in turn controls the release of ADH. In addition, Beatty and Schwartzbaum (1967) demonstrated that following septal lesions rats exhibited hyperreactivity to both positive and negative taste properties of solutions. Compared with controls, they rejected water adulterated with quinine and preferred water sweetened with saccharin. Other experimental data, e.g., Grossman's in 1963, showed that lesions in the amygdaloid complex can result in increases in both food and water intake. As in the hypothalamus, cholinergic stimulation of many limbic structures will elicit water intake whereas adrenegic stimulation will elicit food intake. It has been suggested by some investigators that there is a limbic-hypothalamic circuit which may be considered the thirst motivational system, as well as a limbic-hypothalamic circuit serving as the hunger motivational system. Presumably, both systems receive pertinent information regarding the physiological state of the body from peripheral receptors and then initiate appropriate behaviors resulting in water or food intake in order to satisfy its needs.

Sexual Behavior

Like thirst and hunger, sexual activity depends strongly upon peripheral feedback from receptors. Stimulation of peripheral sexual organs or erogenous (sexually excitable) zones of the body surface produce sexual arousal, which is a centrally mediated phenomenon. Cutaneous input from sexual organs produces responses in the hypothalamus. As in the case of eating and drinking, the hypothalamus is a critical structure for the regulation of sexual behavior, and the limbic system also plays an important role. One respect in which sexual activity differs from hunger and thirst is that it is not essential for the survival of the individual; it is, however, necessary for the survival of the species. Nevertheless, sexual activity obviously does not exist simply because of the need to reproduce. This is particularly the case in man, and it has also been shown in experimental animals that removal of the gonads in either the male or female does not necessarily lead to a loss of sexual acitivity.

During the past two decades one of the foremost investigators in the area of sexual motivation has been Frank Beach. His contention is that sexual excitement becomes increasingly varied and complex as one ascends the phylogenetic scale and that the variety of sexual behaviors in which higher animals engage is correlated with the development of their cerebral cortices. Beach speaks of a "sexual arousal mechanism," which in lower animals is dependent primarily upon hormonal factors but in higher animals is more under neural than hormonal control. In man, therefore, damage to the central nervous system would presumably cause a greater disruption of sexual activity than alteration of the level of circulating sex hormones. In lower animals the opposite would be the case. Further, in higher animals sexual activity is not simply a reflex type of behavior but depends strongly upon learning patterns of sexual response, such as courting behavior.

Relatively little is understood about the peripheral mechanisms involved in sexual excitement. Male and female genital organs contain somesthetic receptors similar to those found in other portions of the body; and although the distribution of erogenous zones varies somewhat from individual to individual, with respect to receptor structure there are no differences between receptors in erogenous zones and those in other portions of the body surface. The input from receptors of the sex organs is apparently of the same nature as the input from receptors of other parts of the skin. Impulses enter the dorsal roots of the spinal cord, where the proprioceptive and touch information ascends the dorsal columns and pain and thermal information ascends the lateral columns. As with proprioception, touch, pain, and temperature in other areas of the body, input from sex organs is distributed to the same thalamic regions. At the somesthetic cortex there is a topographical projection of the body surface; the external surface of the sexual organs has its own representation as does the external surface of the legs, arms, face, back, and so forth. The fact that erogenous zones exist in children indicates that whatever makes certain areas of the body sexually excitable and other areas inexcitable in that regard seems to be a property of the somesthetic system that develops early in life, perhaps even in the embryo. Modification of excitable zones—that is, their extension and refinement later in life—may depend upon learning and memory processes and the kind of experiencs an individual has had.

In lower vertebrates sexual drive is to a large extent under the control of the gonadal hormones. Testicular androgenic hormone level in males and estrogen level in females are mainly responsible for controlling motivational levels. Estrogen levels determine when ovulation will occur, and increased receptivity of the female during ovulation maximizes the probability that fertilization of the ovum will occur. The importance of hormones is demonstrated by the observation that removal of the gonads in rats and other lower species lessens sexual activity when the hormone level falls. However, hormonal replacement by injection of sex hormones can restore sexual activity. It is even possible to initiate puberty prematurely in man and animals of either sex by administration of hormones.

In higher animals such as primates, including man, learning plays a primary role in sexual behavior, and the relative importance of hormones diminishes as compared with lower species. For example, in chimpanzees removal of the gonads has relatively little effect on sexual activity, especially in the male. Sexual activity clearly persists in humans through and beyond menopause even though hormonal levels have fallen considerably.

The hypothalamus is the central structure having key control over sexual behavior. This structure, as we already know, also controls eating and drinking as well as functions of the endocrine system. Endocrine function is closely tied to sexual functions. It has been known for a long time that malfunction in the endocrine system can cause disruption of sexual activity and even abnormal development of the sexual organs themselves because the production of gonadal hormones is controlled by pituitary hormones. The pituitary, in turn, is under the control of the hypothalamus.

Central Mechanisms   Let us consider in a little more detail the role of the hypothalamus and the mediation of sexual drive. The most potent area of the hypothalamus for the mediation of sexual behavior appears to lie in its anterior portion. In 1938 Fisher and his colleagues showed that lesions placed in the supraoptic nuclei resulted in decreased sexual activity in female cats. Interestingly, this is the same area that controls water balance. In 1940 Brookhart found that large lesions in the general region of the anterior hypothalamus produced a loss of mating behavior in guinea pigs. However, this investigator also showed that sexual behavior could be restored by treatment with estrogen. According to an experiment by Maes in 1940, loss of sexual behavior in the female resulting from hypothalamic lesions is independent of effects that could be ascribed only to the pituitary gland, and after removal of the pituitary, sexual behavior continues if the animal is given estrogen treatments. Other work reveals that, whereas lesions of the anterior hypothalamus tend to affect sexual drive, lesions of the posterior hypothalamus tend to affect the functions of the sexual organs directly. For example, it has been demonstrated that lesions of the mammillary portion of the hypothalamus or in the ventromedial nucleus cause atrophy of the gonads, which in turn leads to a lack of sexual activity. The hypothalamus is thus clearly a focal point for mediation of sexual behavior.

Chemical or electrical *stimulation* of the anterior hypothalamus elicits erection in male monkeys, as shown by MacLean and Ploog in 1962. This observation has also been replicated in rats and cats. On the other hand, massive lesions placed in the thalamus produce virtually no changes in copulatory behavior as compared with small lesions placed in the hypothalamus. Even the complete removal of the neocortex and most of the diencephalon in the cat or rabbit causes no major changes in sexual activity according to work by Bard in 1940. It is, therefore, likely that the cerebral hemispheres are not critically involved in the regulation of sexual behavior, particularly in the female. In the male the cortex has been shown to play a more substantial role, particularly with regard to loss of cutaneous sensibility resulting from cortical lesions. Beach, also in 1940, showed in the male rat that, although small cortical lesions do not change sexual behavior, lesions in which more than 60 percent of the cortex was removed lead to a reduction in copulation. In subjects with the largest lesions there was an almost total loss of sexual drive. Furthermore, these effects seemed to be independent of location of the lesions in the cortex. A similar finding was the mass action effects reported by K. S. Lashley for visual functions in the rat. In some animals, such as the male rabbit, sexual behavior remains even with extensive neodecortication, provided the olfactory bulbs are not damaged. Apparently in these animals olfactory cues are critical for maintaining sexual behavior patterns. One of the most dramatic examples of the effect of cortical lesions on sexual behavior came from the work of Klüver and Bucy in 1939. They reported that bilateral removal of the temporal lobe in monkeys markedly increases sexual drive, i.e., produces hypersexuality, and that the drive becomes generalized to animals of the same sex and even animals of other species. These results have not been found in female subjects.

In summary, there is evidence to support the contention that the critical centers for the integration of sexual behavior lie in the anterior portions of the hypothalamus while the posterior portions of the hypothalamus and the pituitary gland are important for maintaining the function of the gonads. The limbic and temporal regions are primarily responsible for organization of the motivational systems which feed through the hypothalamus to produce sexual responses. Although the interplay of the hypothalamus and the cortex is not as clear in the case of sexual behavior as it is for consummatory behavior, a somewhat similar pattern of organization seems to be unfolding.

SUGGESTED READINGS

Arnold, M. B. Emotion and personality. Vol. II. Physiological aspects. New York: Columbia University Press, 1960.

Bovard, E. W. A concept of hypothalamic functioning. Perspectives in Biology and Medicine, 1961, 5, 216–218.

Gellhorn, E. Prolegomena to a theory of the emotions. Perspectives in Biology and Medicine, 1961, 4, 433–436.

Hess, W. R. The functional organization of the diencephalon. J. R. Hughes (Ed.). New York: Grune & Stratton, 1957.

McCleary, R. A. Response-modulating functions of the limbic system; initiation and suppression. In E. Stellar & J. M. Sprague (Eds.), Progress in physiological psychology, Vol. I. New York: Academic Press, 1966.

MacLean, P. D. New findings relevant to the evolution of psychosexual functions of the brain. *Journal of Nervous and Mental Disease,* 1962, *135,* 289–301.

Papez, J. W. A proposed mechanism of emotion. *Archives of Neurology and Psychiatry,* 1937, *38,* 725–743.

Schachter, S. Cognitive effects on bodily functioning: Studies of obesity and eating. In D. C. Glass (Ed.), *Neurophysiology and emotion.* New York: Rockefeller University Press and Russell Sage Foundation, 1967.

Teitelbaum, P., & Epstein, A. N. The lateral hypothalamic syndrome: Recovery of feeding and drinking after lateral hypothalamic lesions. *Psychological Review,* 1962, *69,* 74–90.

Ursin, H., & Kadda, B. R. Functional localization within the amygdaloid complex in the cat. *Electroencephalography and Clinical Neurophysiology Journal,* 1960, *12,* 1–20.

Warren, J. M., & Akert, K. (Eds.). *The frontal granular cortex and behavior.* New York: McGraw-Hill, 1964.

HIGHER FUNCTIONS

CHAPTER 9

"Higher functions" is a loose term for qualities of behavior which are thought to be representative of animals high in the phylogenetic scale, particularly man. A precise definition is hard to make, but it can be approached from either a "mental quality" or a "response" point of view. On the one hand, higher functions are considered to be mental abilities beyond those required for sensory discriminations, simple motor reactions, or the learning of simple tasks. On the other hand, higher functions can be thought of as responses not readily predictable from the immediate environment or from the organism's past history. Perhaps the best course is to assume that everyone has some idea of what is encompassed by the term and let the reader create his own definition as he progresses through this chapter.

First, those functions which are uniquely man's, or are found to be more prevalent in man's behavior than in the behavior of other animals, will be the basis of our approach to higher functions. Second, we will attempt to correlate the development of the brain with the development of higher abilities across several species.

There is justification for our first approach—that is, regarding the higher functions as being more or less associated with man—for man is, after all, the ultimate object of our attention. The second approach is highly problematical in view of repeated failures to establish meaningful or reliable correlations of structure and function (other than sensory or motor function) over the last hundred years and more.

Since it is man who describes men and their attributes, we can distinguish many admirable characteristics associated uniquely with man in the writings of philosophers and psychologists and in our own thoughts: wisdom, love, charity, compassion, insight, consciousness, a sense of right and wrong, and, from a religious point of view, an immortal soul. Of course, a pessimist will use other adjectives, expressing less social desirability, to describe man's nature. For the experimental psychologist, however, many attributes are very difficult to measure and assess. The physiological psychologist has even more of a problem since his aim is to establish relationships between these attributes and the physiological mechanisms responsible for them. In addition, much physiological work is done with animals, and the adjectives used to describe man's behavior become almost meaningless.

The present chapter will consider many "higher functions" which may seem prosaic. This approach is taken out of necessity, but it may have virtue. The behavioristic view of the study of higher functions offers precision of experimental manipulations and of measurement that would not otherwise be possible, and a firmer base from which to consider the related physiological phenomena. Moreover, it may give us a better opportunity to evaluate the rough progression of functions up the phylogenetic scale from the lower animals to man. By using generalizations based upon changes in anatomy and function as different species are explored, one can make more informed guesses as to the changes which are most significant for the higher and the lower forms of behavior.

Our orientation to the topic of higher functions should not be taken as a denial that man possesses love, compassion, wisdom, and the like. In fact, some of these qualities are being investigated at the present time, in ways which allow precision in definition and measurement. But most of them are at present beyond our means of investigation. It is to be hoped that a physiological approach can be made to them in the future.

LANGUAGE

From a behaviorist's point of view, what sets man apart from all lower animals is his ability to use "language," written and spoken. Some psychologists and others might argue that it is the written language that is truly a differentiating characteristic. However, man's ability to communicate abstract ideas and concepts verbally appears unique, although this skill may originate in his use of the written language. With the development of language man is no longer restricted to communication by gestures, signals, and signs. Symbols are used in language to represent events and things but more frequently to represent classes of events and things. Language conveys actions, relationships, generalities, and abstractions. Human life without language is inconceivable, and without the mental characteristics made possible by language, life would probably be devoid of all higher values.

Perhaps the most valuable aspect of language is transmission of information to new generations. Tons of information dating from the origin of written language to the present time are stored in our libraries. Data about man and the world around him, and even his dreams of things as they might be, are available. Because we can understand and use language, we are able to profit from the experiences of millions of people who have lived before us. We do not have to learn by trial and error or by imitation. We do not have to learn at the cost of harsh failures and punishments as do lower animals.

All animals come into the world equipped to learn, but the lower animals cannot take advantage of what has been learned by previous generations of the species. An animal learns things only over its own lifetime, by doing, and each new generation must go through the same doing and learning without benefit of the experiences of those that have gone before. It may or may not be true that man learns faster or can learn more than the lower animals. It is certainly true that man learns more different things than the lower animals because of the ability to use language.

A good deal of speculative thought has been given to how animals compensate for their inability to use language. For example, it is sometimes said that man comes into the world relatively unprotected by those reflexive behaviors known as instincts. Animals possess at birth a large number of instincts—that is, species-specific behaviors—available to help them preserve their own lives and preserve the species. The prolonged infancy during which the human is essentially at the mercy of his environment is pointed to as a singular characteristic of man and is often compared with the earlier maturation of other animals. However, it has been argued, by William James for one, that man has *more* instincts than the lower animals, including those necessary for language. Many other animals do have long periods during infancy when they are as much at the mercy of unfavorable environments as a baby.

Anatomy and Language

It might be hoped that the ability to use language, as well as other higher functions, found in man would be associated with unique anatomical developments. Thorough investigation of the appearance of the outside of the brain reveals nothing unique to man. His brain is more convoluted than the brains of most of the higher animals, but at the same time, the convolutions vary widely in number and extent from one individual to another. Some brains observed at autopsy have shown very few convolutions, yet language and intelligence did not seem unusual. Moreover, the weight of the brain varies among normal people. A person with either a very light or a very heavy brain may be articulate or inarticulate. A microscopic examination of the brain of man reveals no particular set of nerve cells which appears different from sets of cells found in the brains of other primates, and there is a marked correspondence among the patterns of cells found in man and those found in other mammals. Although it has been reported that the left hemisphere, which is associated with speech and language in man, has a small prominence not shared by the "silent" right hemisphere, man's ability to use language probably cannot be attributed to any particular configuration of cells or to any type of neuron specific to man. However, one characteristic of the brain of man *is* unusual, if not unique, as it relates to language functions: the relative localization of language functions in the left hemisphere.

Localization of Language

For a long time, it had been recognized that damage to the left hemisphere had particularly debilitating effects upon language. Gunshot wounds, traumatic accidents of different kinds, tumors, and disruptions of the blood supply (strokes) of the left hemisphere have all been found to produce many disorders related to language. Similar accidents to the right hemisphere had much less effect on language. There is no discrete "point" or set of points which is categorically responsible for language. Figure 9-1 shows that the areas related to language are more or less concentrated in the region toward the juncture of the temporal, frontal, and parietal lobes. But rather considerable differences are found between one person and the next in those areas in which damage will disturb language and speech. There

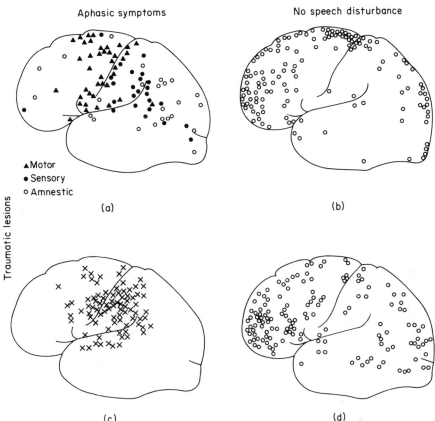

Aphasic symptoms   No speech disturbance

▲ Motor
● Sensory
○ Amnestic

Traumatic lesions

(a)   (b)

(c)   (d)

FIGURE 9-1—Compilation of areas of the brain which when damaged have produced aphasic symptoms. Each symbol represents the center of damage to the left hemisphere, although the extent of the lesion was highly variable. The points on the drawings were compiled by Lenneberg (1967). Figures (a) and (b) were compiled from one study while figures (c) and (d) were compiled from a different research report. Figures (a) and (c) point out maximal damage in the left hemisphere which produced aphasic symptoms. The open circles on figures (b) and (d) represent points of maximal brain damage in the left hemisphere which did not lead to speech disturbances.

are cases in which language functions are bilaterally represented in the brain, but they are very rare.

The work of Roger Sperry and his associates has utilized a special technique involving surgical separation of the two hemispheres of the brain. This has been done experimentally in animals and in humans for the relief of uncontrollable convulsive disorders. In both cases the great band of fibers which connects the hemispheres, the corpus callosum, is cut. In animals the anterior commissure is usually sectioned also, further isolating the hemispheres, and sometimes the optic chiasm is divided, so that visual input from each eye is restricted to a single hemisphere. The two hemispheres thus remain intact but without direct communication with each other. (There are, however, possibilities for one hemisphere's affecting the other through connections in the supporting brain stem.) With such a surgical preparation, it is possible to test the animal or person with visual or auditory input restricted to one hemisphere or the other. Careful testing demonstrates that in man (almost all) language functions tend to be restricted to the left hemisphere. The right hemisphere is mute but can understand some primitive commands; the left can comprehend and respond as if it represented the entire individual.

As we have seen, the dominant motor control area for the right hand is found in the left hemisphere and is related to the crossing over of the pyramidal tracts in the medulla. Conversely, control of the left arm and hand is largely dominated by the right hemisphere. Because of the close relationship between motor control and sensory feedback from a bodily area, most of the information reaching the brain from the right hand goes to the left hemisphere and vice versa. If one is talking with a person who has had this split-brain surgery, a conversation can proceed in a normal fashion. Moreover, if an object is presented to the person and he handles it only with his right hand, and cannot see what is in his hand, he can adequately describe what it is. But if the subject grasps an object in only his left hand and cannot see it, he will not be able to describe what it is. The left hemisphere, which is controlling the language of the person, will often make guesses at what the object might be, and it then becomes clear that the "talking" brain does not have the information necessary to identify it.

One almost gets the impression, about such a patient, that two individuals are inhabiting the same body. The person represented by the left hemisphere is verbal and can engage in symbolic activities like advanced arithmetic and mathematics. The right-hemisphere person seems mute and incapable of manipulation of mathematical symbols but can understand a few basic commands and accomplish the actions required by the commands with the left hand.

An interesting characteristic of the right, minor hemisphere is its ability to organize material spatially. It seems to understand how stimuli relate to one another in term of coordinates of space, i.e., up-down, right-left, to a far greater extent than does the left, major hemisphere. For example, when asked to duplicate a pattern made out of blocks, the split-brain patient does it quickly and efficiently when using the right hemisphere. When forced to use the left hemisphere, he progresses slowly in step-by-step fashion, manipulating one block at a time. The ability to organize the perceptual world in terms of spatial coordinates is, of course, essential to artistic creation and expression. A summary of Sperry's observations is presented in Figure 9-2.

Accepting the functional differences between right and left hemispheres in man, one wonders whether a similar condition exists in other animals. Are there functional differences between the two sides of the brain in animals? The answer is not entirely clear. Traditionally the functions of the two hemispheres in animals have been thought to be identical. But perhaps the right experimental questions were not asked. Some experiments do show differences between the hemispheres in animals. Hand (or paw) and eye

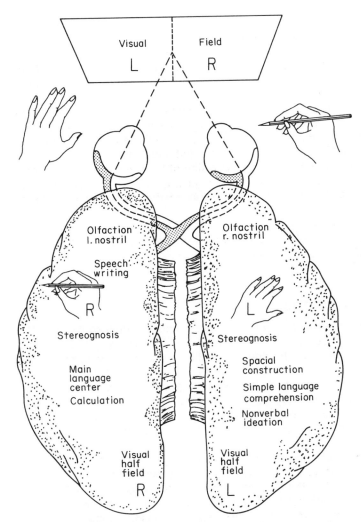

FIGURE 9-2–Schematic drawing of the functional lateralization found in patients with surgical interruption of the corpus callosum. (From Sperry, 1968.)

preferences can be found in the rat. The gross electrical responses to visual and auditory signals (evoked potentials) are sometimes different in the two hemispheres of cats and monkeys, but the significance of these differences is uncertain.

The ability to use language and manipulate symbols is not likely to be produced by a specific configuration of nerve cells or other unique anatomical arrangement. The right hemisphere *is* capable of language, because in some patients in whom the left hemisphere was damaged early in life the right hemisphere has developed the ability to use language and manipulate symbols required for arithmetic. It is as if there is an inborn tendency for the left hemisphere to be used for language. If development is normal and this hemisphere does participate in language skills, the ability of the right hemisphere to do the same thing seems to be suppressed. It should be remembered that some people have language represented in both hemispheres, but they are rare.

The confinement of language to the left hemisphere is most clear-cut in right-handed people. In left-handed people, language has some representation in the right hemisphere. Perhaps because of this tendency for greater bilateral representation of language, the right hemisphere cannot be as exclusively concerned with spatial organization of the visual word as in right-handed people. It is true that left-handed people tend to do less well in psychological tests designed to evaluate the spatial organization of visual stimuli.

In the case of language, we have a morphological correlate of an unequivocal higher function. Nevertheless, we cannot pinpoint the cellular mechanisms of this remarkable ability.

SYMBOLS: A QUESTION

As we have seen in the work of Sperry and his colleagues, the left hemisphere seems to be related to the use of abstract symbols as well as the use of language. There is little doubt that the use of abstract symbols is a property which is highly evolved in man, if not a unique characteristic. The difficulty in the use of methods for evaluating symbolic behavior is that symbols almost certainly require a language. There are many kinds of languages. One kind is the natural language which we learn early in life and with which we communicate. We can, of course, learn new natural and artificial languages too.

Investigations into the use of symbols by higher animals include some six studies of chimpanzees raised in human family situations. There is relatively close agreement in their observations. Up to the age of about 3 years the home-raised animals keep up with children of the same chronological age fairly well in terms of mental achievement tests based on motor performance. At 3 years the mental age of the chimp is not far behind that of the child of the same age; of course the chimpanzee is more advanced in its motor capacities. During development, chimps seldom babble or imitate adult verbal sounds. Most of the sounds they do make are the species-specific sounds, such as screeching and screaming, which they cannot modify into human speech. They seem to need to have sounds "elicited" by their environment.

Some home-raised chimps have been trained to pronounce a few English words in a more or less recognizable fashion: "mamma," "papa," "cup," and perhaps "up." They do somewhat better in comprehending speech and probably can differentiate 50 or more different commands. These animals can express themselves in a limited way by means of gestures, although most of the gestures commonly seen are anticipatory portions of the task in which the chimp is about to engage.

One wonders whether the chimpanzee is capable of understanding language other than that based upon the articulation of human, spoken words. Nonverbal languages exist, such as the American Sign Language used so extensively by the deaf. This problem is currently being studied.

After 16 months of home-based training the chimp Washoe, raised by the Gardners, was able to make and use 19 signs fairly well and probably understood quite a few more signs than it was able to make. Some of the signs convey a complicated meaning, such as "hurry," "sorry," and "please." Although it is too early to fully evaluate the experiment using a gesture language, it seems clear that the human's ability to use speech is a specialized characteristic suited to symbolic communication and that this ability is genetically determined, probably evidencing itself both in neural systems and in speech organs. The failure of the chimp to share this ability prevents it from profiting from language during early development.

Since mathematical symbols represent the vocabulary of the artificial language of mathematics, the statement that man has a unique ability to deal with abstract mathematical concepts is really only another way of saying he has the ability to learn a new language. If man has capacities to deal with symbols which are over and beyond the abilities of animals, a differentiation must be made between the use of symbols and the use of signs. Animals, at all levels of the phylogenetic scale, can learn to understand the significance of signals and can master complicated tasks to obtain symbolic rewards of tokens which can later be exchanged for primary reinforcements. Therefore, neither the use of symbolic rewards nor the use of signs differentiates man from the lower forms of mammalian life.

Abstraction and Concept Formation

Another approach to higher functions in general rests on the assumption that the symbolic behavior of man can be differentiated from the behavior of lower animals in that man can "abstract" qualities from the environment and use these abstractions as a basis for later behaviors. In the 1930s several investigators noted that rats seemed to respond consistently to specific characteristics of training situations when learning a task.

Let us consider a simple learning task and a hypothetical experiment. Figure 9-3 shows an apparatus in which an animal can be trained to discriminate between stimuli projected from behind onto two panels at one end of the box. A response is made simply by pushing on one or the other of the panels. If a correct choice is made, the animal is rewarded with a food pellet delivered through a mechanism located between the two panels. If an incorrect choice is made, no reward is given. After an incorrect response the animal must return to the opposite end to push a lever which begins a new trial. Depending on the design of the experiment, the stimuli are projected onto the choice panels in any fashion desired by the experimenter. To train animals to discriminate "triangles" from "squares" we could present on a given trial one triangle from a set of triangles of different sizes and one square from a set of squares of different sizes. On every trial the animal would have a choice between one triangle and one square, but the sizes of each could vary. A response to a square would always be rewarded and a response to a triangle would never be rewarded.

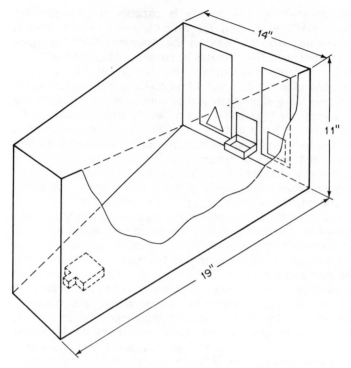

FIGURE 9-3–Testing chamber used by D. Lewellyn and R. L. Isaacson. Rats are trained to push on the plastic panels in front of the symbols. After each response to the back panels the animal returns to the other end of the box (toward the bottom of the figure) to press a bar (*dashed lines*), which begins a new trial. Positions of the numerals are randomly selected on each trial. Food rewards are provided in cup between the two panels for correct responses.

    The animal being trained could respond in several different but systematic ways. Since there are two positions (right panel, left panel) to choose between, it could systematically push the panel at one location. Since the squares and triangles would be randomly varied from side to side, the subject would receive a reward on about half of the training trials.

    The animal could also choose to respond on the basis of the brightness of the stimuli projected on the panels. Since the triangles and squares chosen for each trial vary in size, one will usually be brighter than the other. A subject might always respond to the brighter or dimmer of the projected stimuli. This would be another consistent method of responding leading to rewards on about half the trials, assuming a random selection of sizes of triangles and squares on each trial.

    A third consistent method of responding would be to choose the panel on which a square is being projected, regardless of position or brightness. This would lead to a reward on every trial.

    Of course, more complicated methods are possible. An animal could respond to the right panel if the two panels were rather similar in brightness and the left panel if they were widely divergent in brightness. Probably few animals adopt such complicated approaches to discrimination problems.

When training is begun on problems like this, response patterns are consistent. An animal first may respond to one position or another, then respond to the brighter panel, then perhaps return to responding to squares consistently. In the language of psychology of the 1930s, it evidenced behaviors indicating first a "position hypothesis," then a "brightness hypothesis," then another "position hypothesis," and finally the "square hypothesis." The term "hypothesis" refers to a consistent method of responding and also suggests how the animal's brain might be functioning. Because the term seemed to imply that animals might hold ideas in the same way man does, it became unpopular. However, animals do respond consistently in various ways while learning problems of different types, and so long as the term "hypothesis" is used only in reference to consistent patterns of responding it does describe the behavior of animals in many learning situations.

In actual experiments, monkeys readily learn to choose triangles in preference to other figures, even though the shapes and colors of the triangles are varied, indicating that they have the ability to respond to what must be considered an abstract character of the stimuli: namely, triangularity. Rats have been trained to respond to a triangle and not to other figures. When new triangles were substituted for the triangle used in the original training, the rats continued to respond to the "triangle." Thus they evidently had the ability to abstract something which has to do with triangularity. However, the rats' preference for three-sided figures seemed to be much more specific to the training stimuli than was the monkeys' preference. When tilted triangles were presented, the rats' response of approaching triangles broke down.

One might assume that the behavior of the rat in comparison with the monkey revealed a less well-formed concept of triangularity. This conclusion is not justified. The visual field of a rat is much different from that of a monkey, and its visual acuity is probably inferior. Motivational, procedural, incentive, and response characteristics cannot be equated across species. In our view the conclusions reached by Maier and Schneirla in their *Principles of Animal Psychology* are probably correct:

> *Abstraction may be regarded as the ability to learn to respond to certain limited aspects of a situation. All situations which contain this limited aspect become equivalent to each other and call out the same response. This does not mean that such learning is not of a higher order than learning which depends upon all characteristics of a situation. . . . It is our contention that the abstraction experiments do not demonstrate the presence of functions other than the processes of association and selection [p. 458].*

In short, Maier and Schneirla believe that the experiments studying the abilities of the animals to use abstraction concepts really did not accomplish this purpose. Their conclusions were based upon literature up to the time of the first publication of their book in 1935 and still seem to summarize the situation fairly. As mentioned above, the greater specificity of responses produced by the rat to the triangles as compared with that of the monkey might be due to sensory factors, or procedural differences, or both. In general, we would be tempted to assume that the more a response can be used outside of the specific training condition, the more adaptiveness it might have for behavior. In comparing the behaviors of different species we must remember that each species tends to adapt its behavior to the representative environmental conditions and to its own sensory capacities. No animal exhibits totally unlimited responsiveness to training stimuli in all conditions and at all times. No animal reacts only to stimuli in the specific training situation. There are wide variations among animals, even within the same species, which determine how much or how little the training will generalize beyond the training conditions.

Animals are often presented with unusual and possibly dangerous situations in which a response must be made. Each type of animal exhibits different types of responses to some abstracted properties of the new situation. Moreover, animals, including man, are always engaged in both longer and shorter behavioral sequences. A specific training trial or a specific training period represents only one chapter in a longer story which might be better considered as a day or a week or a longer period of time. The significant duration of "behavioral episodes" varies from animal to animal and is determined by the nature of the animal in terms of age, deprivation conditions, and presence of environmental stimuli. The point is that when some abstracted portion of a stimulus is presented, the response the animal will make depends in considerable measure upon the larger behavioral episode in which it is engaged.

If we cannot, then, establish the ability to make abstractions from the environment as a specific ability of the higher animals, including man, can we use other criteria for distinguishing man from the lower animals? One might think that the ability to form "concepts" was a characteristic of the higher forms of life. Certainly, however, it is not uniquely human. Monkeys can be readily taught to learn what are called *oddity problems.* In these, the monkey must choose one of three objects. On any trial, two of the objects are the same and one is different. The nature of the objects varies from trial to trial, but the situation remains the same: Two objects are always identical and a third is always different. The animal's job is to respond to the "different stimulus." If this ability is taken as evidence that the monkey has learned a concept of "differentness" and that the signal for what is different is not specific to the objects employed (because new objects are used continuously), we must conclude that concept formation is not unique to man. Under most criteria for the definition of concepts, we would have to accept this as a task representing the use of concepts. However, it is now apparent that such problems can be taught to cats and possibly even to rats. Therefore, the use of concepts, at least like those required in solving oddity problems, does not represent any unique characteristic of even higher animals.

In conclusion, the one demonstrable unique property of man as distinguished from other animals is his remarkable ability to use languages. Because of the different ecological requirements imposed upon different species, it is difficult even to say that one animal is more rapid or facile in acquiring or using concepts or symbols than another. This is not to deny that man (and possibly other higher animals) is, in general, better able to use concepts or symbols than other animals. Yet this superiority has not really been established.

Reasoning
The ability to learn new responses is not one of the higher abilities by any definition. Individual animals well below the vertebrate level can learn, as can higher animals with severe brain damage. But are all behavioral changes due to the same kind of basic learning process?

In a series of experiments which have not been accorded their rightful place in the psychological literature N. R. F. Maier investigated the ability of animals to "reason" in contrast with an ability to learn. He defined reasoning as the putting together of several previously learned but otherwise isolated experiences in order to reach a goal. Many types of procedures and situations were used. Perhaps of greatest interest is the *three table problem* illustrated in Figure 9-4.

In the three table problem an animal is allowed to explore all three tables freely, while unmotivated and with no rewards available. Later, when it is hungry, the animal is placed on one of the tables that serves as a starting platform. Previously, the animal had seen that food was available on one of

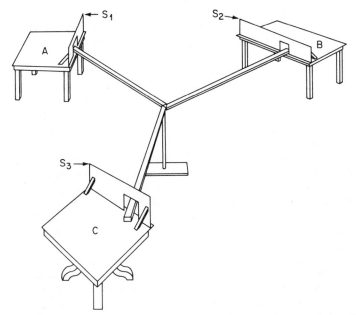

FIGURE 9-4—The three table problem of Maier. The rat can be started from any of the tables and given food or other rewards behind the screen at the front of each table. (From Maier and Schneirla, 1935.)

the other tables. Since it has learned the routes between the two tables, choice of the correct table depends on its ability to locate where it saw food. Naturally, animals generally select the route to the table which had the food.

The procedure can be modified by having the food always presented at the same table, and thus the ability to learn under these circumstances can be studied. In this case the ability to learn to reach the rewarded table and reasoning ability act in a combined fashion. In normal animals the reasoning ability seems to predominate in this task. For example, about 80 percent of normal animals will choose correctly when started randomly from the other two tables. Most of them have learned the location of the food and can take whatever route is available to get there. If the rat is always started from the same table and the food is always available at another table, the opportunity for the joint contribution of learning and reasoning is presented. However, the number of correct responses does not increase very much when learning and reasoning factors are combined in this way. With a slightly different method, reasoning and learning can be pitted against each other. In this case the animal is started for a series of trials from one table (A) and the food is consistently at another (B). After the animal has made a number of correct responses to the table with the food (B) it is placed on the food table (B) but now the food has been removed. It is also placed on the third table (C), which had no food on it before, and shown that now the food is there. For the test trial, the animal is replaced at the starting table (A). A response based on learning and past responses would be an approach to (B), the rewarded response of the past. A "reasoning response" would be an approach to (C), to which the animal has not been responding but which now has the food. When reasoning is pitted against learning in this way, the animal makes about 70 percent correct responses to the table with the food.

One of the most interesting results is found with animals subjected to this testing program after partial destruction of the neocortex. Maier found that destruction of as little as 18 percent of the neocortical surface in almost any location eliminated the rat's ability to use the reasoning solution. On the other hand, the ability to respond on the basis of "learning" remained constant despite the cortical destruction.

The fact that this "learning response" remained intact after cortical destruction is consistent with the ability of animals with relatively large amounts of cortical damage to perform well in simple learning tasks. The fact that cortical destruction effectively eliminated the reasoning basis for responding suggests that reasoning may truly be a "higher function" both in terms of the characteristics of animal behavior and because damage to the neocortical surface disrupts the behavior.

Maier and Schneirla report the work of another investigator, Campbell, who correlated the reasoning ability of rats with their scores on two types of mazes. Animals that learned one maze quickly also learned the other one quickly. The indication would seem to be that some common ability to learn mazes was called forth by the two apparatuses. However, the rate of acquisition of the maze problems was unrelated to the animals' ability to "reason."

This finding tends to support the distinction between learning and reasoning abilities.

Remarkably similar are the conclusions of Professor Beritoff of the Soviet Union, who emphasizes the importance of "conditioned images" in animals and man. He believes that the position of the animal in regard to its environment is a fundamental part of the "conditioned image." The three table problem can be solved on the basis of reasoning only if one assumes that the animal is able to localize the table with the food in space. According to recent work by two of the present authors (Douglas and Isaacson), when animals exhibit what has been called "spontaneous alternation" (the tendency to alter behavior on the basis of past behavior without the involvement of motivation or reward), they alternate *places* in the experimental room they have visited and not the *responses* required to get there.

Moreover, in the learning of avoidance tasks in which an animal must shuttle between a right compartment and a left compartment to avoid shock, it has been demonstrated that the animal really learns two separate problems, going from right to left and going from left to right. All of these experiments tend to stress the importance of the organism's position in the environment relative to the position of pathways and goals. Behavioristic psychology's emphasis of the past 20 years on simple associations between stimuli and responses, which become strengthened through the application of rewards, is inadequate to account for the higher behaviors of animals and men.

CONSCIOUSNESS

There is probably no more firmly held belief than that we are sometimes fully conscious and on the other hand that some acts are accomplished without conscious awareness, e.g., slips of the tongue or routine actions. At the least we believe we can distinguish between being conscious and being unconscious. Sometimes it seems that there is a "twilight zone" when we feel less than completely conscious or awake, and generally we would say that it is possible to distinguish between being awake and being asleep.

We are likely to assume that others have the same conscious experiences we do because the verbal reports of them ring true. Of course, we can never know the state of consciousness of another person or organism directly, but there seems to be a reasonable basis for the inference that similar states of consciousness exist in many if not all people within a given culture.

The subject of consciousness is usually ignored in physiological and experimental psychological textbooks because, being, after all, a private experience, consciousness is a very difficult topic. It is hard even to define it. What is consciousness? It is a feeling we have which is generally of an all-or-none nature. We tend to think of ourselves as being either conscious or not conscious—that is, asleep. Nevertheless, often we are fully awake when we engage in automatic acts to which we pay little attention. For example, we are driving along and discover that we have made a turn which is inappropriate in getting us to the place we are trying to go now but is one we made frequently in the past going to a different location. A mistake like this can occur when we are conscious, but should we say we were conscious when making the wrong turn? In a sense, we have not been attending to driving. The work of Freud and other personality theorists should have convinced us that we engage in many behaviors which are not under constant conscious control, yet, because they stand in a clear relation to certain goals, we are led to conclude that they are, in fact, purposeful. The classic examples used by Freud were slips of the tongue. What are we to say about these? Are they conscious or unconscious?

Part of the difficulty arises from a confusion between the words "consciousness" and "attention." Certainly we do not direct attention to all of the things we do while conscious. The automatic muscular acts used in playing baseball or golf are so routinized that they occur with little intentional control once they have been started. Many things can be done with a minimum of attention—driving a car, for example. Thus the confounding of "consciousness," "attention," and "intention" makes a precise definition of consciousness extremely difficult. Under the circumstances, we shall consider here only those situations in which a more or less clear differentiation can be made between conscious and unconscious states. In spite of its disadvantages, this seems to be the most reasonable approach until greater precision and understanding of the nature of consciousness and its relationship to the other types of behaviors has been acquired.

Neural Mechanisms of Consciousness

One can be unconscious during sleep or unconscious because of an accident or a disease. Often the unconscious state produced by an accident is caused by a reaction of the brain which is secondary to a reaction of the blood circulatory system. A sudden drop in blood pressure deprives the brain of an adequate supply of blood. With an inadequate supply of blood the neurons are no longer provided with the oxygen they need and temporarily cease to function. When circulation is restored, the brain cells will once again become active. This recovery may be gradual or rather sudden, depending upon circumstances.

The blood pressure is normally controlled by reflexive mechanisms located in the brain stem. These mechanisms regulate the strenuousness with which blood is pumped from the heart. The system responds to changes in blood pressure, as sensed by receptors in large arteries near the heart. When blood pressure declines, nerve impulses are sent to the controlling mechanisms of the heart, which increase or decrease the heart's responses. The entire system operates to maintain an optimal blood supply to the brain and to the rest of the body. The brain stem centers for this reflex are controlled in turn by other regions in the hypothalamus. Traumatic damage such as a bullet wound in the hypothalamus or in the upper brain stem can disrupt the mechanism and almost immediately produce a sufficient drop in blood pressure to cause unconsciousness or "blacking out." Moreover, since the hypothalamus controls the blood pressure centers of the brain stem, a means is provided whereby the forebrain (the cerebral hemi-spheres) can come to have strong effects upon blood pressure. The emo-tional systems of the brain, which include the limbic system as well as the cerebral cortex, are in constant interaction with the hypothalamus. Thus, one's resistance to "blacking out" or fainting may be different during different emotional states.

Loss of consciousness due to that dramatic fall in blood pressure is, however, rather unusual. More common is the unconsciousness that occurs during sleep, and research into the sleep mechanisms has been active in the past 10 years. From the study of sleep we may be able to learn more about what underlies the states of consciousness and unconsciousness.

Sleep and Consciousness

In most studies investigating the physiological bases of sleep the naturally occurring electrical rhythms of the brain are recorded on paper or photographic film. This technique requires that small electrodes be attached to the scalp, the surface of the skull, or to the brain surface itself, and the small electrical changes which arise from the brain are fed into electronic amplification systems and can easily be recorded. This method is called *electroencephalography*. Once the records of the electrical activity of the brain are made, relationships can be sought between them and the behavior of the person or animal during sleep or wakefulness.

Even though we have developed the technology to record electrical patterns and rhythms obtained from the brain, we still do not know precisely what they represent. They are not merely the summated activities of the action potentials of the many neurons of the brain. Because the electrodes are very large relative to the size of a single neuron of the brain, the EEG reflects the electrical changes occurring in millions of cells. The EEG indi-cates, to some extent, changes in the excitability of these cells, although it does not necessarily represent their responses, action potentials, which are generated when they fire.

From observations of the EEGs of sleeping individuals, four stages of sleep have been identified. The EEGs of these four stages are shown in Figure 9-5. The waking stage (stage 0) pattern shows many fast, high-frequency, low-amplitude rhythms. This pattern is often called a *desynchro-nized* record. In a relaxed condition much of the high-frequency activity disappears; the record becomes more *synchronized* and relatively smooth with a regular rhythm between 8 and 12 cycles per second which occurs in periodic episodes. This is sometimes referred to as an *alpha pattern*. It appears only when the person is awake but relatively inattentive. It rapidly disappears when visual or auditory stimuli are presented or the person engages in mental activities such as trying to solve a complicated mathe-matical problem. When the person dozes off, the record becomes more and more desynchronized. The alpha pattern disappears, and the EEG records reflect stage 1 of the figure. The record can appear almost free of fast frequencies. Stage 2 of sleep is identified by the presence of "sleep spindles," stage 3 is characterized by the appearance of large-voltage slow waves with some additional spindling, and stage 4 is dominated by large-

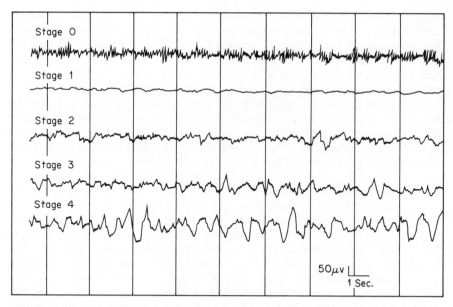

FIGURE 9-5—Illustrations of the electrical activities recorded from the scalp or brain surface during various stages of sleep. (From Webb, 1968.)

amplitude waves of 1 to 3 cycles per second which occur with regularity. People who are asleep go back and forth among these different stages as the night progresses. Stage 4 is generally regarded as the deepest stage of sleep, and it is reached by progression through the lighter stages, that is, from stage 1 to stage 4. Stage 4 is the one from which it is most difficult to wake. Even during sleep a person keeps in touch with the environment. Sounds, sights, and smells may waken him.

There is selectivity to the stimuli which will be most effective in waking up a person. A mother (or father) will be especially sensitive to sounds from a new baby but insensitive to even louder sounds of less personal significance. Moreover, people adjust to the expected sounds of the environment and will be awakened only by novel sounds or sometimes by the reduction of normally anticipated sounds of the night—for example, when an air-conditioning unit *stops*. Even during sleep, they monitor the environment for unusual or significant events. One can assume that the lighter stages of sleep are those in which the stimuli of the environment are more closely monitored.

Two types of stage 1 sleep are recognized. The first is a light sleep, as described before. However, sometimes when the EEG shows stage 1 sleep, other physiological events are found too—for example, rapid eye movements (REM) which are similar to those made when a person is actively observing his environment. At the same time, many of the major heavy muscles of the body become extremely relaxed. This stage of sleep is called stage 1–REM sleep or *paradoxical sleep.* It should be distinguished from regular stage 1 (sleep without the rapid eye movements and without the considerable lessening of muscular tensions).

REM Sleep and Dreaming

Stage 1–REM sleep has been found to be associated with dreaming. People awakened from stage 1–REM sleep are much more likely to report that they have been awakened in the middle of a dream than if they are awakened at other times. Stimuli presented during stage 1–REM sleep are much less likely to affect the subject than in the other stages, with the possible exception of stage 4. As many of us know, when we are asleep such stimuli as the ringing of the telephone tend to be incorporated into the ongoing dream structure. Perhaps this is a mechanism to preserve the sleep and maintain the integrity of the dream, as was suggested by Freud.

The relationship of stage 1–REM sleep to the other stages is not very clear. In many records, subjects lapse into stage 1–REM sleep from stage 2 and not from stage 4, the deeper sleep. The best way to characterize stage 1–REM sleep in comparison with the non-REM stages may be to consider it a qualitatively different type of sleep from the others and not to put it on a continuum with the other stages.

Stage 1–REM sleep can be observed in animals as well as man. If one is watching a rat, for example, which is sleeping during the day (rats spend as much as 80 percent of the daytime sleeping), its going into stage 1–REM sleep is signaled by the great reduction in its body muscle tension. The animal slumps. Moreover, its vibrissae tend to move differently from the way they usually do, for some unknown reason. During non-REM sleep the vibrissae rise and fall in unison, but during REM sleep each hair moves almost independently of the others.

Almost all dog lovers have noticed that dogs often appear to be dreaming while asleep. Fractional parts of responses such as sniffing, chewing, and running can be observed.

It is generally agreed that stage 1–REM sleep is the result of an active process initiated by neural mechanisms in the reticular formation of the brain stem. There is little agreement, however, as to the actual mechanisms and circuits involved. Stimulation or lesions of several portions of the brain—regions of the thalamus, the limbic system, the hypothalamus, and certain regions in the upper brain stem—affect either the behavioral or the electrical components, or both, of the sleep cycle.

The French researcher M. Jovet has discovered an area in the midbrain portion of the brain stem which seems to be critical for the occurrence of REM sleep. When lesions are made in this area, the animal has relatively normal sleep-wakefulness cycles but never exhibits stage 1–REM sleep. Stimulation of certain regions of the thalamus and hypothalamus have been able to induce sleep, and lesions of some thalamic and hypothalamic areas will cause animals to sleep considerably less than intact animals.

The hippocampus, one of the major portions of the limbic system, seems to be involved with sleep also. When an animal exhibits electrical sleep patterns, as recorded from the neocortex, the hippocampus tends to show more desynchronized activity, with fast frequencies predominating, than when the animal is awake. If this active, desynchronized pattern which appears in the hippocampus during at least certain stages of sleep is representative of increased excitatory activities, it is possible that sleep is initiated or maintained through systems operating through this structure.

Perhaps it inhibits certain aspects of the hypothalamic system which are also involved in the activation of the animal. Certainly it would be a good guess that if the hippocampus has something to do with the regulation of sleep the involvement is expressed through its effects upon hypothalamic systems. Furthermore, surgical destruction of the hippocampus in experimental animals results in a tendency to be more active in the evening than normal animals. The rat is a nocturnal animal and spends most of the daytime in sleep. The hippocampal lesions do not change its daytime sleeping very much. At night, when the rat is most active, it still sleeps 30 to 40 percent of the time, but the animals with hippocampal lesions spend much less than this time in sleep.

Interestingly, the areas of the thalamus and the hypothalamus which are involved in the sleep-wakefulness cycle are also those which have been identified as contributing to the amount of activity evidenced by animals under normal, awake conditions. Today we believe that maintenance of effective excitatory levels in both the higher and lower portions of the brain depends upon neural systems which provide general excitation or inhibition of higher centers in other regions.

Activation and Arousal Systems

Activation and arousal systems are sometimes called activating systems, arousal systems, or diffusely projecting, or diffusely activating systems. In general, they are related to three anatomical regions. First, the *brain stem reticular formation,* a network of cells and fibers, extends from the spinal cord to the posterior margins of the hypothalamus along the middle of the neuraxis. Fibers originating from cells in the reticular formation project diffusely to the neocortex and other forebrain areas while also proceeding in more discrete bundles to the hypothalamus and to the diffusely projecting nuclei of the thalamus. The areas receiving fibers from the brain stem reticular formation also represent systems for maintaining high activity levels in the rest of the brain. Second, the posterior regions of the *hypothalamus* also act diffusely on various other forebrain areas. Third, some nuclei in the *thalamus,* the diffusely projecting thalamic nuclei, send fibers to many areas of the neocortex. The activity of all three arousal systems probably interacts to produce the optimal levels of arousal from the entire brain relative to the behavior sequences in which the animal is engaged.

These three regions, which project more or less diffusely toward the neocortical surface, represent what we know about the architecture of arousal mechanisms in the central nervous system. Consciousness requires their collaborative activities although we cannot say that consciousness is their activities. Probably they provide the necessary background for conscious mental activities. We know that lesions or tumors of the thalamus and hypothalamus, as well as those in the brain stem, result in gross abnormalities of sleep-wakefulness cycles. We know that certain stimulants selectively affect the hypothalamus or the reticular formation and cause changes in alertness and arousal. Certain depressants tend to act upon the reticular formation and on the hypothalamus. Many lines of evidence converge to make it reasonable to assume that these areas are concerned with maintaining conscious activities, but we cannot go far beyond mere assumption. We know about the conditions necessary for the occurrence of conscious, awake behavior but little or nothing about what conscious behavior really is.

Abnormal Mental States

Consciousness can include perceptual experiences which do not correspond to the stimulus conditions of the environment. When experiences fail to show a close correspondence to the external world, we call them *hallucinations.*

Hallucinations can be brought about in a number of ways. Probably the most talked-about method today is use of hallucinogenic drugs, such as lysergic acid diethylamide (LSD). We do not know the precise mechanisms whereby LSD alters perception and mental activity, but probably the drug has a chemical structure like that of chemicals which normally participate in controlling the activity of nerve cells or are involved in the actual transmission of nerve impulses from one cell to another at the synapse. Some hallucinogenic drugs tend to mimic the effects of some of the neurochemicals that are released at synapses and produce unnatural excitatory or inhibitory activities. Brain regions associated with the sensory systems seem especially susceptible to the effects of LSD.

Hallucinations can be produced in other ways. Often they occur when the sensory input to an organism is greatly reduced—when a person or animal is placed in a monotonous environment, for example. A monotonous environment would be one such as occurs while driving a car over a long, straight road that has little roadside scenery. Reports from truck drivers, especially in some flat areas of the Southwest, indicate that hallucinations are quite common. Some even lead to accidents when drivers try to avoid hallucinated objects in the road. Airplane pilots also have reported hallucinations when flying long routes in clear air with untroubled circumstances.

Hallucinations are experienced by experimental subjects who pass long periods of time in restricted sensory environments. Sometimes subjects are placed in rooms built to minimize auditory and visual input stimulation, or they are suspended in pools of warm water, or they are dressed in special suits with frames and pads to cushion them from tactual stimulation and prevent sensory information from arising from movement of the joints. In general, the more complete the sensory deprivation, the faster the occurrence of the hallucinations. While this result is frequently reported, there are still some unsolved issues. It is not clear whether all subjects are equally prone to hallucinate under impoverished sensory conditions, and it is not clear what role the suggestion, often made to the subjects before the experiment, that they *may* experience hallucinations plays in the reports of the subjects.

There are several explanations for the hallucinogenic effects of sensory deprivation, based by most investigators upon the presumed spontaneous activity of the nervous system. In the face of diminished input the spontaneous activity of the nervous system "runs loose"—that is, without sensory guidance—and produces various hallucinations. For some reason a particular pattern of neural activity with perceptual components begins and continues unchecked by input from the environment.

Elicited Abnormal Perceptions

Hallucinations can be elicited from the brain by electrical stimulation in at least two areas. They can arise from temporal lobe stimulation while the brain is exposed for surgery. They are very rare, however, being found only in patients suffering from certain types of temporal lobe epilepsy. Electrical stimulation of the visual areas of the occipital lobes can also cause hallucinatory experiences, but only in patients in whom the corpus callosum, that great band of nerve fibers connecting the two hemispheres, has been severed. The cutting of the corpus callosum was discussed earlier in this chapter in connection with the work of Sperry (pp. 255–257). The origiral observations were upon a human subject undergoing brain surgery but they have been extended for finer examination through the use of animals. Dr. Robert Doty of the Brain Research Center, University of Rochester, implanted electrodes into the visual areas of the brains of animals in which the corpus callosum had been sectioned previously. When electrical stimulation was applied to one of the visual areas, i.e., in either the right or left hemisphere, the monkey responded as if it were trying to grasp some nearby stimulus which was not there. The human patient described the sensation as seeing something like a butterfly moving about in the visual field. Of course we do not know what the monkey sees during brain stimulation, but whatever it is, the monkey trys to grab it.

The most fascinating aspect of Doty's experiment is that the electrical stimulation of the visual area produces this effect only in animals with a severed corpus callosum. If the two halves of the brain are interconnected in a normal manner, the animal does not reach out for the imaginary object.

This finding suggests that normally the two sides of the brain cooperate in evaluating the reports produced by either side alone. If one side responds in some manner, behavior is not affected unless there is independent confirmation of the sensory event from neural activity in the corresponding locations on the other side of the brain.

Such an interpretation is highly speculative, of course. We do not really understand how the phenomenon is produced. It should also be recognized that, even though the corpus callosum is cut, the two sides of the brain can influence each other through circuits of neurons going through deep structures of the brain, including the reticular formation.

Delayed-Response Problems

A number of behavioral tasks have been considered at one time or another to be representative of higher mental activities in animals. These include delayed-response problems (sometimes called delayed reactions). In such tasks information is provided which indicates what a correct (rewarded) response will be, but the animal is prevented from making a response for some time. It was once thought that animals higher in the phylogenetic scale could delay their responses longer than animals lower in the scale. Various maximum delayed periods were obtained for different types of animals. Some investigators found that a rat could delay its response no longer than 10 seconds and still perform correctly whereas a gorilla could delay its response up to 2 minutes. Other workers found use of a different procedure could cause a gorilla to delay its response up to as much as 48 hours. Exploration of other species of animals began, and varying procedures were initiated. Very divergent results appeared. The literature now has reports of maximum delays possible for a rat ranging from 10 seconds to 24 hours. Maximum delays of response for a gorilla range from 2 minutes to 48 hours. Obviously the method used to test animals on their ability to delay a response is crucial to the results obtained. Careful consideration of the nature of the tasks presented and the suitability of a task for the behavioral repertoire of the animal makes it apparent that delayed response is not a good task for evaluating higher abilities.

Because of the failure of this behavioral problem to be a good index of higher functions, we cannot attribute any special "higher function" to brain areas in which damage interferes with performance of the task. This is unfortunate in a way, since the areas of the brain which affect performance of delayed-response problems are probably the most studied of any in brain-behavior relationship research. Damage to the lateral surface of the frontal lobe in monkeys produces a severe and permanent impairment in the "standard" delayed-response problem. This behavioral deficit is interesting in itself but certainly does not point to these lateral surfaces as being particularly concerned with any special higher abilities.

Damage to the anterior portions of the frontal lobes in man produces no deficit in delayed-response problems developed for the human but does cause other alterations in behavior. The most common outcome of frontal lobe destruction in man is emotional change. There is a general flattening of affective (emotional) reactions and a reduction in anxiety and worry. Apparently the operation does not effect much loss of intellectual functions immediately after surgery, but a progressive loss of mental ability gradually becomes ever more apparent. It is difficult, moreover, to determine precisely a loss in intellectual ability since the patients were usually under severe psychological or physiological stress before surgery. If they had not been deeply disturbed, surgery would not have been indicated.

Insight

Some psychologists have argued that higher functions must be recognized when an animal's performance improves radically while it is learning a specific behavioral task or problem. This sudden change in the learning curve has sometimes been called *insight.* The idea was that the precipitate drop in errors reflected the animal's gaining understanding of what was required by the problem. Perhaps before insight occurred the animal was operating under the wrong hypothesis. At the point at which the learning curve showed a dramatic improvement the animal was presumed to have come across the correct hypothesis in some way or other.

It is now clear that, over the course of training, performance, even in very simple problems, shows one or more dramatic improvements. With many tasks learning always occurs suddenly. An animal goes from a stage in which he has not learned the task to a "learned state" abruptly. Insight is not characteristic of performance only during the solving of difficult problems, nor is it found only among higher animals. Abrupt changes which are thought to signal moments of insight during learning are easily demonstrated in the rat as well as higher species and occur even in animals with a considerable amount of brain damage. For these reasons, and others, it is unlikely that the sudden drop in errors or, conversely, the sudden improvement in performance referred to often as insight during training is representative of any truly higher function.

The Use of Tools

Other situations have been thought at one time or another to be diagnostic of special higher abilities. One such is the use of tools or instruments to obtain goals. In general, this form of activity is confined to primates and some birds, but the use of tools may have more to do with the manipulative abilities of a species than with a higher-order ability. Comparisons have been made between different types of subhuman primates in attempts to determine whether the use of tools might be a diagnostic criterion for the evaluation of higher functions. The answer is less than clear. As an overall rule, the apes are superior to monkeys in using tools and stacking boxes to obtain rewards suspended from the ceiling of cages. Nevertheless, some exceptionally successful monkey performances have been recorded. The monkey appears to be capable of using tools almost as well as the higher apes, but under many conditions of testing it fails to do as well. When monkeys have been in captivity a long time and have been well treated, they are more likely to exhibit proficient use of tools. The precise variables which adversely influence their performance are unknown, but we must be suspicious of using the ability to make or work with tools efficiently as a criterion of higher mental processes.

THE CORTEX AND HIGHER MENTAL FUNCTIONS

In man, about one-half of the brain's 12 billion nerve cells are located in the cerebral cortex. Traditionally, the functions responsible for higher processes, regardless of what they might be, are ascribed to the cerebral cortex. This is the case even though attempts to find characteristics which might be called "higher processes," other than language, have not been very profitable, except perhaps for the work of Maier on the ability to reason. Nevertheless, it is certainly true that the higher cognitive functions, whatever they are, are almost always attributed to this gray mantle of the brain. Hundreds of books have been written about the structure of the cortex as well as its presumed functions. Regions and subregions numbering in the hundreds have been localized on this surface of the brain in the higher animals. The distribution of fiber systems running to and from the cortical mantle has been studied in exquisite detail. Yet even a reasonable definition of cortex is difficult to formulate.

The distinguished anatomist C. Judson Herrick noted in 1926 that "when the whole evidence is reviewed, we find that there is no single anatomical criterion by which cerebral cortex can be distinguished from other sheets of superficial brain matter in the cerebral hemisphere. . . ."

Herrick pointed out that the neocortex merges with several cortical areas by a series of gradual changes so small as to be undetectable.

Four types of cortex can be discerned among animals. One type is that which is possessed by the fishes and amphibians. Certain regions at the top and lateral walls of the rudimentary hemispheres in these animals exhibit tendencies toward cellular organization something like that of the cortex of higher animals. A second type is found in reptiles and birds, which have a cortex very similar to that in the higher animals although it is relatively small. A third type is found in the mammals, and in the mammals there is a considerable expansion of the neocortical areas. A fourth type is thought to be that of the human, but whether the cellular architecture of man's cortex is really different from the ape's has been much debated. In general, we must conclude that there are no particular differences in cellular architecture between the human brain and the ape brain.

From his comparative neuroanatomical point of view Herrick stressed two points about the relationship of neocortex to the rest of the nervous system. First, the functions of the neocortex have been added to already highly functional systems which are competent to handle most of the activities of the animal. The subcortical systems are adequate for many kinds of learning and retention of that learning. The neocortex influences the more primitive systems of the thalamus, hypothalamus, and lower brain stem regions. It is removed from the more primitive lines of transmission of sensory and motor activities, although in the course of phylogenetic development it does come to assume this role in some degree. Second, all of the cortex and the rest of the brain act in a synergistic system to obtain a fine adjustment of behavior to the environment. All areas of the brain are elaborately interconnected and work with consistent and continuous interactions. For our present purpose, this finding suggests that higher functions are not localized in any particular region of the brain, including the neocortex, but manifest themselves through continuous interactions among the neocortex, subcortex, and brain stem regions. This is the case even for the ability to use language. The noted neurosurgeon Wilder Penfield has pointed out that often surgical lesions of the language areas fail to produce the same degree of language impairment as do traumatic or vascular accidents in the same areas. He attributes this difference to the fact that the surgical lesion is restricted to the outer neocortical layers and does not usually penetrate into the underlying white matter or the subcortical systems associated with these superficial areas, whereas involvement of subcortical regions almost always occurs in accidents. Penfield's observation emphasizes that the normal operation of the neocortex is in active cooperation with other areas of the brain.

The neocortex of higher animals differs in several ways from that of the lower animals. As one ascends the phylogenetic scale, there is a "spreading out" of the nerve cells in the cortex. Neurons appear to be farther apart in the human than in the apes and farther apart in the apes than in the monkey, and so on. Moreover, the nerve cells are probably larger in the higher animals than in the lower. These two factors suggest that a greater amount of space is devoted to dendritic arborizations in higher than in lower animals, for the regions between nerve cells are not empty but are filled with many branching processes, mostly dendrites, throughout the neocortex. Of course, between the neurons there are also supportive glial cells and blood vessels. Furthermore, according to some evidence, the larger the cell body, the greater its dendritic arborization. The significance of these observations is that more extensive dendritic arborization makes more distance available for a nerve cell to receive information from the billions of other cells making contact with the dendritic tree. The hypothesis is that with increased dendritic arborization goes a heightened ability to integrate items of incoming sensory information as well as the input from cells in many other regions of the brain.

Actually, in the brains of higher animals the number of nerve cells is increased, but not by a great deal. Man, for example, has only about 1.25 times as many nerve cells as the chimpanzee. Considering the vast numbers of cells involved, this is not a striking difference. It becomes even less striking when we mark the enormous variability among men in the weight of their brains and in the number of nerve cells they have. Furthermore, many nerve cells perish each day as we age, without a corresponding decline in ability, and there seems to be little, if any, correspondence between the weight of the brain (and presumably the number of nerve cells in it) and intellectual ability.

The higher brains are also not distinguished on the basis of a particularly thick cerebral cortex relative to the total size of the brain. In fact, the rat's neocortical mantle is relatively thicker than man's. The most pronounced change found in comparing higher and lower brains is the great increase in the thickness of the white matter. As will be remembered, the white matter is that part of the forebrain which is made up predominantly of myelinated axons of nerve cells running from one cortical area to another and from the cortex to the subcortical regions. It also includes fibers with myelin which reach into the cerebral cortex from the thalamus and other locations carrying information about the environment. Thus, the major difference found among the neocortices of animals high and low in the phylogenetic scale is in the development of fiber systems: first the fast-conducting, myelinated fibers which appear white when the brain is cut and exposed to view, and second the difficult-to-observe dendritic fibers which permeate the neocortical mantle. Very little is known about how the growth in fiber systems can act to produce those qualities of behavior which we consider to be related to the higher functions exhibited by the higher animals.

The possibility should be recognized that the key to understanding higher functions does not lie in the anatomical characteristics of the brain at all, and that the observations of fiber systems, cell densities, and other factors are not relevant to understanding them. The explanation may lie, for example, in differences in the biochemical makeup of the brains. Perhaps the nerve cells of the higher animals become much more efficient through refinements in the creation of transmitter substances or of substances which remove the transmitter substances once they have done their job. Other sorts of enzymatic relationships could be suggested to account for the superior functioning of the higher animals. It might be speculated that the brain cells of man receive greater supplies of nutrients and other chemicals because of greater numbers of supportive glial cells or more efficient glial cells. Maybe the neurons of the higher animals are more efficient because of enriched blood supplies relative to lower animals. There are many alternative hypotheses, but they remain in urgent need of experimentation and evaluation—a fruitful area for future investigation.

SUGGESTED READINGS

Lenneberg, E. *Biological foundations of language.* New York: Wiley, 1967.

Maier, N. R. F., & Schneirla, T. C. *Principles of animal psychology.* New York: Dover, 1963. Paperback.

Sperry, R. W. Hemisphere deconnection and unity in conscious awareness. *American Psychologist,* 1968, *23,* 723–733.

Webb, W. B. *Sleep: An experimental approach.* New York: Macmillan, 1968.

INDEX

INDEX

abducens nerve, 76
ablation technique, 204
    See also brain damage
absolute refractory period, 43–44
abstraction formation, in man and animals compared, 259–263
acetylcholine, and pain sensation, 155
    as transmitter of nervous system, 55–56
ACh, *see* acetylcholine
acidity, 144
acquisition phase of learning, 182
ACTH secretion, 80
    and emotion, 232
action potential, definition of, 43
    initiation and propagation of, 53–55
activation and arousal systems, 270–271
active avoidance apparatus, *208*
adaptation to taste, 146
adenine, 26–27
adenosine triphosphate, *see* ATP
Adey, W. R., 204
ADH, release, 245
    and thirst, 243–244
adrenal medulla, 75
adrenalin, and behavior changes, 223
    secretion, 75
adrenergic blocking agent, hunger and, 245
affectionate behavior, septal ablation and, 232
afferent nerves, 63
    and brain function, 112
alcoholism, brain damage from, 195–196
alpha motor neurons, 162
    destruction of, 176
    and voluntary movement, 167
amino acids, conversion to protein, 26
    of foreign proteins, 24–25
amphibians, evolution of, 99–100
ampulla, 176

amygdala, 83, 84, 85–86
    ablation of, 229–231
    of cat, *231*
    and emotional behavior, 229–232
    lesions, 203, 241
    and olfaction, 150
    of placental mammal brain, 105
    of reptiles, 100
amygdaloid nucleus, 148
anatomy, of auditory system, 133–136
    of brain, *see* brain
    of cell, *see* cells
    of cell membrane, 29–30
    of gustatory system, 142–143
    and language, 254
    of nervous system, *see* neuroanatomy
    of olfactory system, 146–148
    of visual system, 117–120
anesthetization, reactions to, 221–222
anger responses, amygdaloid complex and, 230
animal behavior, and behavioral episodes, 6–7
    day-night cycles of, 4
    developmental approach to, 15–21
    and differences among animals, 10
    genetic influences on, 10–11, 12–13
    imprinting, 15, *16,* 17
    internal factors controlling, 5–7
    orienting response, 8
    and similarities among individuals, 13–15
    spontaneous activity, 4
    See also animals
animal intelligence, 11–12
animals, and abstractions, 259–263
    brain, right and left hemispheres of, 256–258
    cerebellum ablation in, 78
    cingulectomized, 207–209
    compensation for inability to use language in, 254

Designed by Michel Craig
Set in Helvetica
Composed, printed and bound by American Book–Stratford Press, Inc.
Harper & Row, Publishers

73   7 6 5 4